TRAINING FOR LIFE
A Practical Guide to Career and Life Planning

Seventh Edition

Fred J. Hecklinger

Northern Virginia Community College
Alexandria Campus

Bernadette M. Black

University of Virginia

KENDALL/HUNT PUBLISHING COMPANY
4050 Westmark Drive   Dubuque, Iowa 52002

Contents

Section 1: Acknowledge Your Unique Self 1

Chapter 1: Work Values 3

Chapter 2: Interests 13

Chapter 3: Skills and Abilities 25

Chapter 4: Personal Values 43

Chapter 5: Self-Esteem 53

Chapter 6: Lifestyle Considerations 67

Section 2: Manage Change in Your Life 77

Chapter 7: Career and Life Planning in the 21st Century 79

Section 3: Explore Career Options 135

Section 5: Enhance Work Performance and Satisfaction 263

Chapter 23: How to Be an Effective Worker 265

Chapter 24: Make Time Your Friend 275

Chapter 25: Don't Be Your Own Worst Enemy 281

Chapter 26: Take Care of Yourself 289

Chapter 27: Routine Maintenance—Your Two-Year Work Checkup 297

Chapter 28: The Payoff—Who Decides Whether You've Done Good Work? 307

Section 6: Create Quality and Balance in Your Life 317

Chapter 29: A Look into the Future 319

Chapter 30: Think Positively 323

Chapter 31: Know When It's Time to Change Work 325

Chapter 32: Develop Interests 329

Chapter 33: Take an Active Role in Staying Healthy 333

Chapter 34: Maintain Good Interpersonal Relationships 343

Chapter 35: Make the Most of Your Financial Resources 347

Chapter 36: Continue to Learn 351

Chapter 37: Your Lifestyle Checkup 355

Summary—Create Quality and Balance in Your Life 369

Appendix A: Continuous Career Options Listing 373

Bibliography 375

Index 000

Preface

After more than 45 combined years in the field of career and life planning, we are committed to the following concepts and values.

1. Adults are fully capable of making career and life decisions for themselves.
2. When adults become actively involved in establishing career and life plans, they are happier, more satisfied, and feel more in control of the direction of their lives.
3. Throughout their lives, adults search for personal and career satisfaction and need to carefully analyze each transition along the way.
4. Adults have the power to change, to grow, and to achieve their own definition of success.
5. Life satisfaction comes from successfully integrating career and lifestyle so that they complement each other.
6. Adults can learn to manage their careers and to maintain fulfilling lifetstyles.
7. Adults can progress most effectively by building on their strengths and by seeking to expand the positive options in their lives.
8. The career and life planning process never ends. Planning for retirement is just as important as planning for another career. Planning is important even after retirement in order to maintain a rewarding and fulfilling lifestyle.

We have written *Training for Life: A Practical Guide to Career and Life Planning* to help adults develop their career and life objectives, decide how to achieve these objectives, and take action in making career and life decisions. It is impossible to separate career from lifestyle. Individuals are not one-dimensional. This book deals with career and lifestyle as an integrated whole, taking the reader through more traditional career planning topics of self-awareness, job investigation, and job campaign, while also addressing the equally important topics of change, job enhancement, and healthy lifestyle characteristics.

We believe that adults grow and flourish by taking an active role in planning their careers and lives. This text can be used as a workbook in classes, in individual counseling, in workshops, and as a self-instructional aid. Use a pencil or a pen as you read this book. Fill in the checklists, answer the questions, and take a more active role in the planning of your future.

Acknowledgements

Training for Life was first published by Kendall-Hunt in 1982. Over the past 18 years, our book, through six revisions, has been read by thousands of adults, used as a resource by hundreds of counselors, and helped job hunters who found it on library shelves. We continue to be pleased by its influence and proud of its use by adults who seek to understand themselves and to grow throughout life's journey.

In the early 1980's, the authors were motivated to write and publish a career/life planning text because of the absence of adult-focused career resources. It was important to translate existing career and adult development theories for community college students who struggled with a multitude of transitions.

This edition of Training for Life is dedicated to the courage of all community college students who seek to learn despite many obstacles. We are awed by their desire to achieve as they define success for themselves. Community college students have motivated us and inspired us to grow.

While many career and life planning books and resources designed especially for adults are now available in most bookstores, Training for Life remains a pioneer in the career/life planning field. The breadth of topics, variety of resources, and common sense approach speak to adults who are engaged in planning their future. We are proud of the history, longevity and contents of Training for Life.

The authors are indebted, first and foremost to their immediate families for their loving support and encouragement:
Margaret C. Hecklinger, who has contributed significantly to many revisions,
John M. Hecklinger, Thomas L. Barnes, Allison A. Curtin, and Kevin R. Curtin.

In addition, we express our appreciation to our colleagues and friends within the Virginia Community College System, especially those at Northern Virginia Community College, Alexandria Campus. Our special gratitude goes to Lyn Gross, Career Services Specialist, who has updated resources and references in the past three editions. A special thank you goes to Kendall-Hunt Publishing Company for their editorial expertise.

Introduction

· ·

Training for Life: A Practical Guide to Career and Life Planning can be your ticket to a better, more satisfying future. This book, together with your thoughts, feelings, and experiences, will help you to assess your strengths, interests, and values and to examine your lifestyle. You will be provided with a route to manage your career and to create the lifestyle that is best for you. This book will help you to

- Develop some short- and long-range goals for your career and lifestyle planning
- Gain better control of your life
- Make informed decisions and commitments about your career
- Actively plan your future
- Create your own luck
- Develop a lifestyle plan that will extend into retirement
- Revitalize your present job or career
- Look at the big picture rather than at each part of your life as a separate entity

TRAINING FOR LIFE

Compare your journey through life to a train trip. You are constantly moving ahead, with many stops along the way. With every mile and every new passenger, the train changes. Each new person you meet and each new experience changes you. Just as the train will take on new passengers, employees, and supplies and will eventually let them go, so will you take on new interests, friends, and skills. Some you will choose to keep and others you will let go. But just as the train keeps going, remaining basically the same, so do you keep going. You are changed by your experiences, but you always come back to *you*. *You alone* must make the decisions that significantly alter your journey through life.

As you wait at the train station platform, you are filled with anticipation and thoughts about the upcoming trip. What new experiences will you encounter? What different people will you meet and get to know along the way? What challenges lie around the corner? The tracks are visible only at the beginning. The end is nowhere in sight. The unknown can be an exciting adventure, a knot in the pit of your stomach, or a mix of both. As always, the choice is yours and yours alone. Your trip is uniquely your own.

Just as the train picks up speed, slows down for tunnels and curves, and encounters bumpy tracks, delays, and detours, your journey through life will be marked by fast, slow, smooth, and rough travel. At times the direction in which you are headed may not seem very clear, but it is there, just as the train tracks are there. You may end up going in circles, but you still keep moving, just as time keeps moving. Whenever you come to a junction and have to decide which track to take, you must make a decision. Some of these decisions can significantly alter the direction of your life. *You* run your life, just as the engineer runs the train. You will be responsible for making decisions, but this book can serve as your guide. You must invest time and energy on this journey, but the rewards will be well worth your investment. You will meet many new and interesting people as new passengers embark and familiar faces disembark. Each person that comes into your life, and every unexpected occurrence teaches you some lesson. Be an aware traveler with an eye to adventure and to expanding you experience.

As you go through your career and life planning process, enlist the help of others who are a part of your life: family, friends, and colleagues. They can provide important advice, encouragement, support, and assistance, but they cannot take over your role as engineer. Listen to others, seek their help, and then make your decisions. This book will help you to get the information you need to make critical life decisions and to deal successfully with important life transitions. There are many routes to follow. There is no one right route for all people.

You may even need to create your own train tracks for your trip. However, by using this book and by getting help from others, you will be better able to choose the route that is best for you.

You are now on your journey and have already traveled a long distance. Do you like the direction that your life is taking? Do you feel that you have control over where you are going? You must decide whether to take charge of your trip and be the engineer or simply be a passenger on your train, letting others make the critical decisions for you. The career and life planning process requires work, just as running a train is more work than being a passenger. However, this work can be rewarding and enjoyable. Put the process to work for you as you begin to establish your life and career goals. Start *now* to plan your trip and make the most of all the sights and experiences along the way.

THE CAREER AND LIFE PLANNING PROCESS

What is career and life planning and how can it help you? It enables you to make decisions about the time you spend in your career and your life. By following an organized approach to career and life decision making, you will be able to make more effective decisions now, and in five years, ten years, or twenty years. You will feel that you have more control over the course of your life. You may not always know exactly where you are headed, but by knowing and using the career and life planning process, you can make better decisions when you come to each junction along the way and have to choose between two or more routes.

The career and life planning process involves gathering information so that you can make realistic decisions based on facts and self-knowledge rather than on your own feelings or the suggestions of others. Think back to your last major purchase, perhaps a home or a car. How much time and energy did you spend researching and uncovering information about this purchase? What did you do to get the information you needed?

If you are employed full time five days a week, 50 weeks a year, for 40 years, you will spend approximately 10,000 days or 80,000 hours at work. This is a major part of your life, certainly more important than any house or car purchase. Therefore, it is essential for you to take the time and action that is necessary to plan your career. In addition, take time to plan your nonworking hours so that you can create a fulfilling lifestyle. Your career and lifestyle are basic to your achievement of happiness and satisfaction with life. The investment of your time in the career and life planning process can have great rewards.

Home	**Car**
• Ask neighbors	• Research written evaluations
• Inspect building	• Talk with other owners
• Talk with owners	• Talk with salesperson
• Talk with real estate agent	• Talk with a mechanic
• Talk with former owners	• Test drive
• Spend time in neighborhood	• Go to other showrooms
• Research home values	• Look at competition
• Talk with mortgage officer	• Talk with loan officer
• Inspect vehicle	

Richard Nelson Bolles, who wrote *What Color Is Your Parachute?*, did not define the career and life planning process, but he certainly continues to popularize and advocate the philosophy of self-empowerment. Bolles's book has encouraged many to define career goals and find jobs with some measure of satisfaction while retaining personal dignity and confidence. Bolles has masterfully translated theory into practice. *Training for Life* also translates theory into practice, not by requiring you to write a detailed autobiography, but by providing exercises and checklists that stimulate self-examination and thought. The process is the same, the means vary, and the results will follow after careful and deliberate assessment of yourself.

The importance of the career and life planning process has been demonstrated by people who have studied the work life, career patterns, and personal needs of adults. For example, Abraham Maslow classified human needs within a hierarchy. Basic needs such as food, water, and safety are in the lower part of the hierarchy, while other needs such as love, knowledge, self-respect, and self-actualization form the upper part. People work not only to satisfy the more basic needs but also to fulfill their need for a sense of purpose, for self-worth, and for success. It is important to recognize work as an integral part of this sense of fulfillment. Of course, it is difficult to deal with the higher level needs if the lower level needs have not been met. In practical terms, it is difficult to deal with career satisfaction if one has not met basic human needs.

John Holland noted that people in similar occupations have similar personalities and personal preferences. In making a career decision, therefore, it is helpful for a person to consider careers that attract people with similar interests and personality characteristics. Interest in a career and in the people with whom one works is often the key to motivation. This is the basis of the extensive use of interest inventories in the career planning process. The two names most often associated with such inventories are Edward K. Strong and G. Frederick Kuder.

John Holland developed six descriptive themes that are simple to explain and simple to understand. Based on the assumption that certain kinds of people tend to go into certain kinds of work, Holland's theory has withstood the test of time and has been accepted by many in the field of career and life planning.

David Tiedeman provided a model for career decision making that is based on the individual's ability to find answers within him- or herself. Tiedeman's holistic view of the individual is predicated on the belief that the individual has the power to create a career.

Donald Super's evolutionary view of career development illustrates the dynamic nature of this process. Super identified two major stages in career development: the exploratory stage and the establishment stage. Within these stages, he defined five major tasks:

1. Crystallization—considering career goals and formulating general preferences
2. Specification—investigating career options and ongoing self-examination
3. Implementation—setting out to achieve one's career goals and obtaining a job in the desired field
4. Stabilization—maintaining a position and developing competence in one's career
5. Consolidation—planning ahead for future career growth

Super's framework provides for the interrelatedness of roles—which include child, student, leisurite, citizen, spouse, homemaker, parent, and worker—and theaters—which include home, community, school, and workplace. To Super, career development is an ongoing process, involving continual change and evaluation throughout one's life.

Confirming the ever-changing nature of the adult development process is the work of Daniel Levinson, Nancy Schlossberg, Frederic Hudson, and others who have studied how adults progress through the early, middle, and late adult years. Adults change their personal goals, career goals, and values throughout their lives. It is important to deal positively with change, to reassess one's dreams, and to adjust one's goals at various points in life. This periodic assessment and the action that is taken after the assessment—whether it be to change jobs, find a new career, develop new interests, or set new priorities—is very important in maintaining a positive outlook on life and in avoiding the crises that many adults confront. Erik Erikson maintained that people go through eight developmental stages. The last stage, integrity versus despair, is particularly crucial in dealing with the life and career planning process in the later years. It is very important to integrate one's life, to adjust one's dreams, and to maintain a positive approach to the years ahead, rather than to despair over lost opportunities and life's failures.

Career and life planning is an ongoing process that is important for everyone. It does not stop at a specific age or when you enter the career of your choice. It even continues into retirement. For this reason, *Training for Life* provides chapters on dealing with change, making the most of your job, and on maintaining quality and balance in your life. There is no one right way to start the process, as long as you *do start.* You may wish to begin with Section I and work through the sections in order. However, you may want to start elsewhere in *Training for Life,* depending on where you are in the career and life planning process. Here are some suggestions:

- If you are just getting started and are considering a variety of different careers, start with Section I.
- If you need a job immediately and have an idea of what you want to do in the future, start with Section IV.
- If you have a job and feel that you cannot change jobs right now, but would like to investigate ways that you can make your job better and more rewarding, start with Section V.
- If you are actively considering one or two careers but are not sure what the future holds or what the job market really is like, start with Section III.
- If you feel that you need some kind of change in your life but are not sure just what to change, start with Section II.
- If you are pursuing your career and planning for a fulfilling lifestyle, start with Section IV.

Do not feel that you have to make big decisions right away. Start working on this book. Talk with people. Set some short-term goals. Some examples of short-term goals are:

- Learn a new skill or "brush up" on a skill that you need in your job.
- Make one or two changes in your job that may increase your job satisfaction.
- Update your résumé.
- Make a change in your lifestyle.
- Set up a few informational interviews.
- Take a course in a school or college.
- Investigate other job opportunities.
- Become involved in a community activity that interests you.
- Begin to plan for a second, third, or fourth career.
- Begin to develop a retirement plan.

Use goals like these to help you get started with your career and life planning. The tracks on the following pages represent your trip through Training for Life. Get on the train at the point along the route that is the best for you right now. As you travel, remember that you have control over the direction of your train ride through life. Be the engineer of your personal train and watch the new horizons open up for you as you direct your exciting journey.

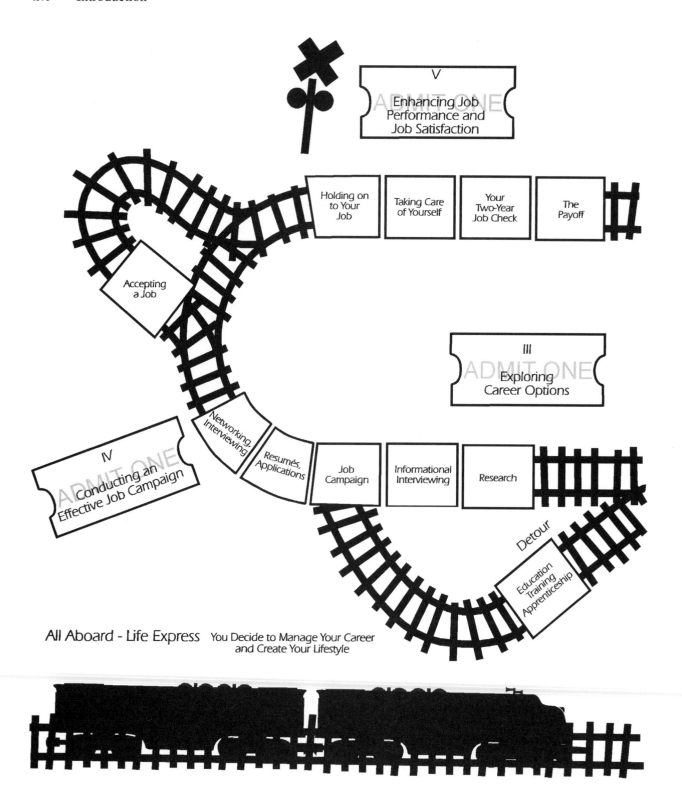

All Aboard - Life Express   You Decide to Manage Your Career and Create Your Lifestyle

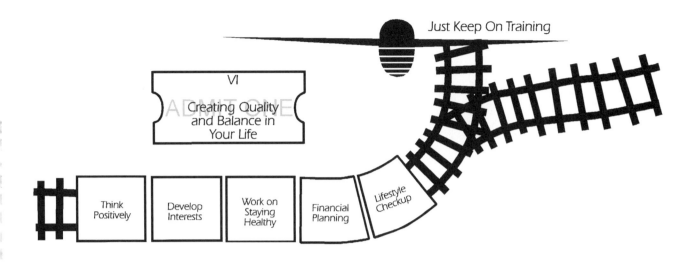

Just Keep On Training

VI
Creating Quality
and Balance in
Your Life

| Think Positively | Develop Interests | Work on Staying Healthy | Financial Planning | Lifestyle Checkup |

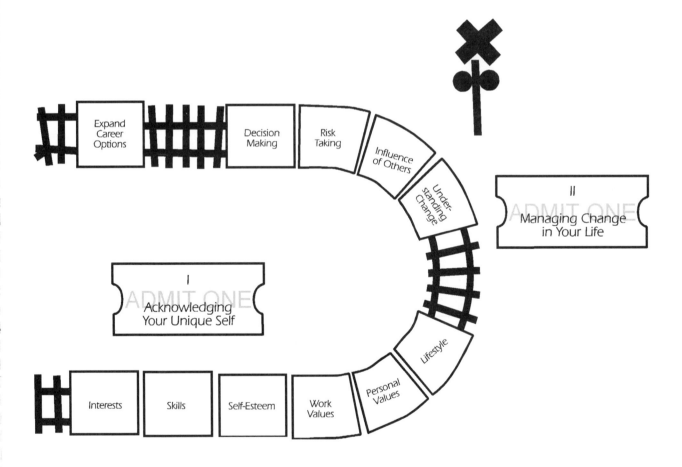

Expand Career Options | Decision Making | Risk Taking | Influence of Others | Under-standing Change

II
Managing Change
in Your Life

I
Acknowledging
Your Unique Self

| Interests | Skills | Self-Esteem | Work Values | Personal Values | Lifestyle |

SECTION ONE

Acknowledge Your Unique Self

This section will help you evaluate several factors about yourself that are important in planning your life and career. Your life is a process of maturing, developing, and growing. You have unique characteristics, needs, and goals. The lifestyle or career that is best for a friend, parent, or relative may not be best for you. It is important that *you* make decisions based on *your own* evaluation of the direction that you want to take in life. To begin this process, ask yourself the following questions:

1. What are my work values? How important are they in choosing a job or career?
2. What are my interests? How do they relate to a career I might choose?
3. What are my skills and abilities? What new skills would I like to develop?
4. What are my personal values? What effect do they have on my career and my way of life?
5. How do I feel about myself and my ability to make changes? How can I enhance my self-esteem?
6. What lifestyle considerations are important to me? How do they relate to a career I may choose?

These questions are important to consider whenever you make life and career decisions. If you are just beginning to decide what career you want, an analysis of these factors can help you to make better choices. If you are thinking about changing careers, it is important to ask yourself these questions before deciding what type of change you want. If you are thinking about starting a new career after having been a homemaker, answering these questions can help you to get started. Use the following information, checklists, and exercises to help you answer these questions. Supplement this with discussions with family, friends, and counselors. There is no one way to begin the life and career planning process. The most important thing is to *do* something—don't procrastinate. Take an inventory of your own unique needs and characteristics. It's a good way to start.

The journey to authentic power requires that you become conscious of all that you feel

Gary Zukav, Seat of the Soul

Work Values

In choosing a career or in making a career change, it is important to consider what you value most about your work. What must your work have to make it rewarding for you? Do you want to be your own boss? What kind of physical working conditions are important to you? What kind of responsibilities do you need? Do you want to work with people or work alone? Is the basic purpose of your work, such as public service, important to you? The answers to these questions and others depend on your work values. The following activities will help you to define your work values.

A. WORK VALUES ASSESSMENT

What should a job be like in order to be satisfying to you? What is important to you may not be important to someone else. Look at the following listing of work values. Use the scale to rate each value in terms of its importance to *you*. Think generally of any career or job that you would like to have and then rate each value as being very important, moderately important, somewhat important, or not important in terms of *your* job satisfaction. Place a check mark (√) in the column that best represents your choice.

Work Value	Very Important	Moderately Important	Somewhat Important	Not Important
Pleasant surroundings My own office Working with a group of people Working by myself A product I can see at the end of the day				
Creating something Regular travel Flexible work hours Being my own boss Opportunity to supervise others				
Opportunity for overtime pay Helping others to work together Running my own business No overtime Working on projects as a member of a team				
Being supervised by someone I respect Good benefits package High salary Little or no supervision Working in a large office with many colleagues				
Working independently Involvement in helping others in the community Regular work hours Working for a large organization Working in a city				
Different things to do every day A regular routine Working close to home Never having to work on weekends Never having to bring work home				

Work Value	Very Important	Moderately Important	Somewhat Important	Not Important
Work that does not interfere with my home life				
Job security				
Working with my hands				
Work that involves writing				
Low pressure on the job				
Work that I can do past age 65				
Work that involves meeting new people regularly				
Convincing others to do something or buy something				
Opportunity for advancement				
Opportunity to change from one job to another in the organization				
Liberal vacation benefits				
Supportive coworkers				
Social activities after work				
The stimulation of a high pressure work environment				
Opportunity to mentor others				
Opportunity for professional development				
Company pays for contunuing education				
Make a commitment to one organization and stick with it				
Have the skills to move from one organization to another easily				
Unions are allowed				
Working primarily outdoors				
Working primarily indoors				
Working where I can travel from place to place in my area				
Work in which I can use my physical skills				
Work where I usually sit at a desk				
Work in which I primarily use my mental skills				
Working with few immediate but potential long-term results				
Work in which I can take a project and follow it through over time				
Work that I can complete at the end of the day				
Public service work				
Work in education				

Work Value	Very Important	Moderately Important	Somewhat Important	Not Important
Work in business Plenty of windows Other:				

Now look back at your assessment of work values and particularly at those you checked as being very important. List them in the spaces below.

1. _____   8. _____

2. _____   9. _____

3. _____   10. _____

4. _____   11. _____

5. _____   12. _____

6. _____   13. _____

7. _____   14. _____

Look at the above list. Put a check mark (√) next to those work values that you feel are *most* important for your career and job satisfaction. Check at least five (more if you wish). What careers are likely to fulfill your most important work values? Write them in the following spaces.

Possible careers to fulfill my most important work values:

1. _____

2. _____

3. _____

4. _____

5. _____

B. YOUR IDEAL (AND NOT SO IDEAL) JOB

Think of your ideal workday. Don't think of a specific job as much as the kinds of activities in which you would be involved, the kind of place where you would work, the type of people with whom you would work, what your supervisor (if any) would be like, how you would spend your time, your hours, and the skills you would use. In the following spaces list as many factors as you can that would make up your ideal workday.

1. My ideal work environment would be: _____

   _____

2. The type of responsibilities I would enjoy are: _____

   _____

3. The type of people with whom I would like to work are: _____

   _____

4. The structure of my ideal workday would be: _____

   _____

5. The skills I would most like to use are: _____

   _____

6. Other aspects of my ideal workday are: _____

   _____

Now think of a workday that you absolutely would *not* want. What skills, activities, people, and situations would you want to *avoid*? Write as many of these as you can in the following spaces.

1. Places that I would not want to work are: _____

   _____

2. Types of work I would dislike are: _____

   _____

3. Types of people I want to avoid are: _____

   _____

4. The type of workday I would dislike is: _____

   _____

5. Skills I don't want to use are: _____

   _____

6. Other things I want to avoid are: _____

   _____

Describe the *type* of organization that you would like to work for. What characteristics and what purpose would the organization have? How would it be managed? List your responses in the following spaces.

1. Size and structure of the organization _____

_____

2. Purpose of the organization _____

_____

3. Management style of the organization _____

_____

4. Other characteristics I want _____

_____

Think of an organization that you would *not* want to work for. What would be some of the characteristics of this organization? List them in the following spaces.

1. Types of organizations I want to avoid _____

_____

2. Purposes I don't agree with _____

_____

3. Management styles I don't want _____

_____

4. Other characteristics I want to avoid _____

_____

Now look back at your responses to the four previous questions. What conclusions can you draw from your responses? What careers might provide you with your ideal workday? What careers should you avoid? What organizations appeal to you and what organizations turn you off? Write your conclusions in the following spaces.

_____

_____

_____

_____

C. How Important Is Your Work?

For many people, work defines much of their basic identity. Everyone works, whether for pay, volunteer, or at home, and for a variety of reasons. Whether work is the most important force in a person's life or just a part of a person's existence, it does play a major role in the lifestyle of most people. Abraham Maslow, a social psychologist, viewed the human personality in light of motivation. His hierarchy depicts individual needs. Maslow assumed that human nature is good rather than bad and that we move in the direction of growth by fulfillment of our needs. Balancing our needs promotes health and encourages spontaneity, freedom, and creativity. Maslow asserted that if we deny or suppress our needs, we become ill. Creative self-expression is an integral part of the personality and the need to express oneself becomes a force in the personality, which continues to encourage-growth and risk-taking. The importance of self-actualization can be seen in Maslow's hierarchy of needs,* which follows.

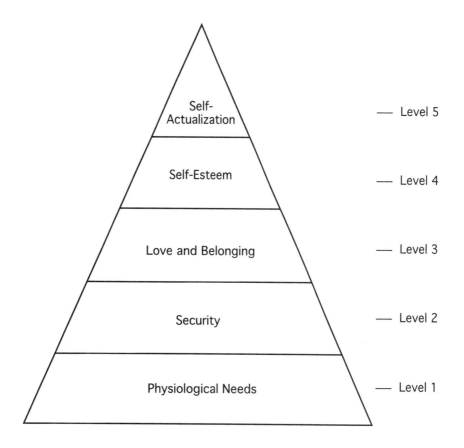

*Maslow, Abraham. *Motivation and Personality*. 2nd ed. New York: Harper and Row, 1970, pp. 35–47.

Most people work to achieve the basic needs in levels one and two. A person must have these needs fulfilled in order to work on achieving the needs at the higher levels. If a person has a sufficient income, physiological and security needs can be satisfied. A person's work enables her or him to associate with other people and to maintain a family, thus contributing to the fulfillment of the needs in level three.

As a person begins to fulfill needs in level four, self-esteem, work takes on even more importance. No longer does work simply provide an income and interpersonal associations. For a person to achieve self-esteem, it is important to develop a sense of confidence, mastery, and achievement in one's life. One gains the respect and appreciation of others for one's accomplishments, and a certain measure of status is achieved. For many people, the primary source of the development and achievement of self-esteem is their work.

If the needs in levels one through four have been substantially fulfilled, a person begins to satisfy the need for self-actualization. This is a difficult need to define, because it varies from person to person and deals with a person's concept of having purpose, or mission, in life. In order to become self-actualized, one must work toward realizing one's potential. Many people begin to reach toward fulfillment of their potential through their work. This need is illustrated by the many thousands of independently wealthy persons who work very hard and are very involved in their work, even though they do not have to work for financial reasons.

Work is a driving force for many people and a source of fulfillment of many individual needs. The importance of work can be demonstrated by surveys that indicate that most retired persons would still prefer to be involved in some form of work. How important is work to you? Keep in mind that it is essential to develop a comprehensive lifestyle in which you gain fulfillment of your needs through a combination of your relationships, activities, and interests. Try to avoid tying too much of your identity and purpose to your work by maintaining a balanced lifestyle. Remember, however, that work plays an important role in your development of self-esteem and in your progress toward self-actualization.

What If You Didn't Have to Work?

Imagine that you are independently wealthy. You have an after-tax income of $200,000 a year from funds that were left to you by a benefactor. Would you work? If so, what kind of work would you do? If you would not work, how would you spend your time? Write your responses in the following spaces.

_____

_____

_____

_____

_____

Now assume that you don't have an after-tax income of $200,000 a year. What could you do to achieve some of the same things that you said you would do if you had that income? What is stopping you from doing them? Write your responses in the following spaces.

_____

_____

_____

_____

_____

Think back to the times in your life when you felt most satisfied and fulfilled. Have you ever felt that you were achieving a sense of self-actualization? When was it? What were you doing and what skills and abilities were you using? Write your responses in the following spaces.

_____

_____

_____

_____

_____

SUMMARY—WORK VALUES

A knowledge of your work values is essential as you plan your life and career. Your work takes up a great deal of the time in your life. What you value about your work may be quite different from what another person values. Analyze your work values before you make career decisions. Look back at your work values inventory and at your responses to the questions on work values. What are your most important work values? What conclusions can you make about the kind of workday you want and about the kind of organization with which you want to work?

Interests

An analysis of your interests can give you insight into careers and lifestyles that can be satisfying and fulfilling. If you can enter a career that is related to your interests, your chances of being successful in and enjoying that career are enhanced. Your interests can also be the key to developing a fulfilling lifestyle. It is unreasonable to expect that most of your interests will be fulfilled by a career. Always try to develop interests outside of work to give yourself a varied and enriched lifestyle. It is therefore important to:

- Identify your interests.
- Evaluate which interests are most important to you.
- Determine how your interests may relate to a career.
- Determine how other interests can be fulfilled outside of your career.

The second step in your career and life planning is to assess your interests and determine how they relate to your career and life plans. The following exercises will help you to evaluate your interests.

A. HOW DO YOU LIKE TO SPEND YOUR TIME?

In the chart below, list fifteen ways you like to spend your time. Think of those things that you enjoy doing, things that you would choose to do if you did not have other demands on your time and things that interest you most. Try to fill in all of the spaces.

Ways You Like to Spend Your Time	Have I done this in the past month?
1.	
2.	
3.	
4.	
5.	
6.	
7.	
8.	
9.	
10.	
11.	
12.	
13.	
14.	
15.	
Others	

Consider your list. Are there ways that you like to spend your time that you could turn into possible careers? Do you know of other people who have turned their interests into careers? History books are filled with stories of courageous individuals who listened to the call of their interests and pursued creative, nontraditional, and sometimes risky career alternatives.

You may wish to keep many interests that you listed as part of your avocation, rather than trying to make a living through them. Turning golf, needlepoint, cooking, or weightlifting into career options may alter their value to you. Your interests nourish and fulfill you and add balance and meaning to your life. You are more than the functions that you fulfill at your work. Your interests expand and broaden you as an individual by providing clearer definition to your life. However, one of the best approaches to selecting a satisfying career is to take something that you already do for enjoyment and turn it into your work. Are there any careers that might relate to the ways you like to spend your time? Write a few alternatives in the following spaces.

1. _____   5. _____

2. _____   6. _____

3. _____   7. _____

4. _____   8. _____

Look at your list again. There are probably many ways you like to spend your time that could not be turned into careers, but are still very important for a fulfilling lifestyle. In the following spaces, list those ways you like to spend your time that you really want to make time for in your life.

1. _____   5. _____

2. _____   6. _____

3. _____   7. _____

4. _____   8. _____

In what ways can you structure your lifestyle to make sure that you will have the time, money, and opportunity to pursue these interests?

1. _____

2. _____

3. _____

4. _____

Look at your list again. In the column on the right, make a check mark (√) after each activity that you have done in the past month.

How many activities did you check? If you did not check many, how can you change your lifestyle *right now* so that you can do more of the things that interest you most? List below some specific changes that you can make *now* so that you can have more time for the things you like to do.

1. _____

2. _____

3. _____

4. _____

For many adults, time seems to be a barrier to fulfilling interests. Remember that the less time that you have, the more important it is for you to make time for your interests. Ignoring your interests over long periods of time can be unhealthy for you and for those who are significant in your life. Attention to your interests leads to self-satisfaction, self-enhancement, and self-empowerment. If you take care of your needs through nurturing your interests, you may well have more to offer your career, your family, your friends, and life in general. Pursuing your interests adds to the energy in your life.

B. DEVELOP A PLAN TO PURSUE YOUR INTERESTS

Once more, look back at your list of ways you like to spend your time. What are five of your most important interests, the things that interest you most and that you definitely want to include as a part of your life either at work or away from work? List them in the following spaces.

1. _____

2. _____

3. _____

4. _____

5. _____

Now try to think of at least four possible ways that you can pursue each of these interests. For example, if you have a major interest in music, you could pursue this interest by being a musician, by working in a music store, by working in administration for a musical organization, by listening to music, by singing in a chorus, by playing in a band on weekends, by attending concerts, by reading about music, by being a music critic, by teaching music, and many others. Creatively expand the possible ways that you might fulfill your major interests.

Interest number one _____

Ways to fulfill this interest.

1. _____

2. _____

3. _____

4. _____

Interest number two _____

Ways to fulfill this interest.

1. _____

2. _____

3. _____

4. _____

Interest number three _____

Ways to fulfill this interest.

1. _____

2. _____

3. _____

4. _____

Interest number four _____

Ways to fulfill this interest.

1. _____

2. _____

3. _____

4. _____

Interest number five _____

Ways to fulfill this interest.

1. _____

2. _____

3. _____

4. _____

C. OCCUPATIONAL ENVIRONMENTS

Do certain types of people go into certain kinds of work? If they do, where would you fit in? It can be helpful to look at your interests and preferences and then compare them with the interests of people in various kinds of work. Some research has shown that your chances of success and happiness in a career are improved if you share similar interests and preferences with others in that career. According to John

Holland,* the world of work can be divided into six categories. People with certain personality characteristics do tend to go into certain types of work. These categories can be called *occupational environments*.

Holland's theory is one of the most widely accepted approaches to understanding career choice. Research has generally supported Holland's basic contention that personality type and occupational choice are related. Holland's theory forms the basis for a categorization of occupations and for a meaningful way to look at the world of work.

The four assumptions of Holland's theory are:

1. Individuals are categorized by strengths and interests into six occupational types.
2. There are six model environments in which unique opportunities exist.
3. Individuals match environments with their unique skills and interests in order to deal with the opportunities that motivate them.
4. Behavior is determined through the interaction of an individual's personality in combination with the unique environment.

Holland encourages individuals to use this structure as a basis for greater in-depth research. It is a beginning, rather than a completion of the information-gathering stage of career exploration. It is very helpful to consider Holland's six occupational themes as you expand and then narrow possible career options. Holland's occupational environments are as follows.

Realistic

People in this category tend to be interested in mechanical things and to have mechanical abilities. Many like to work with objects, tools, and machines. Many tend to be athletic and are interested in activities where they can use their physical abilities. They tend to enjoy working with their hands. They are very practical in their outlook on life and often enjoy working outdoors. They prefer an active life rather than a sedentary lifestyle.

Some examples of jobs in this category are construction worker, carpenter, mechanic, skilled trades, police officer, dental technician, forester, farmer, military officer, and air traffic controller.

Investigative

People in this category are interested in observing and analyzing situations before they act. They like to investigate situations and solve problems. They are very interested in learning and are likely to continue

---

*Holland, John L. *Making Vocational Choices: A Theory of Careers.* Englewood Cliffs, New Jersey: Prentice-Hall, Inc., 1973, pp. 27–36.

their education. They like to evaluate possibilities and are task oriented. They tend to enjoy dealing with abstract problems and have a need to understand how things work and why things are the way they are. They like to design equipment and develop solutions to problems.

Some examples of jobs in this category are engineer, chemist, computer programmer, biologist, economist, social scientist, physician, research worker, physicist, systems analyst, meteorologist, mathematician, dental hygienist, tool designer, optometrist, and x-ray technician.

Artistic

People in this category like to use their imagination in dealing with situations and tend to be quite independent. They prefer an unstructured environment where they can create and use their artistic abilities. They like to innovate. They express themselves in artistic ways and could often be described as being unconventional. They are independent and need room to express themselves and their creativity.

Some examples of jobs in this category are singer, actor, fashion model, actress, musician, interior decorator, reporter, artist, public relations person, author, advertising manager, composer, technical writer, photographer, and music teacher.

Social

People in this category like to work with other people in a helpful and supportive way. They like to inform, teach, enlighten, and train others. They like to help others solve problems and develop their potential. They tend to be concerned with the welfare of others and are very humanistic in their approach to dealing with others. They are often skilled with words and like to be with other people. They tend to be quite sociable and feel responsible for helping others who need assistance.

Some examples of jobs in this category are clinical psychologist, waiter or waitress, minister, teacher, marriage counselor, speech therapist, nurse, personnel director, dietitian, child care director, social worker, bartender, and ticket agent.

Enterprising

People in this category are energetic and like to assume leadership roles. They enjoy being in charge of other people, and persuading others to do something or to buy something. They often work hard to achieve power and status, and financial gain is an important goal. They enjoy material wealth and will work hard to achieve it. They like to manage and influence other people. They tend to be goal directed and welcome the opportunity to advance in an organization or in their own enterprises.

Some examples of jobs in this category are realtor, lawyer, buyer, farm manager, business executive, salesperson, marketing director, bank manager, recruiter, sales manager, insurance investigator, and florist.

Conventional

People in this category like well-ordered activities, and usually enjoy office work. They like to know what is expected of them and appreciate a system in which there are well-defined tasks. They tend to like to work with data and to use numerical and clerical skills. They are interested in following things through in detail and they also like to follow the instructions of others.

Some examples of jobs in this category are bank examiner, bookkeeper, court reporter, computer operator, credit manager, secretary, accountant, and telephone operator.

Where Do You Fit In?

Now look back over the six occupational environments. In which environment would you feel most comfortable? Does one stand out as your clear choice or is it difficult to choose? In the following spaces, write three choices, in order, of the occupational environments in which you would feel most comfortable.

First choice _____

Second choice _____

Third choice _____

Many career resource centers are organized using these six occupational environments. For example, you can go to a resource center and investigate all of the possible careers in the realistic category. It is also interesting to combine categories, since most careers involve a variety of interests and skills. For example, some engineering careers involve both realistic and investigative interests. Some social service careers involve both social and enterprising interests. Use these occupational environments to expand your investigation of possible careers. In the following spaces, write as many careers as you can that would fit into the occupational environments that you chose.

1. _____   6. _____

2. _____   7. _____

3. _____   8. _____

4. _____   9. _____

5. _____   10. _____

D. INVENTORIES AND INTERACTIVE CAREER EXPLORATION PROGRAMS

You may also wish to further explore your interests by taking one or more interest inventories. These will not necessarily tell you what you do well, but they will help you to categorize your interests and to compare them with those of people who are working in various careers. Some of the more widely available interest inventories are described here.

The Strong Vocational Interest Blank

First developed in 1927, the *Strong Vocational Interest Blank* is the most widely used interest inventory today, having received several major updates over the years. Considerable research supports the relationship between a high score on one of the *Strong's* occupational scales and satisfaction in that occupation. The individual who completes the *Strong* is able to compare interests to the interests of people who are happy and successful in specific occupations. In this way, the individual is able to determine trends in the type of occupations that correspond with interests.

The Self-Directed Search

This inventory was developed by John Holland to determine which of Holland's six occupational categories a person prefers. The responses on activities, competencies, occupations, and self-estimates provide a rank order of choices for three of the six categories. The *Self-Directed Search* is self-scored and is complemented by the *Occupations Finder*, a reference booklet of hundreds of occupations that are organized according to Holland's six categories.

The Campbell Interest and Skill Survey

Designed by David Campbell, the CISS is a relatively new assessment that provides an integrated view of your interests and skills. It measures your degree of attraction to seven broad occupational areas and estimates your confidence level in your ability to perform in the same occupational areas. The two scales offer a balanced and comprehensive assessment of interests. The CISS is particularly helpful for adult students.

Kuder Occupational Interest Survey

The *Kuder Occupational Interest Survey,* first published in 1966, shows the relationship between a person's interest profile and those of people in various college majors and occupational groups. Its approach of comparing people on the basis of interests is similar to that of the *Strong*.

Myers-Briggs Type Indicator

This assessment, developed in the 1960s, is based on the assumption that individuals have specific preferences in their personality that determine the way they deal with personal relationships, with information, with work environments, with problem solving, with decision making, and with many other aspects of life. The Myers-Briggs Type Indicator is designed to evaluate preferences in four different areas, from which a type is derived. The four areas are preferences for introversion and extroversion, sensing and intuition, thinking and feeling, and judging and perceiving.

Interactive Career Choice Programs

Advances in information technology have resulted in the development of a variety of computerized and self-instructional programs that provide help in career decision making. Some programs are highly interactive and help the user to assess interests, values, skills, and other factors before obtaining career information. Others primarily offer an efficient method of obtaining educational and career information. The more popular programs are SIGI, DISCOVER, and CHOICES. Many states have special programs, established through Vocational Information and Occupational Coordinating Committees (VOICC), that distribute information about employment projections and salaries within the individual states. New resources for career planning are available through the Internet, World Wide Web, and other on-line sources. See chapters Fourteen and Twenty for information.

Some of the inventories and programs mentioned should be used with the assistance of a professional career counselor. Consider your objectives, your current progress in career decision making, and the career and life planning options available before you decide to take any of these inventories. Share your career process with a career counselor. Together you can decide which, if any, of these inventories are appropriate for your needs. The results of your assessment can be interpreted by your counselor.

If you would like to locate a certified career counselor, a listing has been developed by the National Board for Certified Counselors. You can obtain the listing of certified career counselors in your state, a consumer guide to counseling, and a brochure describing client rights and responsibilities by contacting:

National Board for Certified Counselors
3 Terrace Way, Suite D
Greensboro, North Carolina 27403-3660
Tel. 336-547-0607
FAX 336-547-0017
E-Mail: NBCC@NBCC.ORG
Web Site: http://www.nbcc.org

The following are some suggestions for places to obtain these inventories, computerized guidance programs, and related counseling assistance. Call to check the type of services, cost, eligibility, location, and hours of operation.

- Community colleges
- Libraries
- Career counselors
- Four-year colleges and universities
- Human resource development departments in companies
- High schools
- Adult education programs
- Women's centers
- Private counseling centers
- State employment commissions
- County agencies
- Local chamber of commerce
- Career resource centers

Inventories and career guidance packages will not provide you with quick and easy answers to your career and life questions. As always, those answers lie within you. However, these inventories and interactive career exploration programs can be valuable tools that you can use in the career and life planning process.

SUMMARY—INTERESTS

Your interests hold the key to a rewarding and satisfying life. Any career that is based on your interests may be very rewarding for you. A variety of interests is needed to maintain a well-rounded lifestyle. This becomes particularly important in your later years when work may take on a less important place in your life. Pursue your interests on and off the job, and *develop new interests as you go through life*. It is never too late to develop interests. The time to start is now!

Skills and Abilities

The next step in planning your life and career is to assess your skills and abilities. You normally enjoy doing the things that you do well. It builds your self-confidence and adds to your self-esteem. Everyone has a variety of skills and abilities, and you are no exception. A skill is an expertise that you develop through practice and study. An ability is a special talent that you possess. Your skills are probably easy to list, because you have spent time, energy, and perhaps money in developing them. Some examples might be typing, tennis, writing, or skiing. Abilities are often more difficult to list because most people tend to underestimate their importance. Not everyone can deal with numbers, people, or machines in the exact ways that you can deal with them.

When assessing your skills and abilities, avoid these common pitfalls:

- Don't undervalue your own unique set of skills and abilities. Take a positive approach toward assessing what you can do.
- Don't limit yourself to only your major skills. You may overlook many small but important skills that you use every day.
- Don't dwell on your weaknesses. Too much emphasis on weaknesses or on skills that you do not have can turn into excuses for not doing something with your career or life. Remember that you are paid in a job for what you *can* do, not for what you *cannot* do.

In our society, it has traditionally been more acceptable to acknowledge negative qualities rather than to emphasize positive characteristics. However, it is important for you to know what you are good at and to be able to talk about your strengths to others. Your skills and abilities help you to achieve your goals. They are the key to:

- **Knowing yourself better**
- **Making positive career decisions**
- **Conducting a successful job campaign**

Discover what skills and abilities you possess. Be able to acknowledge them and to articulate them to colleagues and friends. Finally, expand your skills and abilities by developing them to the best of your potential. Richard Bolles organizes skills in three distinct categories.*

- **Self-management skills**
- **Functional skills**
- **Work content skills**

The following exercises will help you identify and understand your unique combination of skills and abilities. You will first analyze some of your past successes and then identify the self-management skills, functional skills, and work content skills that you possess and those skills that you would like to develop.

A. ANALYSIS OF SUCCESSES

Before you categorize your own unique set of skills and abilities, think back over your life and identify at least three successes that you have enjoyed. They can be great or small. The only requirement is that they gave you a measure of satisfaction with yourself. Your successes can be drawn from any area of your life. Take some extra time to review

---

*Bolles, Richard N. *The Three Boxes of Life,* Berkeley, California: Ten Speed Press, 1981, p. 142.

some of the highlights from your most recent past. If you have more than three successes, choose the ones that gave you the most satisfaction. If you are having difficulty thinking of more than one or two successes, look over your personal calendar and take note of the special events you have experienced. That may jog your memory about successes that have given you satisfaction.

As an example, look at Ruth J.'s successes from the past two years. They may give you some ideas about your own recent successes.

Ruth J.'s Successes

Number 1 Success
    With little advance notice and little preparation, substituted for son's soccer coach. The team won the game.
 	
Number 2 Success
    Earned 15 college credits at Capital Communty College, which helped me get a promotion to assistant manager of my division.
 	
Number 3 Success
    Trained my dog, P.J., to become an effective watch and house dog.

Now write three of your successes in the spaces below.

My Successes
Number 1 Success _____ _____ _____ Number 2 Success _____ _____ _____ Number 3 Success _____ _____ _____

You have chosen these three for a reason. Now you will analyze and identify what it was in these successes that helped you feel good about yourself. By exploring your successes you will uncover some interesting information about yourself, and that is what this exercise is all about. First, let's take Ruth's number one success and analyze it. Then, analyze your own successes.

Ruth J.'s Analysis

Number 1 Success
With little advance notice and little preparation, substituted for son's soccer coach. The team won the game.

a.   What motivated you to do this?

Challenge of doing something new, help the coach, help the team

b.   What abilities or skills did it take for you to accomplish this?

Organization, fast thinking, encouragement of others, enthusiasm conveyed to the team, work with team parents

c.   Who is responsible for this success?

Fourteen little boys, the coach, and me

d.   Did you accomplish this alone or with others? Who?

With others—the team members

e.   What were the circumstances surrounding this success?

Outside, soccer field filled with cheering parents and children

f.   What was the payoff (reward) for this success?

Working with eager eight-year-old boys, had the opportunity to contribute to their first win of the season, helped the coach

g.   How did you feel about this success?

Scared at first when I agreed to coach but thrilled with the results. My risk paid off!

Now that you see how this analysis is done, think about your own successes by answering the same questions.

My Analysis of Success #1

I succeeded in:

_____

_____

a. What motivated me was:

_____

_____

b. I used the following skills or abilities in this success:

_____

_____

c. Who was responsible for this success?

_____

_____

d. Did I accomplish this alone or with others? Who?

_____

_____

e. What were the external circumstances surrounding this success?

_____

_____

f. What was my payoff or reward for this success?

_____

_____

g. How did I feel about this success?

_____

_____

My Analysis of Success #2

I succeeded in:

_____

_____

a. What motivated me was:

_____

_____

b. I used the following skills or abilities in this success:

_____

_____

c. Who was responsible for this success?

_____

_____

d. Did I accomplish this alone or with others? Who?

_____

_____

e. What were the external circumstances surrounding this success?

_____

_____

f. What was my payoff or reward for this success?

_____

_____

g. How did I feel about this success?

_____

_____

My Analysis of Success #3

I succeeded in:

_____

_____

a. What motivated me was:

_____

_____

b. I used the following skills or abilities in this success:

_____

_____

c. Who was responsible for this success?

_____

_____

d. Did I accomplish this alone or with others? Who?

_____

_____

e. What were the external circumstances surrounding this success?

_____

_____

f. What was my payoff or reward for this success?

_____

_____

g. How did I feel about this success?

_____

_____

Evaluation of Your Analysis of Your Successes

You can now evaluate your three successes by looking for a pattern in your three sets of answers. Is there a common thread that links your successes? For example, in answer to your first question, are you motivated to help others, overcome great odds, or take risks? Are there similar skills and abilities that keep appearing in each of your highlights? Do you continually attribute your successes to someone else? Are you achieving your significant events alone, as part of a team, or as a leader? Are there certain circumstances that encourage you to succeed such as stress, pressure, competition, projects, or structure? What are your intrinsic or extrinsic payoffs for your success? Consider your own special needs, and look for patterns. These may be significant as you shape your career and life goals.

a.   What motivates me?

_____

_____

b.   What skills and abilities do I like to use?

_____

_____

c.   Responsibility for my success lies with:

_____

_____

d.   I have accomplished my successes with the help of:

_____

_____

e.   Circumstances that motivate me are:

_____

_____

f.   The payoffs or rewards I want are:

_____

_____

g.   My successes make me feel:

_____

_____

B. SELF-MANAGEMENT SKILLS

How do you relate to other people? Are you punctual? Are you organized? How do you perform under stress? Are you enthusiastic? These are all self-management skills. One might call these personality or character traits, because they are a basic part of your nature. However, they actually are skills that are specific to you and do not depend on any particular job or career. They can be enhanced, developed, and controlled, if you wish to do so. For example, you can learn to be more punctual if it is important to you. You can learn to be more organized. You can work to improve your performance in stressful situations.

It is important to consider your self-management skills when planning a career or job change. Try to match your career or job to your skills or to those skills that you plan to develop. If you are a very enthusiastic person, try to find a job in a setting where your enthusiasm will be an asset. If you are attentive to detail, this can be an asset in many job settings. On the other hand, if you know that you do not have a certain self-management skill and do not intend to develop it, try not to choose a job that requires the skill. If you have difficulty getting going in the morning and being punctual, and do not wish to change, avoid taking a job that requires you to show up at 7:30 A.M. sharp. If you have difficulty concentrating, try not to choose a job that requires you to concentrate amid many distractions.

In some cases, a self-management skill that is a disadvantage in one job may be an asset in a different job. For example, flexibility may be detrimental in certain jobs requiring strict accounting practices such as auditing, but flexibility can be a positive skill when working with a community recreation program. If you are adventuresome, you could be an asset to an organization that needs people who are willing to take risks and try something new, but you may feel stifled and out of place in a highly structured organization. If you can identify a career that complements your self-management skills, your chances for happiness and success in the career are enhanced.

As you consider the following exercise, include all of your experience in your past and present work, education, home, volunteer, and other activities. You do not need a certificate or a degree hanging on your wall before you acknowledge that you possess certain skills. The following is a listing of some self-management skills. Go through the list and circle those skills that you possess.

Self-Management Skills

dignified	strong	resourceful	organized
inventive	warm	unexcitable	sensitive
prudent	accurate	attractive	serious
tenacious	aggressive	cooperative	original
progressive	deliberate	broadminded	conservative
teachable	efficient	cool	sincere
discreet	logical	considerate	calm
kind	realistic	flexible	capable
purposeful	trusting	charitable	careful
thorough	independent	positive	conscientious
intellectual	pleasant	enjoyable	cautious
precise	versatile	spontaneous	charming
tactful	alert	moderate	confident
dominant	daring	responsible	successful
quick	loyal	honest	secure
thoughtful	reflective	painstaking	cheerful
informal	trustworthy	sociable	clear-thinking
practical	imaginative	forceful	competitive
strong-minded	persevering	modest	competent
wise	stable	intuitive	clever
academic	ambitious	helpful	introspective
adventurous	curious	outgoing	analytical
adaptable	courageous	sincere	forgiving
determined	energetic	formal	loving
eager	mature	natural	supportive
light-hearted	relaxed	healthy	consistent
quiet	unaffected	original	reflective
tolerant	patient	frank	assertive
industrious	spontaneous	obliging	motivated
polite	fair-minded	self-confident	extroverted
hopeful	methodical	friendly	organized
wholesome	reliable	open-minded	caring
active	unassuming	self-controlled	goal-oriented
affectionate	unaffected	generous	genuine
easygoing	far-sighted	opportunistic	empathetic
likable	meticulous	sensible	creative
rational	reserved	gentle	theoretical
tough	understanding	good-natured	serene
individualistic	firm	optimistic	enthusiastic
poised			

Now look at your list and at those skills that you circled. In the following spaces, write at least five (and as many as ten) of your top self-management skills that you would like to use in a career.

1. _____   6. _____

2. _____   7. _____

3. _____   8. _____

4. _____   9. _____

5. _____   10. _____

Now list at least five (and as many as ten) self-management skills that you would like to develop.

1. _____   6. _____

2. _____   7. _____

3. _____   8. _____

4. _____   9. _____

5. _____   10. _____

C. FUNCTIONAL SKILLS

Functional skills cover the basic tangibles of work. They can be broken down into three basic areas: data, people, and things. These skills involve doing something to something, acting on something, or doing something with someone. They can be thought of as action verbs such as computing, teaching, or operating. These skills are generally transferable from one job to another. Once you have learned a functional skill, you take it with you and can apply it in a different setting. For example, if you are good at analyzing data in one job, you will probably be good at analyzing data in another job.

The following diagram illustrates the three general categories of functional skills. Note that the more elementary skills are at the bottom and increase in complexity toward the top. Each skill usually involves all of those below it. For example, if you want to be involved with people, you can do it at a relatively basic level (helping, serving) or at a much higher level (mentoring, negotiating).*

---

*Adapted from Fine, Sidney. *Dictionary of Occupational Titles.* 4th edition. Washington, D.C.: U.S. Dept. of Labor Employment and Training Administration, 1977, revised 1991, p. 1005.

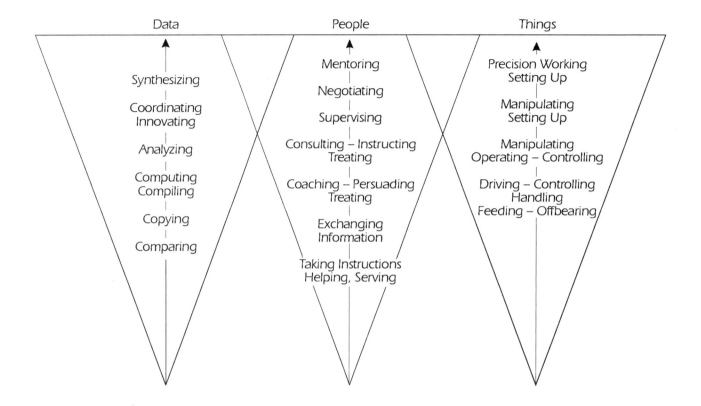

Data — Synthesizing, Coordinating, Innovating, Analyzing, Computing, Compiling, Copying, Comparing

People — Mentoring, Negotiating, Supervising, Consulting – Instructing, Treating, Coaching – Persuading, Treating, Exchanging Information, Taking Instructions, Helping, Serving

Things — Precision Working, Setting Up, Manipulating, Setting Up, Manipulating, Operating – Controlling, Driving – Controlling, Handling, Feeding – Offbearing

• • • • • • • • • •

Remember that certification is not necessary. Acknowledge your strengths with confidence! Be generous to yourself.

• • • • • • • • • •

Functional skills and abilities are the foundation of the expertise that you sell to an employer through your résumé and in a job interview. Identifying and building on your skills and abilities is a very powerful career and life planning strategy. Your task is to recognize and develop your gifts and get paid in a career to develop them even more.

How do you know what you are good at? Think about what skills you have used and enjoyed using the most in any area of your life. How did you feel in using your skills? Did you continue to develop those skills? Are you using your top skills now? Incorporating and building on your existing skills is a lifelong task that is very empowering.

How do you develop skills? Your first job is to recognize that you have skills and abilities without fear of appearing boastful or conceited. You have a right to acknowledge your strengths. Who are people that you have observed in your life that have developed their gifts? What qualities did they possess? Did you admire them for using their gifts?

It is time for you to identify your functional skills. Include skills acquired from your work, education, avocation, volunteer activities, and all other segments of your life in this list. The comprehensive list on the next two pages is just a start. You may have other strengths that you would like to add. Circle the skills that you possess. Check (√) those skills that you would be interested in building for your career and life purposes. Check only those that you would be willing to spend time developing. Enjoy this part of your trip.

Establishing effective priorities
Designing events/publications/structures
Information processing
Record keeping
Recruiting talent
Arbitrating/mediating
Showmanship
Public speaking
Motivating others
Lecturing
Musical talent
Athletic ability
Developing rapport
Motor/physical coordination and agility
High tolerance for repetition
Inspiring trust
Implementing decisions
Leadership
Working well under stress
Risk taking
Policy making
Chairing meetings
Directing creative talent
Project designing/programming
Organizing people
Filing
Fundraising
Developing ideas/programs
Performing
Adept at precision work
Rapid manipulation of numbers
Financial planning and management
Culinary talent
Developing a budget
Making and using contacts effectively
Keen memory for detail
Administering budget
Poise in public appearances
Classifying and organizing data
Following detailed instructions
Sophisticated mathematical abilities
Decision making
Applying what others have done
Adept at conflict management
Ability to handle variety of tasks
  simultaneously and efficiently
Ability to move into totally new situation on
  one's own

Foreign language skills
Arranging social events
Helping and serving others
Summarizing
Scientific investigating
Rapport building
Promoting, planning, and implementing
  change
Briefing
Delegating responsibility
Data processing
Creating visual displays
Adept at confronting others with touchy
  personal matters
Organizing data
Prioritizing tasks
Constructing
Influencing/persuading
Debating
Crisis intervention
Selling
Retrieving data
Interviewing
Landscaping
Traveling
Follow-through
Systematic goal setting
Standard setting
Policy interpreting
Team building
Analyzing quantitative data
Coordinating operations/details and
  administrative tasks
Composing
Inventing
Proofreading
Researching data
Synthesizing data
Problem solving
Public relations
Informing
Sensitivity to others
Coaching
Detective skills
Working with abstract concepts
Mentoring
Scheduling
Troubleshooting

Researching
Supervising
Financial investment planning and decision
   making
Driving
Adapting to new environments
Editing
Translating
Scientific writing
Technical reading and interpreting
Hostessing
Innovating
Visualizing concepts
Speech writing
Recognizing and using skills of others
Conveying enthusiasm
Information gathering
Imaginative publicizing
Abstracting information
Negotiating
Business correspondence
Interior decorating
Managing people/programs
Advising
Writing, creative/concise/humorous/organized
Interpersonal relations
Nursing
Diplomacy
Listening
Telephoning
Accounting
Liaison skills
Conveying understanding/patience/firmness
Reading
Enlightening others
Communicating, oral/visual/written

Thinking quickly
Facilitating personal growth
Empowering others
Counseling
Explaining concepts
Forecasting
Diagnosing
Perceiving needs of others
Entreprenurial
Illustrating
Directing
Observing
Perceiving and defining cause-and-effect
   relationships
Testing
Critiquing
Listening intently and accurately
Understanding legal concepts
Communicating warmth
Teaching
Laboratory skills
Clarifying goals of others
Group facilitating
Organizing programs/conferences
Photographing
Drawing
Investigating
Executing/following through
Mobilizing resources
Clerical skills
Articulating
Problem identifying
Achieving substantial results with limited
   funds
Technical mediating
Others:

Count those skills you have checked _____.

Count those skills you have circled _____.

Of all the functional skills that I possess
   the following are my best.

These are functional skills that I would like
   to develop.

1. _____

1. _____

2. _____

2. _____

3. _____

3. _____

4. _____   4. _____

5. _____   5. _____

6. _____   6. _____

7. _____   7. _____

8. _____   8. _____

9. _____   9. _____

10. _____   10. _____

Self-Evaluation of Skills and Abilities

Instructions: Look through these categories on the following pages and evaluate yourself on each according to this scale.

1 = no ability here at all
2 = enough ability but need help from others
3 = some ability
4 = definite strong ability

Remember that certification by others is not necessary. Acknowledge your strengths with confidence! Be generous to yourself.

A. Communication Skills and Abilities

Writing
_____ informing
_____ editing
_____ translating
_____ researching
_____ formatting
_____ typing
_____ reading
_____ technical writing
_____ foreign languages
_____ persuasive
_____ letter writing
_____ summarizing
_____ record keeping
_____ note taking
_____ writing
_____ critical analysis
_____ clerical skills

Helping
_____ advising
_____ coaching
_____ leading
_____ mentoring
_____ negotiating
_____ interpreting
_____ influencing/persuading
_____ articulating
_____ empathizing
_____ public speaking
_____ training
_____ teaching
_____ convincing
_____ counseling
_____ motivating
_____ supporting
_____ understanding
_____ arbitrating

Creating
_____ composing
_____ designing
_____ illustrating
_____ painting
_____ sculpting
_____ drawing
_____ writing
_____ singing
_____ inventive
_____ observing
_____ imagining
_____ showmanship
_____ aesthetic sense
_____ acting
_____ landscaping
_____ interior decorating
_____ photography

B. Organizational Skills and Abilities

Managing
_____ classifying
_____ systematizing
_____ filing
_____ handling details
_____ problem solving
_____ decision making
_____ orderly
_____ supervising
_____ precision oriented
_____ follow-through
_____ accomplishing
_____ set schedule
_____ controlling
_____ effective
_____ assertiveness
_____ organizing,

Analyzing
_____ budgeting
_____ mathematical ability
_____ investment planning
_____ financial savvy
_____ counting
_____ integrating
_____ comparing
_____ investigating
_____ abstract thinking
_____ reviewing
_____ evaluating
_____ analyzing
_____ critical analysis
_____ calculating
_____ number memory
_____ statistical

C. Technical and Physical Skills and Abilities

Technical
_____ auto repair
_____ construction
_____ drafting
_____ mechanical drawing
_____ electronics
_____ tool oriented
_____ laboratory skills
_____ working with machinery
_____ cartography
_____ medical laboratory skills,
_____ blueprint reading
_____ graphics
_____ keypunching
_____ computer operation
_____ programming

Physical
_____ athletic talent
_____ coordination
_____ active
_____ finger dexterity
_____ hand-eye coordination
_____ assembling
_____ physically strong
_____ outdoor activities
_____ exploration

Look back at your list and circle those skills and abilities that you rated "4." Write them in the following spaces.

1. _____
2. _____
3. _____
4. _____
5. _____

6. _____
7. _____
8. _____
9. _____
10. _____

Now combine your two lists of functional skills and abilities. Think about what skills you would like to use in your career and in your other life activities. List as many as you wish.

1. _____   11. _____

2. _____   12. _____

3. _____   13. _____

4. _____   14. _____

5. _____   15. _____

6. _____   16. _____

7. _____   17. _____

8. _____   18. _____

9. _____   19. _____

10. _____   20. _____

D. WORK CONTENT SKILLS

The third type of skills, according to Bolles, are work content skills. These skills relate to a specific job and are normally very specialized. Work content skills usually require you to remember something very specific in order to do a job. They tend to be less transferable from one job to another than are functional skills. You develop these skills as you move from job to job. Some you may retain; others you may lose.

Examples of work content skills are knowing how to fill out a particular set of government forms, knowing how to take apart a specific brand of refrigerator, knowing the sales patterns of a department store, knowing the steps to take when inspecting a building, knowing how to operate a printing press, and knowing the names of all the customers on a sales route. You may use functional skills in developing work content skills. For example, a good memory will help you to remember the names of the customers on a sales route that you have taken over.

It is important to be aware of your work content skills, particularly those that you can use in other settings. In addition, when you apply for a job, beware of job descriptions that list many specific work content skills that are really transferable functional skills. Many employers describe jobs in terms of much more specific skills than are in fact required. You may actually have the skills that are necessary for the job.

Now think of some of your work content skills and list them in the following spaces.

1. _____   6. _____

2. _____   7. _____

3. _____   8. _____

4. _____   9. _____

5. _____   10. _____

SUMMARY—SKILLS AND ABILITIES

You now have a listing of your skills in the three areas. It is not essential that you know all of your skills, but it is important to acknowledge that you do have all three types of skills and that you can describe major examples of each. Of the three types of skills, functional skills are probably the most important to articulate, because they are very transferable from one experience to another. There is a tendency in describing a job to list the job requirements in work content terms when actually most of the skills required are functional. Try to analyze any job or new experience for the actual skills required and avoid going for new training to obtain skills that you already may possess.

In evaluating a job for the skills required, ask yourself the following questions.

1. Self-management skills: What types of personal characteristics do I need for this job?
2. Functional skills: What kind of actions do I need to do this job well?
3. Work content skills: What kind of special knowledge do I need to do this job well?

> The whole secret of a successful life is to find out what it is one's destiny to do, and then do it.
>
> *Henry Ford*

Personal Values

What matters most to you in your life? In Chapter 1, you assessed your work values in order to determine the types of work and working conditions that would be best suited to your needs and goals. In this chapter, you will assess your personal values. These values relate to all parts of your life and form the basis of your decision making. Values can be abstract or specific as illustrated by the following examples:

family	creativity	financial achievement
friendships	security	material possessions
helping others	honesty	a satisfying career
religious commitment	pleasure	good health

Whether you realize it or not, every time you make a choice about doing one thing as opposed to another, you make a value decision. Most major decisions involve value conflicts. If you a get a job offer in another town, you have to move. Career values may conflict with family and friendship values. When you have a decision that involves two or more conflicting values that are of major importance to you, the decision can be extremely difficult to make. You can, however, make these decisions more effectively if you have some idea of *what your most important values are and the priority that you give to each.*

The following exercises will help you to understand what personal values are, which personal values are important to you, and how you rank them. Your values are expressed through your actions. If you can bring your actions and life choices into harmony with your values, you will feel more in control of your life and more satisfied with the decisions you make. Your personal values can also play an important role in the type of career that you choose and in the career decisions that you make throughout your life.

A. PERSONAL VALUES AND ACTION

The following is a list of personal values that are important to many people. Read them briefly. Are some more important to you than others?

justice	independence	honesty
family	healthy life	environment
leisure	personal appearance	work
friendships	recognition	financial security
social consciousness	innovation	intimacy

The following is a list of ways that you might actually put these values into action. Taking the values just given, match them with the appropriate action. Write the value in the space provided.

Action	**Values Represented**
• You do volunteer work to help others less fortunate than you.	_____
• You spend a good deal of time getting yourself ready to go to work in the morning.	_____
• You get upset when one person takes credit for what another has done.	_____
• You like having your own home and living by your own resources.	_____
• You enjoy doing new things and like to encourage others to try something new.	_____
• You carefully schedule time to do things with your children and your spouse.	_____
• You work to become an authority in your field and you enjoy this status.	_____

| **Action** | **Values Represented** |

- You demonstrate an interest in others and actively maintain personal contacts. _____
- You exercise,, watch your diet,, and don't smoke. _____
- You have several activities outside of your job that you do for your enjoyment. _____
- You volunteer at the wildlife organization and nature center. _____
- You are preparing for a comfortable retirement. _____
- You refuse to cheat on your income tax. _____
- You renew your wedding vows with your spouse of 25 years. _____
- You take pride in the service that you provide your customers. _____

The answers are probably quite apparent, but it is important to note that the values indicated are fulfilled by action, not by feelings or general statements. It is one thing to *say* that you value something, but it does not become a real value until it becomes translated into *action*.

B. PERSONAL VALUES ASSESSMENT

The following is a list of personal values. Go through this list and rate the personal values in terms of their importance to *you*. Place a check mark (√) in the category that best represents your feelings about how important the personal value is to you.

Personal Value	Very Important	Moderately Important	Somewhat Important	Not Important
Good health Many close friendships Having a large family A fulfilling career A long life				
A stable marriage A financially comfortable life Independence Being creative Intimacy with another				

Personal Value	Very Important	Moderately Important	Somewhat Important	Not Important
Having children A variety of interests and activities Freedom to create my own lifestyle Having a house A happy love relationship				
Fulfilling careers for me and my spouse Contributing to my community Abundance of leisure time Happiness Ability to move from place to place				
A life without stress Strong religious involvement A chance to make social changes To be remembered for my accomplishments Helping those in distress				
Freedom to live where I wish A stable life Time to myself Enjoyment of arts, entertainment, and cultural activities A life without children				
A life with many challenges A life with many changes Opportunity to be a leader Opportunity to fight for my country A chance to make a major discovery that would save lives				
A good physical appearance Opportunity to establish roots in one place To write something memorable A chance to become famous To help others solve problems				
To make lots of money A stable environment for my children Other:				

Whenever you make an important or difficult decision, it usually involves choosing between conflicting values. In order to help you to make career and life decisions, it is necessary that you have some idea not only of your most important personal values, but also of the priority that you give them. In the following spaces, list at least ten of your most important personal values from your personal values assessment.

1. _____   6. _____

2. _____   7. _____

3. _____   8. _____

4. _____   9. _____

5. _____   10. _____

Now look at your list. In the space below, list your top *five* personal values *in order of priority*, with number one as the most important.

1. _____   first priority

2. _____   second priority

3. _____   third priority

4. _____   fourth priority

5. _____   fifth priority

You have assigned priorities to your most important personal values. Now ask yourself the following questions and write your answers in the spaces provided.

1. Does your life right now reflect your values? Is the time you spend consistent with your priorities?

2. If the time you spend in your life right now does not reflect your personal values, how can you change your life so that the time you spend is more in keeping with your values?

3. Are there some parts of your life that you would like to change but that you cannot right now? If so, what is your timetable for bringing your lifestyle more into harmony with your values?

4. What kind of career or career change would be most in keeping with your personal values?

5. Think about someone whom you have known and respected, someone who may have served as a role model for you. What special personal qualities did that person have?

6. Which of these special qualities would you like to develop?

C. PERSONAL VALUE DECISIONS

Values can be discussed and considered from a theoretical point of view. However, you really make a value decision whenever you take action. The following questions illustrate decisions that must be made. These decisions involve value conflicts. There is no right or wrong answer. Answer them from your own perspective, using your own personal values.

1. You and your spouse are employed. You enjoy your work very much and are heavily involved with it. You have no children. Your spouse received a job offer in a city 300 miles away. It is an excellent job and your spouse really wants to take it. You don't want to leave your job. What would you do?

List the values involved in this decision.

2. Your son has a basketball game at 7:00 P.M. It is the last game of the year and you have promised your son that you will be there. At 5:00 P.M. your boss comes to your office and says that there is a project that must be done right away. You know it will take 3 to 4 hours to complete. What would you do?

List the values involved in this decision.

3. You have worked hard all week. You haven't had much time to spend with your family. You love golf and your friends ask you to play golf on Saturday. Although you do not have anything specific scheduled for Saturday, you know that the golf game will take up most of the day. What would you do?

List the values involved in this decision.

4. You are working with records. Your supervisor comes to your desk and tells you to destroy certain records because it will be in the company's best interests to do so. You know that it is illegal to destroy these records. What would you do?

List the values involved in this decision.

5. Your child is sick and has a fever. You have a very important meeting at work and there is no one who can take your place. Your spouse is out of town. You might be able to get a sitter, but it would be difficult to do so and you are worried about your child's condition. What would you do?

List the values involved in this decision.

6. You are happy in your work and you have children. Your like to spend time with them. A promotion has been offered to you, but it would involve your working most Saturdays. What would you do?

List the values involved in this decision.

7. You have just come into a certain amount of money. Your present car is sufficient to meet your needs, but you would like to get a new one. Your family would like to take a trip to Europe. There are not sufficient funds to do both. What would you do?

List the values involved in this decision.

8. You have just completed college and have accepted your first job. You are living with your parents but you want to move out to a place of your own. Your parents really want you to stay at home for a while longer. You would save money by staying at home. What would you do?

List the values involved in this decision.

9. You have worked hard all week and it is now Friday afternoon. You and your spouse have three separate social engagements to attend over the weekend. It is important to your spouse that you attend. You would really prefer to stay at home and relax. What would you do?

List the values involved in this decision.

10. You have been working at the same job for twenty years and you're very tired of it. You make a good salary and have family responsibilities. You would really like to change careers but you feel that it would call for substantial sacrifices for members of your family. What would you do?

List the values involved in this decision.

SUMMARY—PERSONAL VALUES

You are constantly making value decisions, whether you are aware of it or not. If you assess your most important personal values and prioritize them, you will be better able to make decisions and will feel more in control of your life. You will also feel more comfortable with your decisions after you have made them. If you are not now living your life according to your values, it will be helpful to consider can change the way you how you spend your time so that your lifestyle can become more consistent with your values. As you go through life, your values may change and your priorities may change. Take time every so often to assess your lifestyle to see if it is in keeping with the personal values that are currently a priority in your life.

Self-Esteem

A. WHAT IS SELF-ESTEEM?

Your self-esteem is based on how you feel about and value yourself. Do you appreciate all the facets of yourself? Self-esteem means different things to different people. If you feel good about yourself and feel comfortable about where you are in life and where you are going, you probably have developed positive self-esteem. Self-esteem may be related to appreciating your physical appearance, contributing through work, achieving a title of influence, helping others, growing as a person, enjoying interpersonal relationships, and earning money. Your self-esteem is your evaluation of these and other areas of your life.

It is important to feel positive about yourself. Developing self-esteem provides you with a strong foundation for the development of healthy relationships, contributions through work, balance in life, risk taking, satisfactory decisions, and self-acceptance. Remember that self-esteem is related to your values and is therefore very personal. The following are some basic concepts about self-esteem.

1.   It is important for you to develop self-esteem because it will help you in all areas of your life.
2.   Develop *your own* mechanisms for maintaining self-esteem. Learn to "pat yourself on the back" for an achievement rather than depending on others for that reward.
3.   Although developing self-esteem from within is important, you can also derive it from others. It is nice to hear others compliment you on your appearance, your job, your beliefs, and your decisions. Positive comments from others can add to your self-esteem.
4.   You can take specific action to enhance your self-esteem. Locating supportive friends, going on a diet, trying something new, obtaining positive feedback on the job, or just smiling more often so that others smile back at you are all actions that you can take to increase your self-esteem.

B. WHERE DOES YOUR SELF-ESTEEM COME FROM?

The following activities are designed to help you assess the sources of your self-esteem.

1.   When do you feel positive about yourself?

Think about the times that you feel positive about yourself and about what you have done. What are the sources of those positive feelings? What are you saying to yourself when you are feeling positive? How are you perceived by others when you are feeling positive? In the following spaces, describe activities and occasions in which you feel positive about yourself. This can be in the present or in the past and the categories are provided as a guideline. Don't be limited by them.

Your physical appearance

_____

_____

_____

Relationships with others

_____

_____

_____

Your work

_____

_____

_____

Involvement with organizations

_____

_____

_____

Learning experiences

_____

_____

_____

Sports and physical activities

_____

_____

_____

Use of knowledge and skills in different ways

_____

_____

_____

Other sources of positive feelings

_____

_____

_____

2. When do you feel negative about yourself?

Now think about the times when you have experienced negative feelings or disappointments. What are the sources of these negative feelings? What are you saying to yourself when you are feeling negative? How do others respond to you when you are feeling negative about yourself? Write your thoughts in the following spaces.

Your physical appearance

_____

_____

_____

Relationships with others

_____

_____

_____

Your work

_____

_____

_____

Involvement in organizations

_____

_____

_____

Learning experiences

_____

_____

_____

Sports and physical activities

_____

_____

_____

• • • • • • • • • • •

Feeling some fear about this process of evaluating yourself is normal. Keep going. Be brave.

• • • • • • • • • •

Use of knowledge and skills in different ways

_____

_____

_____

Other sources of negative feelings

_____

_____

_____

Now review your responses to compare the positive and the negative feelings that you have listed. When do you feel positive about yourself? What factors are present when your self-esteem is high? Write several of them in the following spaces.

_____

_____

_____

_____

Look back over your negative feelings and experiences and consider the factors that tend to undermine your self-esteem. What conditions are present when you feel negative about yourself? Write them in the following spaces.

_____

_____

_____

_____

What can you do to increase the positive factors that enhance your self-esteem and decrease the negative factors that undermine your self-esteem? Developing your self-esteem is a lifelong process that is well worth the effort. Now, look at self-esteem in another way.

3. What is your perception of self-esteem?

The messages you received about yourself as you grew up helped to determine your adult self-image. As an infant, you were ego-centric and totally absorbed in yourself. You were not born with beliefs about yourself, but rather, you were born with a _clean slate_ and developed your self-esteem through interaction with others. In this section, you will be asked to consider how you perceive self-esteem in others. By doing this, you will learn more about your personal definition of self-esteem.

What is self-esteem on a practical level, and how does it show up in your everyday life? Consider what low self-esteem looks like to you and then consider the same questions for high self-esteem.

How does someone reveal low self-esteem? In the space below, list some of the characteristics of a person with low self-esteem.

_____

_____

_____

What does a person with low self-esteem say? In the space below, describe what this person sounds like.

_____

_____

_____

In your opinion, how does a person with low self-esteem feel?

_____

_____

_____

Think of a person, real or fictitious, whom you consider to have low self-esteem. How does that low self-esteem manifest itself in the person's daily life?

_____

_____

_____

Now think of a person whom you know that you feel has high self-esteem. In the space below, describe that person.

_____

_____

_____

What does the person with high self-esteem look like? What characteristics does the person with high self-esteem possess?

_____

_____

_____

What does the person with high self-esteem say? What does the person sound like?

_____

_____

_____

In your opinion, how does the person with high self-esteem feel?

_____

_____

_____

How does the person's high self-esteem manifest itself in the person's daily life?

_____

_____

_____

Self-esteem is often overlooked in the process of considering career and life options. Researchers have repeatedly confirmed that the way you feel about yourself is linked to career and life satisfaction. It is important to understand the concept of self-esteem and how it relates to your life. Your behavior is affected by your self-esteem.

Lack of time, constant noise, and plain, everyday life may obscure your inner feelings and thoughts. The radio in the car, the television at home, the needs of others, the demands of work, the push and pull of finances, and unceasing chores fill our lives with duties, responsibilities, and often pandemonium. Yet it's important to free up time to explore your values and evaluate your self-esteem. This review can benefit all the areas of your life.

C. YOUR SELF-ESTEEM TREE

First, consider your uniqueness by completing the following sentences on the Self-Esteem "I" Tree. The branches of your tree bear many buds. Imagine that it is spring and the buds are about to bloom. Each blossom is unique and beautiful, just as your thoughts and feelings are special. A single bud is special, but when you step back and notice the entire tree full of buds, the view is breathtaking. Your uniqueness is similar to the tree's beauty.

Create some quiet space and time in your life to really explore your uniqueness by completing the following Self-Esteem "I" Tree. Listen to your inner self and respond with the first idea or words that come into your mind. Those first reactions are the correct ones for you.

Consider the individual branches of your tree one at a time and then step back and admire the entire tree, complete with the buds. Just as the buds are fragile, your self-esteem is very delicate and vulnerable to outside forces. The harsh, cold wind and elements can damage the blooms on the tree. Criticism, negative joking, constant comparisons, embarrassments, rejections, and negative labels damage your self-esteem until you begin to question yourself, believe the negativity, and even incorporate the negative thinking into your behavior. Then the negative on the outside becomes part of you.

You can become your worst critic, ignoring your needs, feelings, and goals. Care of yourself becomes secondary or even last on the long list of things to do. A tree requires watering, sun, pruning, and fertilizing in order to thrive, bloom, and grow. Similarly, your self-esteem requires even more tender and loving care. Why is it that caring for other living things is natural, but caring for self-esteem is so over-looked? Your self-esteem requires at least as much if not more care from the primary caretaker—you.

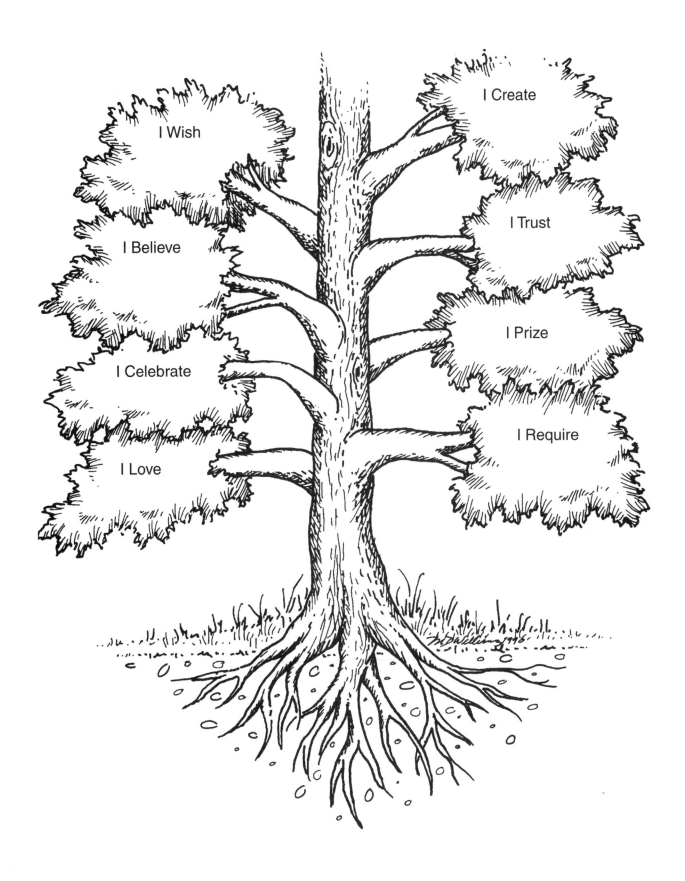

D. Labels, Poisoners, and Cultivators of Self-Esteem

Sometimes feelings keep you from accomplishing a desired task or goal. An appropriate analogy to the theme of self-esteem is the flight of the honeybee. The honeybee is a curious insect. Aerodynamically, the honeybee is not supposed to fly, because the weight of its body is greater than the wings should be able to carry. The bee does not know this, and no one has successfully informed the bee. It flies and completes its mission by pollinating blossoms, never knowing that technically it should not be able to fly. What may be holding you back from accomplishing your mission? Are any negative labels, thoughts, fears, or criticisms sticking with you and keeping you from accomplishing your goals?

Carrying around old labels can be a heavy burden. Sometimes, you confirm that these labels are correct by creating circumstances that support your belief in them. Labels can limit you if you stop short of achieving your goals.

What are some of the positive labels that you had growing up? Some examples are pretty, cute, handsome, fun, sweet, helpful, smart, popular, leader, sharp, cool, neat, coordinated, quick, mature, mannerly, well-behaved, good, thoughtful. Write some of the positive labels that you heard about yourself.

_____

_____

_____

What are some of the positive labels you choose to describe yourself now?

_____

_____

_____

What are some of the negative labels that you endured as you grew up? Some examples are four-eyes, smart aleck, slow, selfish, homely, shy, loud, bad, dummy, stupid, lazy, too tall ("too" anything), goody-two-shoes, wise guy, clumsy, weak, nerd, geek, and metal mouth. Write some of the negative labels that you heard about yourself.

_____

_____

_____

What are some of the negative labels that you choose to describe yourself now?

_____

_____

_____

Just as you would not consider poisoning a growing, healthy tree, it would be a sheer waste to poison flourishing self-esteem. Consider the following obstacles to self-esteem that poison the spirit and kill creativity. This list has been adapted from the work of Sidney Simon, a noted author and authority on the issues of self-esteem.*

Self-Esteem Poisoners

- Underestimating your abilities as a reason not to try
- Believing that you do not deserve better
- Magnifying every setback as proof of failure
- Expecting perfection immediately
- Creating a self-fulfilling prophecy of unworthiness
- Engaging in addictions that eventually control everything
- Moving in a self-destructive pattern that spirals downward
- Passivity to decisions and events
- Guilt and shame
- Derogatory thinking about yourself and allowing others to confirm these negative thoughts

Do you find yourself engaging in any one of these behaviors? If so, place a check mark next to each poisoner that seems to block you. The poisoners and the negative labels that you have identified may be held over from childhood and adolescence or may have been acquired in your adult years.

What can you do to reverse the effects of these self-esteem poisoners and labels? Developing and nurturing your self-esteem is important, just as you would care for your trees or plants. Make your self-esteem work for you and not against you in the career and life planning process. The following suggestions may help you to plan a strategy for growing and nurturing your self-esteem. This list has also been adapted from the work of Sidney Simon. Check those that you would like to encourage in your own life.

*Simon, S. B. *Getting Unstuck: Breaking through the Barriers to Change.* New York: Warner, 1989, pp. 51–119.

Self-Esteem Cultivators

• • • • • • • • • • •

I know there are
aspects about
myself that
puzzle me, and
other aspects that
I do not know.
But as long as I
am friendly and
loving to myself,
I can courageously
and hopefully look
for the solutions
to the puzzles and
for the ways to
find out more
about me.
—Virginia Satir*

• • • • • • • • • • •

- Find positive mentors and role models.
- Risk by expanding horizons—learn something new.
- Seek and build emotional supports.
- Reclaim lost power—make the difficult decision.
- Stop blaming others, anyone, anything, everyone, the world.
- Recognize individual uniqueness in yourself and in others.
- Create human warmth by joining.
- Acknowledge your values and allocate your time accordingly.
- Be productive. Start by achieving the little goals.
- Write your goals and fulfill them—start small and work up.
- Visualize a path clear of obstacles.
- Visualize high self-esteem, and feeling positive.
- Keep a journal in which you explore your present dilemmas, feelings, and thoughts.
- Give positive feedback to significant others in your life.
- Use the following sentence starters: I appreciate your . . .

  I value your . . .

  I respect your . . .

  I prize your . . .

  I admire your . . .

- Request positive feedback from significant others.
- Reprogram your negative thoughts with positive ones.
- Replace your old "shoulds" with "wants."

---

*Satir, Virginia. *Self-Esteem.* California: Celestial Arts, 1975.

E. YOUR ACTION PLAN TO ENHANCE YOUR SELF-ESTEEM

Review your plans for improving your self-esteem and make a commitment to yourself and at least one other person that you will address one or more of the sixteen self-esteem cultivators. Write those that you have selected and list several specific actions that you can take to increase your self-esteem.

_____

_____

_____

_____

_____

_____

The purpose of life is undoubtedly to know oneself.

—*Mohandas K. Gandhi*

Lifestyle Considerations

What kind of life do you want to live? Do you want to live in a specific part of the country? Do you want to live in a rural setting or in a metropolitan area? Do you want to be involved in community activities, or do you want to be left to yourself? Do you want to live near your relatives? Do you want to have cultural activities available to you, or would you rather live where you have ready access to the outdoors without many people around?

In considering any career or life decisions, it is very useful to evaluate what lifestyle considerations are important to you. If access to entertainment and cultural opportunities is important, you would probably want to live in a metropolitan area. This may affect the type of career decision you make. If you wish to live in a rural area, then you should choose a career that will allow you to locate there. If you want to travel often, you may wish to choose a career that involves frequent travel.

A. LIFESTYLE ASSESSMENT

The following listing of lifestyle considerations will help you assess which are most important to you. Go through the list and place a check mark (√) in the appropriate category, indicating how important that lifestyle consideration is to you. There may be only a few that are very important. If so, you have more flexibility in forming a lifestyle that is compatible with the considerations. If, however, certain lifestyle considerations are very important to you, these may have a very significant influence on your career and life planning.

Lifestyle Considerations	Very Important	Moderately Important	Somewhat Important	Not Important
Live in a rural setting Live close to work Be able to walk to work Own my own home Live in a moderate climate				
Be active in my community Live in a suburban setting Live in an apartment Live close to cultural and entertainment opportunities Go out to eat often				
Travel frequently Live in a warm climate Live where children can walk to school Live where my spouse can have a good job				
Live near relatives Live where the weather changes from season to season Live in a constant climate Have time to pursue my interests Have friends nearby				
Have a garden Have a house and yard to work on Live near a college Have a second home Live near the water				
Live close to stores Live in a wooded setting Be involved with sports of my choice Participate in family-oriented activities				
Live where I don't have to spend time with neighbors Have time to myself Spend time with my neighbors Work on projects around my house				

Lifestyle Considerations	Very Important	Moderately Important	Somewhat Important	Not Important
Do things alone or with my spouse Have a big house Live in a stable neighborhood Spend time with arts or crafts Go places on weekends				
Stay at home on weekends Be very involved in social activities Do volunteer work Be active in church work				
Do things often with friends Go to movies, plays, and concerts often Other:				

Now look back at your list. In the following spaces, write five to ten of the lifestyle considerations that are most important to you.

1. _____   6. _____

2. _____   7. _____

3. _____   8. _____

4. _____   9. _____

5. _____   10. _____

How can you structure your life and career in the future so that you can fulfill these lifestyle priorities? What influence would they have over your choice of a career or over your choice of where and how you want to live? Write your responses in the following spaces.

_____

_____

_____

_____

In summary, your total lifestyle is very important to your life satisfaction and to your general mental and physical well-being. It is important to maintain a variety of interests and activities outside of your work that can form the basis of a well-rounded lifestyle. Make specific plans for achieving not only your career goals but also the lifestyle of your choice. In future years, it may be difficult for many people to fulfill their needs for self-esteem and self-actualization primarily through their work. A well-developed, balanced lifestyle may hold the key to future success, happiness, and fulfillment.

Try to realize, and truly realize, that what stands between you and a different life are matters of responsible choice.
—Gary Zukav, *Seat of the Soul*

SUMMARY
Acknowledge Your Unique Self

 You have now evaluated your work values, interests, skills, personal values, and lifestyle preferences. This knowledge can help you to make life and career decisions based on what you need and what you want. Knowing yourself is the essential first step in effective career and life planning. To summarize what you have found out about yourself in Section I, it may be helpful to return to the questions asked at the beginning. Review your original responses throughout the section as you complete this summary.

What are my work values?

In the following spaces write at least five of your most important work values.

1. _____   Other: _____

2. _____   _____

3. _____   _____

4. _____   _____

5. _____   _____

How do your work values relate to a career or lifestyle you might choose? Write your answer in this space.

What are my interests?

In the following spaces write at least five of your major interests.

1. _____   Other: _____

2. _____   _____

3. _____   _____

4. _____   _____

5. _____   _____

How do these interests relate to a career or lifestyle you might choose? Write your answer in this space.

What are my skills and abilities?

In the following spaces write at least five self-management skills and at least five functional skills that you have or would like to develop.

Self-management skills

1. _____   Other: _____

2. _____   _____

3. _____   _____

4. _____   _____

5. _____   _____

Functional skills

1. _____   Other: _____

2. _____   _____

3. _____   _____

4. _____   _____

5. _____   _____

How do your skills relate to a career or lifestyle you might choose? Write your answer in this space.

What are my self-esteem cultivators, and what action can I take to build my self-esteem?

1. _____   Other: _____

2. _____   _____

3. _____   _____

4. _____   _____

5. _____   _____

What are my personal values?

In the following spaces write at least five of your most important personal values, in order of priority.

1. _____   Other: _____

2. _____   _____

3. _____   _____

4. _____   _____

5. _____   _____

How do your personal values affect your choice of a career or lifestyle?

What lifestyle considerations are important to me?

In the following spaces write at least five of your most important lifestyle considerations.

1. _____	Other: _____
2. _____	_____
3. _____	_____
4. _____	_____
5. _____	_____

In order to achieve this lifestyle, what type of career do you need? What other actions must you take? Write your answer in this space.

Now proceed to Section II, Manage Change in Your Life, where you will explore how to use the information about yourself from this chapter as you begin to consider the changes that are before you.

ADDITIONAL RESOURCES

General Resources for Career and Life Planning

Bernstein, Alan B., and Schaffzin, Nicholas. *The Princeton Review Guide to Your Career.* New York: Princeton Review Publishing Co., 1998.

Boldt, Laurence. *How to Find the Work You Love.* New York: Penguin Books, 1996.

Bolles, Richard N. *The Three Boxes of Life.* Berkeley, California: Ten Speed Press, 2000.

———. *What Color Is Your Parachute?* Berkeley, California: Ten Speed Press, 1999.

Borchard, David C., et al. *Your Career: Choices, Chances, Changes.* Dubuque, Iowa: Kendall-Hunt Publishing Company, 1988.

Cabrera, James C., and Albrecht, Charles F., Jr. *The Lifetime Career Manager.* Holbrook, MA: Adams Media Corp., 1995.

Carter, Carol. *Majoring in the Rest of Your Life.* New York: The Noonday Press, 1995.

Crystal, John C., and Bolles, Richard N. *Where Do I Go from Here with My Life?* Berkeley, California: Ten Speed Press, 1993.

Fadiman, James. *Unlimit Your Life: Setting and Getting Goals.* California: Celestial Arts Books, 1989.

Feingold, S. Norman. *Futuristic Exercises: A Workbook for Emerging Lifestyles and Careers in the 21st Century.* Maryland: Garrett Park Press, 1989.

Germann, Richard, and Arnold, Peter. *Job and Career Building.* Berkeley, California: Ten Speed Press, 1990.

Guterman, Mark S. *Common Sense for Uncommon Times.* Palo Alto, CA: CPP Books, 1994.

Harris, Marcia B., and Jones, Sharn L. *The Parent's Crash Course in Career Planning.* Chicago: VGM Career Horizons, 1996.

Helmstetter, Shad. *Choices.* New York: Pocket Books, 1990.

Hirsh, Sandra, and Kummerow, Jean. *Lifetypes.* New York: Warner Books, 1989.

Holland, John L. *Making Vocational Choices: A Theory of Careers.* Florida: Psych. Assess. 1992.

Hopson, Barrie, and Scally, Mike. *Build Your Own Rainbow.* San Diego, CA: Pfeiffer & Co., 1993.

Jackson, Tom. *Not Just Another Job—How to Invent a Career that Works for you—Now and in the Future.* New York: Random House, 1992.

Kaplan, Robbie. *The Whole Career Sourcebook.* New York: AMACOM, 1991.

Krannich, Ron, and Krannich, Caryl. *Discover the Right Job for You.* Virginia: Impact Publications, 1991.

Kroeger, Otto. *Type Talk.* New York: Delacourte Press, 1989.

Lakein, Alan. *How to Get Control of Your Time and Your Life.* New York: New American Library, 1989.

Leider, Richard J. *Life Skills-Taking Charge of Your Personal & Professional Growth.* Paramus, NJ: Prentiss Hall, 1994

Linquist, Carolyn, ed. *Where to Start Career Planning.* New Jersey: Peterson's Guides, 1991.

Michelozzi, Betty. *Coming Alive from Nine to Five: The Career Search Handbook.* California: Mayfield Publishing Company, 1991.

Powell, C. Randall. *Career Planning Today.* Dubuque, Iowa: Kendall-Hunt Publishing Company, 1990.

Rubin, Theodore I. *Overcoming Indecisiveness: Eight Stages to Decision Making.* New York: Avon Books, 1986.

Scott, Cynthia, and Jaffe, Dennis. *Managing Personal Change: Self Management Skills for Work and Life Transitions.* California: Crisp Publications, 1989.

Shingleton, John. *Career Planning for the 1990s: A Guide for Today's Graduates.* Maryland: Garrett Park Press, 1991.

Sturman, Gerald. *The Career Discovery Project.* Colorado: The New Careers Center, 1993.

Timm, Paul. *Successful Self Management.* California: Crisp Publications, 1987.

———. *Your Perfect Work—The New Career Guide to Making a Living, Creating Life.* New York: G.P. Putnam's Sons, 1996.

Zunker, Vernon G. *Using Assessment Results for Career Development (Fourth Edition)* Pacific Grove, CA: Books/Cole Publishing Co: 1994.

Self-Esteem Resources

Alberti, Robert, and Emmons, Michael. *Your Perfect Right: A Guide to Assertive Living.* Virginia: Impact Publications, 1990.

Beattie, Melodie. *Beyond Codependency*. Minnesota: Hazelden, 1989.

———. *Codependent No More*. Minnesota: Hazelden, 1989.

Blumenthal, Erik. *Believing in Yourself*. One World Publications, 1997.

Branden, Nathaniel. *How to Raise Your Self-Esteem*. New York: Bantam Books, 1988.

———. *Six Pillars of Self-Esteem*. New York: Bantam Books, 1995

Bradshaw, John. *Creating Love*. New York: Bantam Books, 1992.

———. *The Family*. Florida: Health Communications Inc., 1988.

Briggs, Dorothy C. *Celebrate Yourself*. New York: Doubleday, 1986.

———. *Your Child's Self Esteem*. New York: Doubleday, 1975.

Burns, David D. *Feeling Good: The New Mood Therapy*. New York: Harper, 1999.

———. *Ten Days to Self-Esteem*. Quill, 1999.

Buscaglia, Leo. *Living, Loving, and Learning*. New York: Fawcett, 1985.

Cavanaugh, Eunice. *Understanding Shame*. New York: Johnson Institute, 1989.

Colgrove, Melba. *How to Survive the Loss of a Love*. New York: Bantam Books, 1991.

Covey, Stephen. *The Seven Habits of Highly Effective People*. New York: Simon and Schuster, 1990.

Dyer, Wayne W. *Real Magic*. New York: HarperCollins, 1992.

Frey, Diane, and Carlock, Jesse. *Enhancing Self-Esteem*. Indiana: Accl. Development, 1989.

Gurman, Mark S. *Common Sense for Uncommon Times*. California: CPP Books, 1994.

Hay, Louise L. *You Can Heal Your Life*. California: Hay House, 1988.

Heldemann, Mary. *When Words Hurt*. New York: Ballantine Books, 1989.

Jampolsky, Gerald. *Love Is Letting Go of Fear*. New York: Cogent Publ., 1989.

———. *Out of Darkness into the Light: A Journey of Inner Healing*. New York: Bantam Books, 1990.

Jeffers, Susan. *Feel the Fear and Do It Anyway*. New York: Columbine Books, 1988.

Kiersey, David, and Bates, Marilyn. *Please Understand Me II*. California: Prometheus Books, 1998.

———. *Please Understand Me II: Temperament Character Intelligence*. California: Prometheus Books, 1998.

Lerner, Harriet. *The Dance of Intimacy*. New York: HARPC, 1990.

———. *The Dance of Anger*. New York: HARPC, 1989.

McKay, Matthew. *When Anger Hurts*. California: New Harbinger Books, 1989.

———. *Self-Esteem*. New York: St. Martin's Press, 1987.

McKay, Matthew, and Fanning, Patrick. *Self-Esteem*. California: New Harbinger, 1987.

———. *Self Esteem* (2nd Ed.) Oakland, CA.: New Harbinger Publications, 1992.

Minchinton, Jerry. *52 Things You Can Do to Raise Your Self-Esteem*. Arnford House, 1995.

Murphy, Joseph. *The Power of Your Subconscious Mind*. New York: Prentice-Hall, 1988.

Orenstein, Peggy. *School Girls: Young Women, Self-Esteem & The Confidence Gap*. New York: Doubleday, 1994.

Peck, M. Scott. *The Road Less Traveled*. New York: Touchstone Books, 1988.

Sanford, Linda, and Donovan, Mary. *Women and Self Esteem*. New York: Penguin Books, 1985.

Scarf, Maggie. *Unfinished Business*. New York: Ballantine Books, 1989.

Simon, Sidney. *Forgiveness*. New York: Warner Books, 1990.

———. *Getting Unstuck*. New York: Warner Books, 1989.

———. *Vulture*. Massachusetts: VALUES, 1993.

Viorst, Judith. *Necessary Losses*. New York: Fawcett Books, 1987.

Waitley, Denis. *Seeds of Greatness*. New York: Pocket Books, 1988.

———. *The Psychology of Winning*. New York: Berkley, 1992.

———. *Winner's Edge: The Critical Attitude of Success*. Berkley Publications, 1994.

Williamson, Marianne. *A Return to Love*. New York: HarperCollins, 1992.

Manage Change in Your Life

What would life be like without any changes? Pretty dull, wouldn't you think? It is hard to imagine a life without change, but sometimes too much change or change that you cannot control can be very stressful. In addition, it is important to be able to initiate changes when you feel that you are ready to change something in your life. This chapter will help you to understand that:

- Change is normal.
- Your needs and expectations change as you go through life.
- You can prepare yourself to deal effectively with change.
- You must take the primary responsibility for managing change in your life.
- Making changes often involves taking risks.
- It may take you a good deal of time and effort to work through a major life transition.

In your career and in other parts of your life, it is important to be able to manage changes that you cannot anticipate and to prepare for changes that you initiate. As the engineer of your train trip through life, you should have the skills and the knowledge to steer your train safely through the conditions and situations that confront you on your trip. Your first step is to understand what change, or transition, is and how you can prepare for and control change in your life. Change will be a major factor in the workplace in the 21st century. This section on change will begin with an investigation of career and life planning as we begin the new millennium.

Career and Life Planning in the 21st Century

What will work be like during the 21st century? What changes will technological developments bring to the job market and to career and life planning? What will happen to people and jobs as a result of organizational "reengineering," which refers to changing most operating procedures to make optimum use of new technologies? This chapter will explore some of the ideas put forth by various writers about the world of work in the 21st century. It will then summarize the major factors on which most writers agree and will offer some practical suggestions on how to prepare for working as we begin a new century.

A. THE WORLD OF WORK IN THE 21ST CENTURY

William Bridges, in his book *Job Shift*,* describes the first great job shift that occurred when people moved from rural, farm oriented work to the jobs of the factories and large organizations. This shift brought about the growth of cities and fundamental societal changes. The tradition that involved an interweaving of home life and work life, with much individual control about how one spent a work day, was replaced by the individual's acceptance of a "job" with a great deal of structure and repetition. The second great job shift, according to Bridges, is taking place now. People have become accustomed to having a job in an organization that provides them not only with money, but also with security, benefits, colleagues, and a sense of identity. With the developments in technology in which many traditional job functions can be handled much more effectively by computers or machines, organizations are reducing the number of jobs needed for the organization to function. In addition, with the rapidly changing needs in the world of work, organizations are less likely to make long-term commitments to individuals in terms of traditional jobs. Rather, they will contract with people to do specific work, often for a limited period of time. This second great job shift, according to Bridges, can be characterized by the term "dejobbing." Workers will be valued based on what they can contribute to an organization, their flexibility in accepting new approaches to achieving goals, and their ability to learn, to create, and to work with teams in completing projects.

This fundamental change in the world of work is the result of quantum changes in the role of technology in the workplace. In *The End of Work*,** Jeremy Rifkin describes a future in which automated machinery, robots, and increasingly sophisticated computers that can perform most simple repetitive tasks will make vulnerable to elimination over half the existing jobs in the American labor force.** Rifkin indicates that this major revolution in the work force is still to come, since less than half of the companies around the world have begun to make the transition to the new machine culture. He draws attention to the concept of re-engineering in which organizations are eliminating layers of management, combining job categories, and training employees to use a variety of skills, as well as simplifying all administrative and production processes using the latest technologies. As a result, productivity has risen while jobs have been reduced.

---

* Bridges, William. *Job Shift—How to Prosper in a Workplace without Jobs.* Reading, MA: Addison-Wesley Publishing Co., 1994, p. 38.
**Rifkin, Jeremy. *The End of Work.* New York: G. P. Putnam's Sons, 1995, pp. 5–7.

Ronald and Caryl Krannich, in *The Best Jobs for the 21st Century*, emphasize the need for people to prepare for high levels of uncertainty in the coming millennium. They predict a slower rate of economic growth, slower growth in the workforce, fewer high paying jobs, more low paying service jobs, fewer people climbing the corporate ladder, less loyalty to employers and organizations, and a greater need for workers to learn new skills, acquire new experiences, and to be job mobile. They stress the importance of hard work and education and make the following prediction about the future:

> The best jobs of the future will go to those who empower themselves with a capacity to shape their future. They take responsibility for their employability. They dream possible dreams because they are well educated, work hard, and know they must be prepared for constant change in the economy, the job market, and their work life.*

Krannich and Krannich question the assumption of many that people will stay at home to work out of their home offices since this is so isolating. However, they do predict the coming of the decentralized work place along with 30 other future changes in the world of work.**

Barry Glassner, in *Career Crash—The New Crisis and Who Survives*, describes a process that a person needs to go through when moving from one job to another or when dealing with a loss of a job due to some of the changes that are taking place in the world of work. He refers to this uprooting event as a "career crash" and describes a three phase process of "cutting loose, hanging out, and moving on,"*** which will normally take place gradually.

In *Career Selector 2001*, James Gonyea predicts that people will have three to six careers in their lifetimes and many more "jobs" in different settings. He cites as one reason for corporate downsizing the perception among many employers that the employees who stay around longest become less productive while earning higher salaries. He predicts that more people will leave traditional jobs to become home-based entrepreneurs and that people will have to take more individual initiative in developing their own health, retirement, and other benefit programs. He emphasizes that people in the future will not be able to count on an employer to provide their security. The age of worker enti-

---

* Krannich, Ronald L., and Krannich, Caryl Rae. *Best Jobs for the 21st Century*. Manassas Park, VA: Impact Publications, 1998, pp. 2–3.
** Krannich and Krannich, p. 51.
***Glassner, Barry. *Career Crash—The New Crisis and Who Survives*. New York: Simon & Schuster, 1994, pp. 186–189.

tlement is over. This security must come from a person's ability to make career adjustments when necessary.*

Tom Gorman has coined the term "Multipreneuring"** to describe the most useful approach to the world of work in the 21st century. Gorman relates the current changes in the workplace to those of evolution, in which some species must die to give way to new species. The industrial age employment system dominated by large organizations which took care of the salary and benefits of the workers is being replaced by a free agent information age system in which organizations and people are called on to continually prove their economic value. He predicts a basic change in the concept of a job in which working relationships become more transaction based rather than relationship based. A person will be more likely to be seen as a service provider who will sell services on an open market and whose economic value must be obvious. Organizations will have more flexible structures and rapid changes will be normal. The overriding influence of technology changes will be pervasive.

In summary, these predictions for the world of work in the 21st century are not ones to bring a sense of comfort and security. We may well be at the beginning of the most fundamental changes in work and our society in our history. How should one approach this uncertain future? It may be possible to hunker down in a relatively secure job and wait to see what happens. However, the changes will take place. Many of the predictions may not turn out to be as revolutionary as some would make them, but the person who actively engages in career and life planning, learns about the future trends, and integrates self and work knowledge will be better positioned to adapt to an uncertain future. The next part of this chapter will summarize these trends.

B. A Summary of the Major Workplace Trends in the 21st Century

The writers whose work is referenced in this chapter paint a picture of fundamental change in the workplace as we begin the 21st century. Here is a summary of the major trends expected to take place in the near future. Carefully consider these and other trends as you develop your career and life plans.

1. The development of ever-more sophisticated computers and information systems will have a profound influence over all phases of work and life outside of work.

---

* Gonyea, James. *Career Selector 2001*. Haupauge, N.Y.: Barron's Educational Series, Inc., 1993, p.4.
**Gorman, Tom. *Multipreneuring*. New York: Fireside, 1996, pp. 20–22.

2. Any job that involves primarily simple, repetitive tasks stands a good chance of being eliminated.

3. Middle management positions that involve supervising people who do simple, repetitive tasks are also likely to be eliminated.

4. Organizations will be able to precisely track productivity and efficiency and these will be primary factors in monitoring work performance.

5. Work that involves direct service to people combined with information retrieval or simple repetitive tasks will change, as more of the repetitive functions are handled by computers.

6. Organizations will be less likely to make long-term commitments to employees. They will be more likely to contract out specific work tasks to individuals or subcontracting organizations. This is termed "outsourcing."

7. Organizations will be less likely to provide comprehensive benefit packages to large numbers of employees.

8. Individual workers will be required to assume increasingly more responsibility for maintaining their own benefits such as health insurance, life insurance, and retirement plans.

9. Individual workers will be called upon to demonstrate specific skills that they can bring to an organization, either to maintain employment or to be hired to perform specific work functions.

10. Many newly created jobs will be at the lower levels of income and status.

11. Many people who have worked for organizations for twenty or more years will find that they are required to leave the organizations earlier than they wished due to downsizing or forced early retirements.

12. Many people will have to accept less than their "ideal" job.

13. Career change will become the norm for the majority of workers, who can expect to have three to six career changes and a variety of work settings during their working lives.

14. There will be significant opportunities for entrepreneurs who can use technological advances to provide new services and new ways to approach traditional functions.

C. CAREER AND LIFE PLANNING IN THE 21ST CENTURY— WHAT YOU CAN DO

The fundamental changes that are taking place in the world of work are already causing a great upheaval in the workforce as traditional jobs are eliminated and organizations seek to operate more efficiently. Long-held values of commitment to employees by providing secure jobs and benefits are being challenged. Technological developments will continue to bring about profound change. What can *you* do to prepare yourself for your life and career? Here are some guidelines.

1. Carefully consider your own unique self. Assessment of your work values, interests, skills and abilities, personal values and lifestyle preferences is just as important as ever. You must know your priorities and skills as you face the uncertainties of the changing workplace.

2. Develop a concept of yourself as an entrepreneur. Know what skills and attributes you offer to the workplace and be able to articulate them. Think of yourself not as a job-holder or job-seeker but as someone uniquely qualified to make specific contributions in the workplace.

3. Do everything you can to learn about and make use of new technologies. If you are working, take advantage of any special training programs on new equipment and software. If you are not working, take both credit and non-credit courses in order to update your technological skills.

4. In any work that you do, volunteer to take part in any team effort, project designed to enhance workplace productivity, or initiative to explore new approaches to getting work done.

5. Embrace change. Always be willing to try new approaches to old problems, to take on new responsibilities, and to retrain in order to enhance your skills. Learn so that you will earn.

6. Take charge of your own future. Take advantage of any self-directed savings, retirement or other individualized benefit plans available where you work. Have your own savings plan to provide security when you are making a transition from one work setting to another.

7. Develop good interpersonal skills and know how to work as a member of or leader of a team. Show a genuine interest in others and be supportive of them. These interpersonal skills will always be highly valued by organizations, especially when combined with the ability to make use of the latest developments in technology.

8. Be willing to move from one phase of work to another or from one organization to another. This is especially important if you are working in an area where technological developments may either decrease or eliminate the number of jobholders. Always keep an eye on the future.

9. Realize that, even with good planning, you may find yourself in transition from one area of work to another, between organizations, or from one geographical area to another. To effectively work through major career and life transitions, you may need to seek the assistance of a qualified career counselor who processes options with you. The other chapters in this section will provide help in dealing with change.

10. Many work settings in the future may be very isolated. You may find yourself at some time cut off from co-workers and other interpersonal contacts, especially if you do a great deal of your work at home. Support systems are extremely important to help you initiate and maintain interpersonal contacts. People tend to take for granted the interpersonal support that they receive in a work setting. You may need to replace support if it is not available where you do your work.

11. Define yourself in broad terms. Throughout this book you are encouraged to consider plans for your career *and* your life. This will be increasingly important in the 21st century as you will be called upon to develop your own identity outside of a traditional job. In past generations, many people tied too much of their identities to their jobs. As we begin the 21st century, it will be even more important to establish your identity in terms of the skills and contributions that you can make in the workplace, but also in terms of your interests, your family, your contributions to others, your faith, and in the many other components of your lifestyle.

12. Maintain a home base where you can have a sense of order and comfort. In the ever-changing workplace, there will be many uncertainties and stressful situations. It will be helpful if you can establish a means of finding respite. It may be your own home, your family, your friends, your church, your special interest, your volunteer work, or a combination of some or all of these. It is important to be able to return to places, people, and activities that provide an opportunity for renewal.

Summary

The importance of playing an active role in your career and life planning has never been greater than it is today, and it will become even more essential in the future. You will be less likely to find a "job" that you can stay with throughout your work life, providing consistent security, salary, and benefits. It will be necessary for you to articulate your skills, abilities, values, and goals and to relate these to a rapidly-changing workplace. It will be necessary to embrace change and to be able to take risks in order to grow in your career. The following chapters in Section II will help you to understand how you can make change work for you as you face the future.

Getting Ready for Change

The Dutch anthropologist, Arnold Van Gennep, published in 1908 a book entitled *The Rites of Passage.* In this book, Van Gennep described how traditional societies structured life transitions. Rituals dealing with birth, puberty, separation from a group or society, marriage, incorporation back into a group with new roles and functions, and death were seen by Van Gennep as important ceremonies marking significant occasions in life. He saw these occasions as being made up of three phases: separation, transition, and incorporation.*

_____

*Van Gennep, Arnold. *The Rites of Passage,* trans. Monika B. Visedam and Gabrielle L. Chaffee (1908, reprint) Chicago: University of Chicago Press, 1960.

William Bridges, in his book *Transitions–Making Sense of Life's Changes,* describes three natural phases of a transition. He named the first phase "Endings," followed by "The Neutral Zone," and the third phase "The New Beginning." Bridges described in detail these three phases which affirm that transition is the key to personal development and growth.*

Frederic M. Hudson, in his book *The Adult Years–Mastering the Art of Self Renewal* described a cycle of change that continues without stopping throughout our lives. he made a distinction between "mini-transitions" which deal with minor restructuring of one's life, such as a move or job change, and a "life transition" which involves a major disengagement from most aspects of your present lifestyle and a re-evaluation of goals, relationships, work values and relationship with the outside world.**

According to Dr. Nancy Schlossberg of the University of Maryland, a *transition* is any event or time passage that results in a change in how you see yourself, the world around you, and your relationships with others. You cannot always predict the sequence in which transitions occur, but you can expect many to take place in your lifetime. There are some transitions that you can anticipate because they take place slowly and involve some planning. Some examples of this type of transition are marriage, the birth of a child, and earning a college degree. Other transitions may be unexpected, such as the death of someone close to you or the sudden loss of a job.

Some transitions are easy to deal with; others are much more difficult. How *you* react and how successful you are in dealing with a transition depend on three basic factors.

1. Your perception of the transition
2. Your personal characteristics
3. Your support systems

It is important to learn how you can deal more effectively with the transitions in your life. The following outline is based on work done by Dr. Nancy Schlossberg.***

---

* Bridges, William. *Transitions.* Reading, Mass.: Addison-Wesley Publishing Company, 1980.
** Hudson, Frederic M. *The Adult Years–Mastering the Art of Self Renewal.* San Francisco: Jossey-Bass Publishers, 1991.
***Schlossberg, Nancy K. "Model for Analyzing Human Adaptation to Transition." *The Counseling Psychologist,* 1981, Vol. 9, No. 2, pp. 2–17.

A. Your Perception of the Transition

How do you look at a particular transition? When you are faced with a change in your life, it is important to evaluate how you feel about the change and how it affects you. Your attitude about a transition makes a big difference in how successful you are in dealing with it. Some of the factors to consider are:

1. Do you see the transition as a gain or as a loss?

Every change in your life involves some gain *and* loss. Do you approach change with eager anticipation or with great reluctance? A change that at first seems to be a major loss may, in the long run, turn into a major gain. For example, if your job is unrewarding, but you are reluctant to leave, and the organization for which you work goes out of business, you may eventually end up with a job that is much more rewarding. Try to look at the positive aspects of each transition you face.

2. Do you have control over the transition?

Did you cause the transition to happen or did it happen to you? You will react differently if you feel that you have some control over what is happening to you. Examples of transitions you control are choosing to change jobs, choosing to marry someone, and choosing where to live. Examples of transitions over which you have little control are serious family illness, your child's choice of a spouse, and the loss of financial aid due to a change in government policies. Often, you may in fact have more control than you think. When dealing with a transition over which you feel you have little or no control, try to identify those factors over which you do have some control and work on them.

3. Is the source of the transition internal or external?

Does the transition come from you or from others and conditions around you? Internal sources can be such factors as changes in your health, in your values, or in your career goals. External sources might be an imposed change in job responsibilities, children leaving home, or the loss of a close friend. You may feel more in control if the source of the transition is internal. However, it is also important to evaluate how you can control and respond to a transition when the source is external.

4. Is the timing of the transition on-time or off-time?

You expect certain changes in your life to take place at certain times. Examples of this would be retirement in the early or mid sixties and children going to college after graduation from high school. These are usually anticipated and planned for. On the other hand, there are changes that may be off-time. Examples of this would be forced early retirement or the loss of your spouse through separation or early death. Off-time transitions can be more difficult to deal with, especially if you have a strong feeling that certain changes should take place at certain times in your life.

5. Does the transition come suddenly or gradually?

You can plan a gradual transition, such as children leaving home, a coming marriage, or the birth of a child. It is more difficult to plan for a transition such as a heart attack, an accident, or a sudden loss of financial resources. Also, a promotion or inheritance may present the need to make difficult decisions immediately.

6. Is the transition permanent, temporary, or uncertain?

If you and your spouse have a newborn child and it is your first, you can expect the transition in your lives to be quite permanent. If you move from one city to another, the loss you feel and the strangeness of being in a new place will most likely be temporary. If you have an accident or health problem and the prognosis is uncertain, it is more difficult to plan ahead. This type of transition may be much more difficult to deal with.

7. What is the degree of stress involved?

If you feel that you have no control over a change in your life, it is likely to be more stressful to you. Also, sudden change creates more stress than gradual change. If you have people who can provide help and support as you work through a transition, you can reduce the amount of stress you feel. Anything you can do to gain some control of your situation will also reduce stress.

B. YOUR PERSONAL CHARACTERISTICS

How do your own personal characteristics affect the way you deal with transitions in your life? In evaluating how you can more effectively manage change, it is important to consider several factors that relate specifically to you.

1. **Your sex and sex-role identification**

   Generally, women are better able than men to tolerate stress, and women have fewer stress-related illnesses. If you are a man and see yourself as the primary breadwinner for your family, the loss of your job may hit you harder than if you see your role of provider as a shared responsibility with your wife.

2. **Your health**

   If you are not physically or mentally well, it will be more difficult for you to deal with a major transition. For this and other reasons, it is important to stay physically active and to obtain assistance, if necessary, to work through any emotional concerns that you may have.

3. **Your age and life stage**

   If your organization makes you retire early, it is an unexpected transition to make in your life stage. If you are in your forties, you may be reluctant to make a career change because you feel that you should be more "stable" at your age. If you are a woman reaching 40 and want to have your first child, you may have misgivings because you feel that you are "too old." This type of age-referenced behavior can often be very self-defeating and restricting.

4. **Your mental approach**

   Do you look at a glass of water and see it as half full or half empty? You can take a negative, even catastrophic, view and look on the dark side of most changes. However, you can look at change as a new opportunity and concentrate on the positive aspects of any transition.

5. **Your values orientation**

   If you intensely value work as the number one priority in your life and then lose your job or don't receive an expected promotion, it will hit you much harder than if you have a more balanced set of family, work, and leisure values. If you have strong ties to your extended family and to your community, it may be very difficult for you to accept a job in another part of the country.

6. **Previous experience with a transition of a similar nature**

If you have already had one child, the process of pregnancy, birth, and early childcare is usually easier the second time. If you have been out of work and have had to conduct a job campaign, it is usually easier if you have to do it again. If you have dealt successfully with a crisis in your life, you can probably handle another crisis more effectively.

C. Your Support Systems

What kind of support is available to you when you are dealing with a transition? It is important to obtain the help that you need and not always try to "go it alone." It is also important to have your support systems established *before* you really need them. Possible sources of support are as follows.

1. **Interpersonal support systems.**

If you have family support, a network of friends, or some intimate relationships, you have good sources of support for dealing with a transition. It is important to develop and maintain your interpersonal support systems as a normal part of your lifestyle. Remember that this support system does not have to involve a lot of people. Even one close friend, your spouse, or a family member who can help you through some difficult transitions can make a world of difference.

2. **Institutional and community support systems.**

In addition to your own interpersonal support systems, it may help to use some of the services available in the community. Examples of these services are community agencies, workshops, counseling and mental health services, special-interest groups such as AA, the Widow-to-Widow Program, and Parents Without Partners, college and adult education courses, and church groups. Do not be reluctant to ask for help. The assistance and support can be critical to your successful progress through a difficult transition.

Summary—Transitions

In the next section of this chapter you will look at some of the major transitions that you may face at various stages in your life. Before you read on, however, let's summarize some of the major considerations when you face change.

1. **You need to be aware of three basic factors.**

    - Your perception of the transition
    - Your personal characteristics
    - Your support systems

2. **You need to realize that it may take a long time to adapt to a loss or to a major transition.**
3. **You need to make use of the resources available to you and to set up support systems ahead of time.**
4. **Your attitude is important as you integrate a transition in your life. It is helpful to look at the positive aspects of a transition and to work on them.**
5. **There are different types of transitions. Some can be completed easily. Others may take much more time and effort.**

D. YOUR OWN TRANSITIONS

Before you continue reading, use the following spaces to list four transitions that you have gone through in the past ten to fifteen years. Then assess how you dealt with each transition and how you might have better handled it. How did you perceive it? How did your personal characteristics influence your handling of the transition? What kind of support did you have? How long did it take to work through the transition?

Transition 1: _____

How did I deal with this transition? _____

_____

_____

How could I have better handled this transition? _____

_____

_____

Transition 2: _____

How did I deal with this transition? _____

_____

_____

How could I have better handled this transition? _____

_____

_____

Transition 3: _____

How did I deal with this transition? _____

_____

_____

How could I have better handled this transition? _____

_____

_____

Transition 4: _____

How did I deal with this transition? _____

_____

_____

How could I have better handled this transition? _____

_____

_____

Now move on to chapter 9, Understanding Change.

Understanding Change

What changes have you experienced in the past ten years? It's natural for adults to have changing needs and changing roles. This has increasingly become a matter for study by psychologists and others. In the past, most of the emphasis in studying human developmental needs was placed on young children and teenagers. Adults were considered to be relatively stable unless some serious change, such as mental illness, arose. This attitude was consistent with the relatively stable lifestyle that was promoted and perceived as "healthy" for most adults—a stable job with the same organization over a number of years, a family, house, car, and all the trappings of a consistent, successful lifestyle.

Many people, however, are reluctant to accept a societal definition of what a good adult lifestyle should be. People do change and often need something different, or something more. It is important for you to evaluate where you are in your development and to analyze some of the forces within you that may be calling for change. Also, consider that the economic environment and the world of work are changing, and you will need to change in response to these forces. The following is a summary of the various life stages that most adults go through in one way or another. Please remember that the descriptions and time periods are general. Each individual does go through various life stages, but the time sequence and intensity of the changes may vary greatly from person to person.

A. The Early Adult Years (Ages 20–40)

The early part of this period involves much testing of skills and establishment of the individual's independence and identity. Parents play a less important role in influencing an individual's decisions or lifestyle than they did before. Peer groups are more important as the individual searches for personal identity. There is a tendency to reach out toward others in an attempt to develop intimacy in relationships. In some cases this is fulfilled by marriage. In other cases, close friendships meet this need. This period is usually marked by the end of full-time education and the beginning of full-time work. The individual may hold a variety of jobs, because working environments and job skills are tested. The need to start at the bottom of the ladder in many organizations and the often slow movement into areas of increased responsibility can be a source of frustration. Many individuals have a need to move quickly and may not be accepting of older people and "the establishment." Another potential source of frustration can come from the scarcity of career-oriented jobs due to economic downturns and organizational downsizing. Some young people may feel that they must accept jobs they consider to be unfulfilling or beneath their skills and education.

This period is marked by the dreams and possibilities that go with a feeling of an unlimited future. So many opportunities exist that there is often little concern with long-range planning. There is usually a desire to create an independent life structure and an identity separate from parents and previous family associations. Often during this period, an individual benefits from having a "mentor," who provides acceptance, support, and assistance in the individual's development.

Although many individuals set up housekeeping on their own well before the age of 20, this period marks a time when possessions of significance may be acquired as the individual moves into a home of her own. There may well be limited financial resources, which sometimes can lead to impatience in achieving tangible goals, such as a home. An individual may be tempted to remain at home with parents in order to stretch financial resources, and this can delay the establishment of independence that is one of the major life tasks of this period.

Family skills are often tested during this time, most frequently through a marriage relationship and by the effort it takes to make such a relationship work. In contrast to earlier generations, individuals may choose a wide variety of relationships and lifestyles. Single-parent homes are more common, as are long-term relationships that do not necessarily involve marriage. Blended families with children from previous marriages and adoptions by couples or by single individuals are examples of the variety of relationships that are generally perceived as acceptable by society. Perhaps one of the most significant developments in recent years has been the crumbling of the stereotypes about what a "typical" family or relationship should be like. Individuals feel more free to develop lifestyles based on their own needs and values, rather than on what they think they "should" do.

In summary, the early part of this period can be one of rapid growth and development, a period in which opportunities seem great—so great that there may be frustration over the rate with which some goals are achieved. This is a period of testing, learning, and developing skills and identity as an adult.

As one enters the thirties, there may be a reevaluation of life's purpose, and an individual may question early decisions that were made regarding self, career, and family. It is important to sit back, evaluate, and consider changes that can be made. An individual's values may change considerably from the twenties to the thirties, and these should be taken into account in considering change. For many individuals, progress in their careers and in other life endeavors has brought a greater degree of self-confidence and self-worth. Recognition has been gained for accomplishments on and off the job, and the individual has the satisfaction of making more of an impact. There may well be more payoffs from work in terms of higher status, prestige, pay, and a feeling of success. Others may just be starting their careers or changing to new careers. Some may not like the work they are doing but may be reluctant to initiate a change. Some may look to outlets other than work for fulfillment. In many cases, workers in this period of life spend a lot of time on the job.

Family responsibilities can consume a lot of time and energy during this period. Given the need to juggle work, family and other responsibilities, there may not be much time for an individual to pursue personal interests or for a couple to spend time together or to develop and maintain relationships with friends and extended family members. If there are children in the household, there are constant challenges of all kinds, from getting them to soccer games on time to dealing with moodiness during the teenage years. If one is involved in a marital or other relationship, it is very important to save some time for the relationship and to maintain effective communication. There may be changing roles as both partners in a relationship pursue their career and life goals. No longer is it expected that the female partner will stay home with the children and defer to the male partner's career needs. The resulting integration of roles can enhance communication.

Physical changes begin to take on a greater significance during this period. It is easier to put on weight. Hair may begin to disappear or turn gray. Physical strength and capabilities may not be quite the same as before. For the first time, the individual is reminded that there is an aging process. There is a tendency to compare progress in career, family, and status with that of friends and relatives, and of others one's age. This age-referenced behavior can be overcome by concentrating on one's own needs, goals, and values. Many individuals need to have some evidence of success, whether it be through job status, acquisition of material goods, accomplishments of children, or through other means. As one approaches the late thirties, there may be a feeling that it is important to make things happen now.

This may be the most dynamic of all life periods. It begins with relative youth and ends with middle age. More issues are confronted during this period than during any other, and the decisions that are made can determine an individual's lifestyle for years to come.

B. The Middle Adult Years (Ages 40–60)

This period could be characterized as the "half-empty or half-full" period, meaning that one's outlook toward life can make a huge difference in the way that one progresses during this time. Researchers have determined that at some point in their forties, individuals tend to begin thinking in terms of time they have left rather than time from birth. Others have emphasized the need to reevaluate one's dreams and life goals, to integrate one's successes and disappointments, and to establish new goals and dreams. As the general population ages, whole sections of gift shops displaying "over-40' items have appeared. Most of the items contain a lot of black and humorously reflect the stereotypes of aging. There is no problem with having fun during this transition. The problem comes when the individual begins to believe the stereotypes. This is often associated with the so-called "midlife crisis,' in which an individual has great difficulty integrating his progress through life and may act out in unproductive ways.

Some people may experience rich career growth during this period, while others are able to relax and help others to grow, drawing on the depth and richness of their experience. Still others may be frustrated by the lack of career growth potential and may seek a change in their jobs or careers. There may be fewer opportunities for change, but it is important to deal realistically with the opportunities that are available, rather than falling into a pattern of job dissatisfaction or lethargy. There is the opportunity to establish new career goals, which may involve being a mentor to others, using skills outside of one's job, or becoming involved in new directions within one's profession.

Changes outside of one's career may include the growing independence of children and the opportunities to reach out to others and to cultivate new friendships. As one's responsibilities with work and family diminish, there can be more time to devote to outside activities and relationships. More time can be devoted to the relationship with one's partner or friends. Although researchers once thought that the transition of children moving away from home would be very difficult for many people, this is not the case. There is much more of a problem when children do not move out and establish their independence or when they return after having been on their own.

Although the early forties can be a time of upheaval, the mid to late forties can be a period of settling down. If the individual can come to a realistic reassessment of dreams and goals and can make decisions and modifications to career and lifestyle, there is the opportunity for increased self-acceptance and greater enjoyment of life. The individual may be more willing to settle down, may be less driven, and may be more able to relax. There may be less perceived pressure to achieve, less of a rush to reach major goals, but instead a desire to enjoy life. Leisure time becomes more important. There may be fewer family responsibilities and possibly more friends. There is a reaching out for new friendships and for new ways to achieve satisfaction in life. This is an opportunity to develop new paths and new dreams, to adjust to them and to set a new life structure. By dealing positively with midlife, an individual can find new ways for life to become more enjoyable and rewarding. Hobbies and other interests can take on a whole new meaning and importance in life.

The latter part of this period is marked by a mellowing process, in which there can be softening of feelings and relationships, with more emphasis on everyday joys, minor achievements, and irritations. Some individuals attempt to deal with the aging process by returning to some of the things they feel symbolized the happiness of their youth. This denial of reality can often bring frustrating and unhappy results. Other individuals, having dealt with midlife changes and having gone through the settling down of the late forties, enter this period with few regrets. New experiences, friendships, and activities are tried with varying results. The individual is now definitely a member of the "older" generation and may have difficulty accepting this fact. Some approach advancing years with a sense of discouragement and withdrawal, whereas others see this as an opportunity for new freedoms, with fewer family responsibilities.

An individual's career may have reached a plateau by this period. There may continue to be challenges, but they may be of a more modest nature. Some deal with this by entering second careers where the challenges of starting something new provide stimulation. A realistic evaluation of alternatives is necessary during this period. Not all opportunities are open and the individual must realize this.

Although there may be fewer family responsibilities, with children grown and independent, the new role of grandparent can be a comfort and provide new opportunities for family involvement. There may be concern over the care for aging parents and for finding facilities to meet their needs. For those who have partners, the new role that developed in the forties continues in this period, with more opportunities to do things together and to share activities and interests with friends. The woman may now have the need to assert herself more and to find individual fulfillment through work and independent activities, while the man may be more content to take an active role in family affairs. This role reversal in the later years is common to many cultures. As the individual goes through the fifties, there can be two distinct approaches. One is to view the period with resignation, withdrawal, and discouragement, and to face the aging process with negativity and fear. The other approach is to see this period as an opportunity to try new things and to make new friendships, unencumbered by some of the responsibilities and demands of earlier years. It is the time to ask "what is the quality of life I want in the time I have left?"

C. THE LATER ADULT YEARS (AGE 60 AND OLDER)

Many people face retirement during this period, but the concept that people retire at age 65 and take it easy is a misleading stereotype. In most jobs, there is no longer a mandatory retirement age. Even though people can work as long as they wish, the average age at which people retire has not risen significantly. Individuals simply have more options and now have the opportunity to exercise those options regarding retirement or career change. Many retire much earlier than age 60 in order to change their lifestyle or to enter a new career. It is possible to enter retirement with a sense of loss of self-worth if an individual defines too much of herself in terms of career role, but there are many opportunities, with or without paid work, to maintain a rich and varied lifestyle in the sixties and beyond.

Some of the major developmental tasks during this period are to decide when and whether to leave one's career, what kind of lifestyle to pursue, how to deal with the aging process, maintaining relationships with one's partner and others, and planning for the future. As in the transition of the forties, it is possible to fall into a negative pattern of dwelling on lost opportunities and longing for the return to the "good old days." One of the most important tasks is to integrate one's life experiences and to move on to new experiences and new opportunities.

As the population changes, there are increasing work opportunities for people in their sixties. Many gain fulfillment from part-time work, because it allows more flexibility in a weekly schedule. Others use the extra time as an opportunity to help others or to use their skills in a variety of volunteer activities. It is important to assess what needs are fulfilled by an individual's work and to develop a plan to fulfill those needs through a variety of activities. A diversity of interests can help to fulfill very important needs.

The most common concern of people over 60 is whether they will be able to remain financially secure in their later years. This is certainly important, given the fact that people are living longer than in past generations. Issues such as health care, housing, safety, long-term care, and inflation take on an added degree of importance when an individual considers a lifestyle based on a retirement income. Long-term planning is essential. Health factors become much more important during this period of life. Individuals must realize that they can play an active role in maintaining good health practices and can actually increase their chances of living longer. (See Section VI.) One of the most important needs of this period is to be prepared for change. A flexible, positive attitude, good health practices, and good support systems can help an individual to deal with the changes and losses that can mark this period.

Summary

As you read the characteristics of the various life stages, you may see certain ones that apply to you. Life is complex, and not everyone goes through these stages at the same time. Also, what may be a particularly critical time for one person may be an easy time for another. We all go through various stages but with greatly different degrees of intensity. Why look at life stages? It is important to acknowledge that they do exist and that everyone is affected by them in some way. There may well be crises between stages, and these challenges can be a positive stimulus for change and growth. It is important to be aware of the changes within you and how they affect you. Too often we think of external changes as the most significant points in our lives—graduation, marriage, having children, or getting a job. These are important, but there are other more subtle changes constantly taking place. Crises can produce growth. A problem can be turned into a new opportunity, or it can be met with an attitude of defeat. It is important throughout life to accept challenges in order to grow.

D. Your Own Life Stages

Look back over the descriptions of the life stages. Where are you? List some of the problems or decisions you are now facing.

1. _____

_____

2. _____

_____

_____

3. _____

_____

_____

4. _____

_____

_____

5. _____

_____

_____

6. _____

_____

_____

E. Change in the World of Work

In chapter seven, you learned about the career and life planning needs for the 21st century. The following is a summary of some of the major factors to consider when you plan for changes in your career now and in the future.

1. **Most people will change careers several times.**

   As people progress throughout life, they will be more likely to change careers, and changing careers three to six times in a lifetime will be the norm rather than the exception. This increased likelihood of career change is a result of changing values of workers and rapid changes in job expectations.

2. **"Jobs" as they have been defined will change significantly.**

   Organizations will increasingly look for people who can perform specific kinds of work for a given period of time. They will be less likely to make a commitment to an individual to take on a job title. Careers may involve working simultaneously for several organizations, performing work projects.

3. **Greater emphasis will be placed on transferable skills.**

   Jobs will require people to use skills such as analyzing, reading, writing, communicating, computation, and problem solving. These are skills that a person takes from one job to another, and they will become more important as a higher level of job functioning is required.

4. **Careers will require more adaptive skills.**

   Changing technologies and societal needs will require organizations to restructure jobs more often than in the past. People who hold these jobs will be expected to adapt to new procedures and new challenges.

5. **Lifelong learning will be essential.**

   Workers must be committed to acquiring new knowledge and skills by continuing their education and professional development both inside and outside the workplace.

6. **Workers will be more involved with quality and productivity.**

   The distinctions between management and workers will decrease. Teams of workers will share responsibility for the results. Workers at lower levels will participate in the overall program rather than passively performing only their specific functions. Rotation of job responsibilities among members of a team will become commonplace.

7. **New jobs will require more education and higher levels of skill.**

The greatest growth in new jobs will be in those that require some post-secondary education. A higher premium will be placed on two- and four-year education prior to entry into a job and on increased on-the-job training. Jobs will require more sophisticated skills. The more menial, repetitive tasks will be handled by computers and machines.

8. **Assessment of time and values will be important.**

As the workplace changes, workers will need to regularly assess the demands on their time and now these relate to their work and personal values in order to deal effectively with potentially stressful work environments.

9. **Workers will be called on to make more decisions.**

Computers will take care of a great deal of the tedious work that occupied much of the time of millions of workers. Decisions about products and services will be the responsibility of more and more workers.

10. **The service sector will grow most rapidly.**

Jobs related to services, such as education, health care, retail, government, finance, and transportation, will expand more rapidly than jobs related to producing goods, such as manufacturing, construction, agriculture, and mining. Many new jobs will be at entry level in terms of wages and responsibilities.

11. **The makeup of the workforce will change.**

Five of every six new people entering the labor market will be women and minorities. There will also be a gradual aging of the workforce.

12. **Flexible work patterns will continue to expand.**

Creative responses to work and home schedules will grow. Flex-time, sabbaticals, job sharing, part-time work, home-based work, and alternative work schedules will become more common in a variety of organizations.

In summary, the world of work will change dramatically and will require higher levels of skills, the ability to adapt, and the willingness to become involved in the total job picture rather than in one's own narrow specialty. The ability to manage change will be an important asset, and as the world of work changes, exciting opportunities will arise for those who are prepared to change.

F. THE FUTURE

An often-overlooked source of job market information is the growing literature on the future. Our society is changing rapidly. New careers are emerging in areas such as artificial intelligence, robotics, and other fields related to our transition to an information society. Changes in demographics, such as the increasing average age of the population in our society, will bring significant changes to the workplace. Totally new career areas will appear, and some existing career areas will experience rapid growth. Other career areas will decline, and of these, some may disappear altogether.

In planning for change, it may be helpful to take some time to investigate future trends in the world of work and in society in general. The time spent in exploring the future can be both enlightening and practical, because it may help you to identify new career opportunities and to better prepare yourself for the changes that lie before you. Here are some resources on expected trends.

ADDITIONAL RESOURCES

Bridges, William. *Job Shift–How to Prosper in a Workplace without Jobs.* Ready, MA: Addison-Wesley Publishing Co., 1994.

Campbell, Colin. *Jobscape: Career Survival in the New Global Economy.* Indianapolis, IN: JIST Works, 1998.

Cornish, Edward, ed. *Exploring Your Future: Living Learning and Working in the Information Age.* World Future Society, 1996.

Davidson, Jeff. *Market Yourself and Your Career.* Holbrook, MA: Adams Media, 1999.

Drucker, Peter. *The New Realities.* New York: HarpC, 1990.

Farr, Michael J. *America's Fastest Growing Jobs.* Indianapolis, IN: JIST Works, 1999.

Farr, Michael and Ludden, LaVerne, *Best Jobs for the 21st Century.* Indianapolis, IN: JIST Works, 1999.

Feingold, S. Norman. *Futuristic Exercises: A Work Book for Emerging Life Styles and Careers in the 21st Century and Beyond.* Maryland: Garrett Park Press, 1989.

Field, Shelly. *100 Best Careers for the 21st Century.* New York: MacMillan, 1996.

Field, Shelly. *100 Best Careers for the 21st Century.* California: IDG Books, 1999.

Harkavy, Michael David. *101 Careers: A Guide to the Fastest Growing Opportunities.* New York, John Wiley & Sons, 1998.

Krannich, Ronald and Krannick, Carol. *The Best Jobs for the 21st Century.* Manassas Park, VA: Impact Publications, 1998.

Naisbitt, John. *Megatrends.* Illinois: Nightingale-Conant, 1989.

Rifkin, Jeremy. *The End of Work.* New York: G.P. Putnam's Sons, 1995.

Scheel, Randall L. *Introduction to the Future.* California: ETC Publications, 1988.

The Top 100: The Fastest Growing Careers for the 21st Century. Chicago: Ferguson Publishing Co., 1998.

Toffler, Alvin. *Future Shock.* New York: Bantam Books, 1971.

———. *Third Wave.* New York: Bantam Books, 1984.

Wegmann, Robert. *Work in the New Economy.* Indiana: AACD/JIST Works, 1989.

Yate, Martin. *Career Smarts; Jobs with a Future.* New York: Ballantine Books, 1997.

Only in growth, reform and change, paradoxically enough, is true security to be found.

—Anne Morrow Lindberg,
The Wave of the Future

Influence of Others

How can other people help you deal with change? Too often, individuals perceive family members, coworkers, and others as impeding or discouraging change. What influence do others have over you and how can you develop support systems to help you manage change in your life? This section will describe three categories of people who can be of great help to you as you deal with life's changes.

- Your personal board of directors
- Your support groups
- Your network of personal contacts

A. Your Personal Board of Directors

As you evaluate the influence of others over your ability to make decisions, consider which people to include on your personal board of directors. These are the special people to whom you can most easily and most productively turn when you need help in making decisions. You can depend on these people to really listen to you and to understand your needs—you know them well and trust them. They can focus on helping you consider what is best for you. They are the people whose opinions you respect, to whom you can turn for advice, steady counsel, insight, and an honest assessment of your options. They are people who will set aside their own agendas and concentrate on *your* needs.

Your personal board of directors may include selected family members, but you should think carefully about which family members you wish to include. Remember the requirement that they be able to concentrate on your needs in making a decision. Your personal board of directors may include some of your closest friends. It may include a professional career counselor or therapist, someone who has served as your mentor, or someone to whom you can turn for counsel, support, and advice at your place of work. Your personal board of directors are those people who provide an anchor for you and whom you can depend on and trust to be there when you need them. You may call on certain members of your board for certain kinds of decisions—you don't have to convene the whole board for every matter that comes up. Some may help with decisions regarding your career, some with family issues, and some with personal decisions. It is important to include several people on your board but to choose them carefully. They can be a tremendous resource as you make decisions and manage change.

The diagram on the following page represents your personal boardroom. Write on the chairs the names of the people who sit on your personal board of directors. Don't be concerned if you have some empty chairs. Take special note of who sits to the immediate right and left of you. These members of your board have significant impact. Also take special note of all those at the table. Is there someone who should be closer to you, whose help you wish to enlist more than you have so far?

Are there others whom you would like to include on your personal board of directors? Are there areas in your life where you need someone to fill an empty place on your board? If so, make an effort to identify people who can serve on your board in the future. Evaluate your board frequently, because you never know when new challenges will require special assistance. Remember that counseling professionals can help to fill gaps that may exist. Unlike a corporation, you do not have to publish the names of the members of your board. Individuals

may not even know that you consider them to be members of your board. What is important is that you identify those individuals on whom you can count for quality assistance in time of need.

B. Support Groups

Support groups are different from your personal board of directors, but they can be very important to your ability to handle change in your life. Support groups can provide you with the opportunity to share your thoughts, to exchange ideas and concerns, to grow with others, to obtain encouragement, and to develop friendships. Support groups differ from your personal board of directors in that they may not provide direct assistance to you at the same level of intensity, but they can provide a very important outlet to help you deal with a variety of life decisions. There are many types of support groups. The following is a list of some of them.

- Family members
- Classmates
- Neighbors

- Colleagues at work
- Friends
- Church groups

Special-needs groups such as:

- Alcoholics Anonymous
- Service organizations
- Personal growth groups
- Political action groups

- Weight-control groups
- Teams and sports groups
- Career planning groups
- Travel clubs

Support groups are very important to us as we go through life. Sometimes we take for granted the support that we receive from people and the positive effect on our lives of simply being with others.

There is evidence that having support groups and being open to developing a variety of relationships with others can help you to live a happier and longer life. In the following spaces, list some of your support groups. Don't be concerned if you can't fill all of the blanks.

1. _____   6. _____

2. _____   7. _____

3. _____   8. _____

4. _____   9. _____

5. _____   10. _____

What additional support groups can you develop? Do you have any special needs that you can help to meet through a support group? Remember that there is a great deal of evidence demonstrating the value of support groups in career planning; dealing with problems such as smoking, alcohol, and other addictions; handling stress; dealing with family issues; personal growth; and in making many other important life decisions.

C. INTERPERSONAL NETWORKS

It is always important to keep open to new ideas, new relationships, and new opportunities. One very good way to accomplish this is through networking. Whenever you go to a meeting, a social gathering, a conference, a trip, or any other occasion that puts you in contact with people, take the time to meet other people and to learn about them. Whether the occasion be job related, common interest, or just getting to know someone, you can expand your network of contacts, learn more about other people and their ideas, and consequently learn more about yourself. Networking can help you to grow as an individual. It offers you resources that you can refer to as you progress through your life and career. You can identify people who have the potential to become colleagues, friends, or even members of your personal board of directors.

Where do you network? Just about anywhere!

- Conferences
- Meetings
- Social gatherings
- Friends of friends
- Families of friends
- Contacts with the public
- On-line interest groups through the Internet
- Volunteering
- Interest sessions
- Associations
- Informational interviewing
- Seminars
- Classes
- E-Mail

Networking can be fun and it can be very helpful as you make career and life decisions. You will find out how others have approached decisions and you will meet people who can give you valuable information. You may even meet people who will be in a position some day to hire you. However, perhaps the greatest value of networking is that your life will be enriched as you expand your personal contacts and are exposed to new ideas and new relationships. You will be able to incorporate creative and innovative approaches that you learn about through networking into your present work and lifestyle. How can you expand your network of personal contacts? Write some possible approaches in the following spaces.

_____

_____

_____

_____

_____

_____

_____

_____

_____

_____

_____

D. FINDING A MENTOR

Many people who have studied adult development have emphasized the importance of a mentor as a positive factor in dealing with career and life decisions. A mentor is someone who can provide you with insight, support, reflection, and sound advice. You may even wish to consider having more than one mentor. While your career growth can benefit from your having a mentor, it may be possible to have a mentor for different parts of your life, such as your creative self or religious self. How do you choose a mentor? Here is a list of qualities to look for in a mentor. However, do not expect your mentor to possess all of these qualities.

Qualities of a Good Mentor

Consider the following when you look for someone to be a mentor.

1. A mentor is someone who listens. A mentor can give advice, but also *listens to you* and tries to understand what *you* want and need.

2. A mentor is usually secure. A good mentor has most likely reached a level of comfort in her life and career. This allows the mentor to give more to you without being overly concerned about her own position. This is especially important if you and your mentor work for the same organization.

3. A mentor is not too self-referent. Many people respond to an idea or to a question by describing what they did or what happened to them. While this can sometimes be very helpful, a good mentor will try to understand what is going on in *your* life and career and will center on *your* needs.

4. A mentor will have the ability to make time to see you. Although you will not be talking with your mentor every day, you should be able to have regular access to your mentor, in person or by telephone. However, be careful not to become overly dependent on your mentor.

5. A mentor is someone who has a genuine interest in you and a desire to help you grow.

6. A mentor should be a moderate risk taker. A mentor who values the status quo above all may not be able to provide the support you need when you are thinking about making a change or taking a risk.

7. A mentor should be politically astute. A mentor who knows the ins and outs of an organization or a professional field is a valuable resource. By sharing how to accomplish things in an organization, the mentor can provide thoughtful and useful assistance.

8. A mentor should be able to grasp the big picture. A mentor should be able to look at the total organization or situation and at your relationship to it. A mentor who has a very narrow focus may not have the perspective you need.

9. A mentor should be someone who shares your values. Look for a mentor whose ideas are compatible with yours. You do not have to think alike, but it is preferable that you both be comfortable with the basic concepts such as the relationship between work and your private life and the qualities needed for a successful career.

10. A mentor should be someone who is flexible in dealing with people and ideas. A mentor should not be someone who applies rigid standards and who feels that there is only one right way to do something.

Where to Find a Mentor

You can find a mentor just about anywhere, but here are some suggestions.

1. On your job. Your mentor could be your supervisor, if your supervisor has many of the qualities of a good mentor.

2. On your job, but not your supervisor. Often, someone who is not in the immediate chain of command that affects you may be able to be a good mentor, since the person would be familiar with the organization but would have some distance from your immediate work situation.
3. A friend. Any friend who has the qualities of a mentor can act as your mentor.
4. A colleague in a similar organization. Sometimes, a good mentor can be someone who works in a job situation that is similar to yours so that she can better understand the dynamics of your work environment.
5. A family member. A family member who has the qualities of a good mentor could easily be your mentor. However, remember that family members often tend to favor stability in decision making and often find it difficult to be objective in providing help.
6. A colleague in a professional organization. A good way to find a mentor is to go to professional meetings and develop a network of colleagues. Through this network, you may find a person to be a mentor.
7. A teacher. A former or current teacher can often provide the perspective and support that you need from a mentor.
8. A former colleague. A good way to find a mentor is to keep in touch with someone with whom you have worked in the past. This person will have the benefit of having known you in the workplace but will have a different perspective from someone with whom you presently work.

A good mentor can be someone of either sex and any age. A mentor does not have to be older, although often an older person would have been able to develop more of the qualities of a good mentor as described. It is important to remember that there is a limit to the time that you can expect a mentor to give and to the type of issues that you ask a mentor to help you address. Try to be sensitive to the number of times you contact your mentor. Don't endanger your relationship by making too many demands on your mentor's time. In addition, there are some issues with which you may need additional help. When you are experiencing significant personal, emotional, or career problems, you may wish to seek professional counseling. Your mentor can provide valuable support during such times, but only as a part of your overall support system.

Summary—Influence of Others

It is important to seek the support of others as you make decisions throughout life. Some people may have a very large personal board of directors, many support groups, and a large network. Others may choose to have a much smaller board and fewer support groups. It is not important whether you have a huge network of support. What matters is that you have some people to whom you can turn to for support in making decisions and in dealing with a variety of life issues.

It is also important to remember that you are your number one supporter and that you have the ultimate responsibility for making a decision. It is important to control the influence that others have in your life and to choose your sources of support wisely. In the end, you must listen to your inner self and make your decision based on your own needs, the information you have obtained, and the help you have received from others. Do not expect others to make decisions for you. That is unfair to them and to you. Be your own best friend when it comes to making your final decision. You will find that your confidence will grow, spurred on by the support that you receive from others and by the decisions that you make for yourself.

Taking Risks

As you go through life, it is important to continually evaluate your options and to explore alternatives. It may take you a long time to get the information you need. However, there will come a time when you have to make a choice, and this may involve some risk.

This point, where you must make a decision about your direction, can be compared to a junction in the route of your train through life. You have to choose which track to follow. This is a place where many people stop the career and life planning process. Unable to choose, they wait at the junction, unwilling to risk going in the wrong direction. They would like to know exactly what lies ahead in both directions, but they cannot see that far. They would like to experience the trip without making the commitment to take the train along the track. They feel that there may be too much risk involved in making a choice. But is there also risk in remaining at the junction? To take no action is to make a decision by default, and, indeed, there is risk in doing nothing.

115

A. How Willing Are You to Take Risks?

In order to make a decision about your future, it is important to evaluate the risk that *you* are willing to take. Some people are much more able than others to take risks involving their careers, due to fewer family responsibilities, financial situation, skills to fall back on, and other factors. Other people are simply more willing to risk, to take a chance, and to take action without knowing fully what the outcome will be. In fact, it is impossible to know completely the future outcome of major decisions.

In all growth, there is usually some risk. Taking risks does create stress, but what would a life without stress be like? It would probably be very dull and would not involve much growth. In order to grow, we often must put ourselves in stressful positions by taking risks. The potential for change is in all of us, but it is up to each individual to decide how much risk to take for each change. We can do excellent research before making a major decision in order to decrease the unknown factors and reduce the amount of risk. But the final decision must be made, and it will usually be impossible to eliminate all risk. After all, as Helen Keller wrote: "Life is either a daring adventure or nothing." Here are some questions to help you evaluate the results of risks you have taken.

1. What are two of the greatest risks that you have taken in your life?

   _____

   _____

2. Why were these risks? What did you stand to gain? What did you stand to lose?

   _____

   _____

   _____

   _____

3. What happened as a result of your taking these risks?

   _____

   _____

   _____

   _____

4. What responses did you encounter from others before, during, and after you took these risks?

_____

_____

_____

_____

5. How did you feel after you took these risks? Did it affect your self-confidence in any way?

_____

_____

_____

_____

B. TEN GUIDELINES FOR TAKING RISKS

It is important to remember that change will occur whether we like it or not. At times it may be worth taking a risk to maintain control over the direction of your life. It is important to develop possibilities and a perspective on the future so that you can determine the value of taking risks to achieve personal goals. The following are some factors to consider in taking risks.

1. Get the information you need before you take a risk. Don't take an unnecessary risk because you are uninformed.
2. Ask yourself about the worst things that could happen as a result of taking a risk. It is important to estimate the possible loss in order to determine the magnitude of risk involved.
3. Carefully consider your motivation for taking a risk. Why are you doing it? Avoid taking a risk just to prove yourself to someone else. Reserve risk taking to accomplish your own personal goals.
4. Before you take a risk, list what could go right and what could go wrong. Evaluate the positive consequences against the negative consequences.
5. Don't procrastinate, but take action deliberately, without undue haste.
6. Make a schedule for the action that you plan to take.
7. Be committed to your course of action. Once you have decided to take action, seek success. Approach your goal positively.

8. Be ready to make adjustments. While approaching your goal with a positive attitude, stop or change direction if you become too stressed or if you meet too many unforeseen difficulties.

9. Be ready to take responsibility for your own actions. Don't blame others or situations if you fail to accomplish your goal.

10. Be realistic and don't be unreasonable in your expectations of yourself. Only take risks to accomplish goals that are consistent with your ideals and your life plans.

C. RISK ASSESSMENT

Now think about *one* risk that you may want to take in the near future. Ask yourself the following questions.

1. What is the risk that I may want to take?

   _____

   _____

2. What do I stand to gain by taking this risk?

   _____

   _____

3. What might I lose by taking this risk?

   _____

   _____

4. Why do I want to take this risk? Is it consistent with my goals and ideals?

   _____

   _____

5. What information could I obtain or actions could I take to decrease the risk or uncertainty?

   _____

   _____

6. What kind of schedule should I set for myself?

There are many types of risks. Some may be worth taking, others definitely not. What risks do you wish to consider taking as you take your train through new territory?
Risks I am willing to take.

_____

_____

_____

Risks I am not willing to take.

_____

_____

_____

I have learned that success is to be measured not so much by the position that one has reached in life as by the obstacles that he has overcome while trying to succeed.

—Booker T. Washington,
Up From Slavery

12

Decision Making

So far in Section II, you have learned that change is normal throughout life, that you can prepare for change, that you can improve your ability to deal with change by seeking assistance from others, and that you must, at times, be ready to take a risk to accomplish a goal. The next step is making a decision. Life represents a series of decisions—what courses to take, what job to take, what relationships to enter, where to live, what car to buy, and many others. People make these decisions in different ways. It is important for you to understand how you make decisions and how you can take action to improve your decision-making skills.

A. Elements of Decision Making

Think about making decisions in the past. When you were a child, were you encouraged to take risks and make some of your own decisions, or were most decisions made for you? Do you put pressure on yourself to make the *right* decision and therefore feel anxious when you have to decide? Do you enjoy making decisions, or does it make you feel uncomfortable? Do you find yourself using any of the following decision-making strategies?

Impulse. Go with your first reaction. Decide quickly, with little thought given to the process. This technique can actually be effective with some types of decisions, such as what to wear in the morning.

Escape. Avoid a decision or make up an answer to deflect an inquiry. This approach is often used when relatives ask about what you plan to major in or what you plan to do after you graduate. It is also used extensively during the difficult process of job hunting.

Procrastination. Delay until someone else makes the decision for you or until the option before you disappears. In delaying, you actually decide by default to do nothing. An example of this approach would be to cut out job ads from the newspaper and then not follow up on any of them.

Compliance. Let someone else decide for you. When you use this approach, you hand over control of your life to others. An example of this approach is to go along with a plan for an evening with another person or a group without expressing your desires.

Agony. Consider every detail of every option over and over again. Get wrapped up in the pros and cons until you get stuck and give up. Overthinking a decision can be used as an excuse for not taking action.

Play It Safe. Always pick the alternative with the lowest level of risk. This strategy may work well as you drive a car or fill out your annual tax return, but by consistently choosing safety as a primary factor in making decisions, you may close out many options for growth and enrichment of your life.

Consider the approaches you use to make decisions and under what circumstances you tend to use these strategies. Your choice of a decision-making strategy may work very well with certain decisions and not with others. The consequences of using inappropriate decision-making strategies can be very negative, particularly if you tend to consistently use these inappropriate approaches.

Your trust in yourself as a competent decision maker is built slowly over time, and setbacks are an inevitable part of that process. Start with small decisions to build your confidence. One way to become successful in making decisions is choosing a decision strategy that fits the circumstances. The decision about which restaurant to go to for dinner, which could be made on impulse, cannot be equated to a career decision, which requires a planning process. Your level of confidence will grow, as will your ability to control your life.

It is possible to become so overly concerned about the outcome of a decision that no action is taken. Stagnation, fear of failure, and even fear of success are emotional blocks to effective decision making. The elusive goal of seeking perfection in any decision that is made can deter progress. Often it is not possible to predict the outcome of a decision. Base the rightness of your decision on the process you follow and not on the outcome. As you apply good decision-making techniques, positive outcomes are more likely to follow.

Making a major decision usually causes anxiety, because there is often some risk involved, and there is the potential to lose something in the process. However, as one goes through life, it may well be necessary to lose something in order to grow. A lobster must shed its shell to grow a new and larger shell. In the interim, the lobster is at greater risk from predators, but the shell must be replaced with a larger one if the lobster is to grow. As you make career and life decisions, be prepared to lose something in order to grow.

Decisions are:

- Choices made from among alternatives
- Actions taken
- Commitments of resources that cannot be retrieved (for example, something that you buy that is not returnable)
- Controlled by the decision maker (what the choice will be and how it will be made)
- Measured in terms of a good decision or a bad decision by how well the process was used, not by the outcome

B. THE SIX RULES OF EFFECTIVE DECISION MAKING

1. Define the decision to be made.

Believe it or not, many of us do not identify precisely what we wish to decide before we start a decision-making process. This can cause frustration and confusion. What is it that you want to decide? If you are unhappy with your career or lifestyle, what do you want to change? Do you want to change careers, change where you work, or change some other part of your life? Don't be impatient to decide how you want to change or what your final decision will be. Rather, spend some time considering just what it is that you want to decide.

Examples:

a. Your job has good points and bad points (as most jobs do). You find yourself feeling frustrated and unhappy. You don't quite know why. You know that you need to make a decision about your job. You define your decision as follows: do I change careers, do I change the place where I work, do I work to improve things where I am, or do I keep feeling frustrated and unhappy?

b. Your commute to work takes you more than an hour each way. You do not like it and find that you are irritable much of the time. You define your decision as follows: do I look for a better job closer to home, do I move closer to work, do I find a different way to commute, or should I grin and bear it?

You may have several things going on in your life. Try to separate them into specific areas and then define decisions that need to be made in each area. You will probably feel more in control and less confused.

2. Identify the obstacles you face, and deal with them.

We all have difficulties making important decisions, but it is more difficult to make some decisions than to make others. It may be helpful for you to take stock of what obstacles you face in making a decision. Some typical obstacles to decision making are as follows.

- The decision you need to make is not defined. You don't know what it is you want to decide.
- You do not have enough information on which to base a decision.
- You are impatient and want to make a decision right away, even though you may not be ready to decide.
- You tend to procrastinate. You may find yourself putting off major decisions.
- You may be faced with a variety of internal obstacles, such as fear of taking a risk, self-doubt, lack of confidence, fear of failure, and concern over making the wrong decision.
- You may be faced with external obstacles, such as family responsibilities, time, geographical location, and money.
- You may be reluctant to take charge of making your own decisions, preferring to let others do it for you or simply by letting things happen. This is decision making by default.

3. **Get adequate information before you make a decision.**

Many people try to make a decision without having accurate and complete information. In order to make a decision, you must be able to evaluate several alternatives and then make a choice. You cannot evaluate alternatives unless you have complete information about each. In the case of a career choice, this is particularly important. Before choosing a career, you need to collect information. You need to know many things about a career, a job, a car, a spouse, a house, or a boss before you select one.

4. **Before you make a decision, always compare at least two alternatives.**

It is difficult to simply decide to do or not to do something in the absence of any alternatives. It always helps to have something that you can compare. Think of comparison shopping. It would be pretty dull if you were looking for a new car and had only one choice. It would be downright depressing if you only had one style of house from which to choose. When you make a decision, consider your alternatives. List the advantages and disadvantages of each. Talk with other people. Obtain more information, then decide. Your chances of making a satisfying decision will be much greater than if you considered no alternatives.

5. **Know your most important personal values and rank them in terms of their importance to you.**

Major decisions always involve choosing between important personal values. If you want to take a new job that involves moving to a different part of the country and your family doesn't want to move, you are faced with a very difficult conflict between career and family values. Such decisions are never easy, but they can be facilitated by your knowing your most important values *in the order of their importance to you.*

6. **The time comes when you have to make it happen. You should decide. Don't let others, or events, decide for you.**

Some people like to delay decisions as long as possible, feeling that things will eventually "work out." Sometimes they do, and sometimes they don't, but it is rather easy to fall into a habit of making decisions by default. People who do this eventually feel that they have no control. Events take control over them. This can lead to frustration and a sense of helplessness. This approach does provide an easy out, however, because people who use it can blame what happens to them on events and on others. You must actively take charge of your decision-making process by defining the decision, getting information, and choosing among your alternatives. If after considering all of the alternatives open to you, you decide to do nothing, then it is still a valid decision arrived at after careful consideration. You are much more likely to be satisfied with your situation than if you simply did nothing by default.

C. Avoiding Pitfalls in Decision Making

There are several kinds of pitfalls that you may encounter as you make decisions in your life. If you find yourself having problems making a decision, ask yourself the following questions. They may help you to identify the sources of difficulty.

1. Are you *motivated* to make the decision?

   You have to want to make the decision. It should not be imposed by others. Is this decision something that you really feel is important? If not, perhaps you should reevaluate whether you really should be making this decision.

2. Are you *creating obstacles* for yourself?

   Are you approaching the decision with a negative attitude? Do you fear making a wrong decision so much that you won't do anything? Are you stereotyping yourself (I'm too old, I'm not smart enough) so that you feel you cannot accomplish something?

3. If there are external obstacles, *how significant are they?*

   You may have some real obstacles to making a decision, such as family responsibilities, time, and money. However, you may be able to get around these. They may not be as formidable as they seem. Are you using these as an excuse not to take action?

4. Do you have the *information* you need?

   You cannot make an adequate decision without knowing about the alternatives you face. What are the merits and problems of each alternative? Don't try to make a decision without first having plenty of information. If you don't have enough information, develop a plan to obtain it.

5. Have you set a *timetable* for yourself?

   It is easy to put off making a decision. Try to set some realistic goals. Make commitments to yourself and to others. Keep your decision-making process on schedule. Set interim goals for obtaining information and evaluating alternatives.

6. Are you trying to make *several decisions at the same time?*

Each change in your life creates stress. Some stress is healthy, because it helps you to grow. Too much stress can be unhealthy and can keep you from making effective decisions. If you are faced with several decisions at once, try to prioritize them and deal with them one at a time.

7. Do you have your *values* in perspective?

Every decision involves conflicting values. Do you know what your most important values are in order of priority? If not, take time to analyze your values and rank them. This may help you to make your decision.

8. Do you have enough *alternatives?*

Too many alternatives can be confusing, but you should have at least two alternatives for each decision you face. If you do not, this could be the reason you are having problems making a decision. Creatively look at your alternatives and then get the necessary information so that you can choose between them.

9. Have you allowed yourself *incubation time* to consider the decision?

Sometimes it helps to think about all aspects of a decision before you take action. It is still important to have a timetable and to avoid procrastination, but give yourself time for careful thought and reflection.

10. What is your *anxiety level?*

Some anxiety can be good—it keeps you from being too reckless. However, anxiety can prevent you from taking action. Can you decrease your level of anxiety by controlling those elements of risk that are controllable? Realizing that some risk is involved, ask yourself what the worst thing is that could happen. Realizing that the worst may not be all that bad, you may be able to decrease your anxiety and move ahead.

D. KNOW YOUR DECISION-MAKING STYLE

Not all people make decisions in the same way. Some people like to analyze carefully their alternatives and then make the decision by themselves, drawing on their own investigative and inner resources. Others like to discuss alternatives with friends. Others prefer to look at the possibilities and then to go with what "feels" right. They like to rely on their intuition as much as an analytical process. Others prefer to get help from a professional such as a career counselor. Some people like to write down alternatives so that they can see them on paper. Others prefer to talk about alternatives rather than to write them down.

There is no single way for everyone to make decisions. Information is provided on these pages to help you with the decision-making process, but you must eventually proceed in the way that is best for you. Think about decisions that you have made in the past and answer the following questions.

1. List two or three decisions that you have made in the past about which you have a positive feeling.

    _____

    _____

    _____

2. In the following spaces, write a few comments on why you felt positive about these decisions.

    _____

    _____

    _____

    _____

    _____

3. When you made these decisions, did you:

    (check those that apply)

    _____ consult with others?

    _____ obtain professional help

    _____ choose from among alternatives?

    _____ accumulate considerable information before deciding?

    _____ make the final decision yourself?

    _____ make the final decision in conjunction with others?

    _____ follow someone else's advice?

    _____ let someone else make the decision?

    _____ write down alternatives and the positives and negatives of each?

    _____ use your intuition in making the decision?

Look back at your responses. What kind of a decision maker are you? Do you like to involve others? Do you like to get as much information as possible? Do you prefer to use your intuition? Do you like to read about your alternatives or talk about them with others? If you prefer a certain approach to decision making, and if it works well for you, then use that approach when the time comes to make a decision. Remember to use the approach that best suits your personal style. As you go about making decisions, remember the following guidelines that apply no matter which approach you use.

1. **Define the decision to be made** and determine what alternatives are open to you.

2. **Obtain sufficient information** about each alternative so that you can make a knowledgeable decision.

3. **Evaluate the alternatives** in terms of the information received, then choose the one that is best for you.

4. **Make a plan** to put your decision into effect and follow through with your plan.

As you go through this process, be aware of the potential pitfalls described earlier and deal with them as they appear.

• • • • • • • • • • •

One grows or dies. There is no third possibility.
—Oswald Spengler

• • • • • • • • • • •

E. DECISION-MAKING OUTLINE

The following outline is provided to help you decide between two alternatives. If you have more than two alternatives, make copies of this outline and then compare each alternative with another. Narrow down your alternatives to two, then compare your two final options. If you need to get more information before choosing between two alternatives, go ahead and get the information, but don't procrastinate.

Decision-Making Outline

	Alternative A	Alternative B
Briefly state each alternative		
Advantages of each alternative		
Disadvantages of each alternative		
Unpredictable factors of each alternative		
Risks involved in each alternative		
What is the best thing that could happen?		
What is the worst thing that could happen?		

Now look back at your responses. Based on the relative merits of each, put a check mark after your choice;

Alternative A_____   Alternative B_____

SUMMARY
Manage Change in Your Life

· ·

Change is normal as you go through life. Invite change; manage it based on your needs and values. It is possible to prepare for change by considering your personal characteristics and by having your support systems in place. Risk taking is an important element of change. Be ready to welcome risks while managing the amount of risk involved in any change. By understanding how you prefer to make decisions and by learning about decision-making techniques, you can reduce your anxiety about the unknown and increase your level of confidence in decision making. Change can make your life exciting and full of opportunities if you are ready for it and are willing to accept the challenges.

ADDITIONAL RESOURCES

Banning, Kent, and Friday, Ardelle. *Time for a Change–The Re-Entry & Re-Career Workbook.* Lincolnwood, Il: VGM Career Books, 1996.

Banning, Kent, and Friday, Ardelle. *Planning Your Career Change.* Illinois: National Textbook, 1987.

Barlow, Diane. *Moving and Relocation Sourcebook.* Michigan: Omnigraphics, 1992.

Bastress, Frances. *The Relocating Spouse's Guide to Employment Options and Strategies in the U.S. and Abroad.* Maryland: Woodley Press, 1989.

Beyer, Cathy. *Surviving Unemployment.* Colorado: New Careers Center, 1993.

Bingham, Mindy. *Changes: A Woman's Journal for Self Awareness and Personal Planning.* California: Advocacy Press, 1987.

Bingham, Mindy, and Stryker, Sandy. *More Choices.* California: Advocacy Press, 1987.

Bird, Caroline. *Second Careers.* Boston: Little, Brown & Co., 1992.

Birsner, E. Patricia. *Mid-Career Job Hunting.* New York: Prentice-Hall, 1991.

Bloch, Deborah. *How to Make the Right Career Moves.* Illinois: NTC Pub. Grp., 1990.

Bloomfield, William. *Career Action Plan.* Meridian, 1989.

Bridges, William. *Managing Transitions.* Massachusetts: Addison Wesley Publishing, 1991.

Burton, Mary Lindley, and Wedemeyer, Richard A. *In Transition.* New York: Harper Ellins Publishers Inc., 1991.

Coad, Cynthia. *Your Full Future: After the Empty Nest.* Indiana: Accelerated Development, 1989.

Davidson, Jeff. *Market Yourself and Your Career.* Holbrook, MA: Adams Media Corp, 1999.

Deroche, Frederick W. *Now It's Your Move: A Guide for the Outplaced Employee.* New Jersey: Prentice-Hall, 1984.

Dubin, Judith. *Fired for Success.* Colorado: New Careers Center, 1990.

DuBrin, Andrew. *Bouncing Back.* New York: McGraw, 1991.

Elcort, Martin. *Getting from Fired to Hired.* New York: Macmillan, 1997.

Fadiman, James. *Unlimit Your Life: Setting and Getting Goals.* California: Celestial Arts, 1989.

Gerberg, Bob. *An Easier Way to Change Jobs–The Complete Princeton/Masters Job Changing System.* Englewood, Co: Princeton/Masters Press, 1993.

Gilligan, Carol. *In a Different Voice.* Massachusetts: Harvard University Press, 1983.

Gross, Andrea. *Shifting Gears: Planning a New Career for Midlife and After.* New York: Crown, 1992.

Hakim, Cliff. *We Are All Self-Employed.* San Francisco: Berre TT-Koehler Publishers, 1994.

Helfand, David. *Career Change.* Chicago: VGM, 1999.

Helmstetter, Shad. *Choices.* New York: Pocket Books, 1990.

Jacobsen, Mary. *Hand Me Down Dreams—How Families Influence Our Career Paths.* New York: Harmony Books, 1998.

Jud, Brian. *Coping with Unemployment.* Colorado: New Careers Center, 1993.

Koltnow, Emily. *Congratulations: You've Been Fired.* New York: Fawcett, 1990.

Krannich, Ronald L. *Careering and Re-Careering for the 1990's.* Virginia: Impact Publications, 1991.

Krannich, Ron. *Change Your Job, Change Your Life.* Virginia: Impact, 1997.

Levinson, Daniel J. *The Seasons of a Man's Life.* New York: Ballantine Books, 1986.

May, John. *The Rif Survival Handbook.* Washington, D.C.: The Tilden Press, 1982.

Menchin, Robert S. *New Work Opportunities for Older Americans.* Englewood Cliffs, NJ: Prentice Hall, 1993.

Mendelsohn, Pam. *Happier by Degrees.* Berkeley, California: Ten Speed Press, 1986.

Otterbourg, Robert K. *It's Never Too Late–150 Men and Women Who Changed Their Careers.* New York: Barron's Educational Series, Inc., 1993.

Peterson, Linda. *Starting Out, Starting Over–Finding the Work That's Waiting for You.* Palo Alto, CA: Consulting Psychologists Press, Inc., 1995.

Rubin, Theodore I. *Overcoming Indecisiveness.* New York: Avon Books, 1986.

Scott, Cynthia, and Jaffe, Dennis. *Managing Personal Change.* California: Crisp Publications, 1989.

Sheehy, Gail. *Passages: Predictable Crises of Adult Life.* New York: Bantam Books, 1984.

————. *Pathfinders.* New York: Bantam Books, 1982.

Simon, Sidney. *Getting Unstuck: Breaking through Your Barriers to Change.* New York: Warner Books, 1989.

Tanenbaum, Nat. *The Career Seekers.* Georgia: Working Press, 1990.

SECTION THREE

Explore Career Options

Whenever you decide to change or choose a career, it is extremely important to learn as much as possible about the job market. As you learned in Section I, the first step in career planning is to know yourself. The second step is to learn about the world of work. Many people will choose a job on a whim or because a job just happens to be available. Sometimes this approach works, but often it leads to a career blunder. You know that you have made a career blunder when you find yourself on your new job for a day, a week, or a month and you discover that this is not the job or career for you. When this happens, you are faced with learning a new job and adapting to a new environment while at the same time starting the job search all over again. A career blunder can undermine your self-confidence.

Can anything prevent career blunders? There are no guarantees that you can totally avoid career blunders. However, this section will help you to consider the relationships among different kinds of work and the careers that may be most suited to your needs and values. Gathering information is your best weapon against career blunders. The better you understand your personal and career requirements, the fewer your chances for career blunders. This section will help you to learn more about the world of work. It will show you how to get information about careers, and it will help you to look at how you go about making decisions and taking risks to accomplish your goals.

In the world of work in the 21st century, it is essential to continually investigate your options and to actively search for those organizations that can best use your skills. You will need to continually update your knowledge about your areas of interest and about the constant changes that are taking place. You will need to identify new skills that will be required and new information to obtain. More than ever before, you will need to have the responsibility for keeping yourself up to date and positioned to deal with changing career needs. The techniques described in this section will help you to accomplish this goal.

Your Career Options List

What careers have you considered? Have other people recommended possible careers for you? Which of your interests could be turned into careers? In this chapter, you will expand your career options by developing several lists of career alternatives. You will then narrow your alternatives by looking at each career in terms of your own needs and by using information that you obtain about each career. To begin, try to think of as many careers as possible that interest you. Don't discount creative or unusual career options. Limiting your investigation to only those careers that are familiar to you can constrict your future career selections. Be open in considering different career alternatives. The following suggestions may help you to expand your list.

A. Look Back into the Past

Start with what you wanted to be when you were a child. What did you see for yourself when you were between 5 and 15 years old? If it's difficult to remember, ask someone who knew you when you were growing up. In the following spaces, list some of the careers you thought about when you were growing up.

_____   _____

_____   _____

_____   _____

_____   _____

_____   _____

B. Consider Career "Dreams"

In the following spaces list all of the careers that have interested you in the past ten years. Include those that you have dreamed about but have never considered possible. Add freely to this list as you think of possible career choices.

_____   _____

_____   _____

_____   _____

_____   _____

_____   _____

C. Get Ideas from Others

Enlist the assistance of three people who know you well. Ask them to suggest possible careers for you to investigate based on their knowledge of your personality, interests, and skills. You may wish to ask them to think about your request for a couple of days rather than giving you quick answers.

_____   _____

_____   _____

_____   _____

_____   _____

_____   _____

D. Consider Your Unique Self

Consider your responses in Sections I and II. Based on your analysis of your interests, work values, skills, personal values, and lifestyle considerations, what careers might you want to explore?

_____   _____

_____   _____

_____   _____

_____   _____

_____   _____

E. Consider Your Choice of Occupational Environments

Consider your choice of occupational environments (realistic, investigative, artistic, social, enterprising, and conventional as described in chapter 2). Which were your first two choices? Most career resource centers have lists of careers that match each of the six occupational environments. Which careers in the occupational environments of your choice interest you most?

_____   _____

_____   _____

_____   _____

_____   _____

_____   _____

F. Make Use of Interest Inventories

Consider taking an interest inventory that may provide a list of possible career choices based on your interest profile. Some suggestions are:

> _The Strong Vocational Interest Blank_
> _The Self-Directed Search_
> _The Career Assessment Inventory_
> _The Kuder Occupational Interest Survey_
> _The Campbell Interest and Skill Survey_

These inventories are normally available at college, community, and private counseling services. In addition, many career resource centers in college, high school, and community libraries have computerized systems with which you can identify potential careers based on your interests, values, and other factors. If you are able to take an interest inventory or to use a computerized choice system, write in the following spaces the careers that best matched your interest profile. Write a career in this space even though you may have listed it previously.

_____	_____
_____	_____
_____	_____
_____	_____
_____	_____

G. Do Some Brainstorming

Another way to expand your career options list is to play the following brainstorming game with a few friends. As you investigate the world of work, consider the following factors.

1. What skill do you wish to use in your career? Do you want to work primarily with:

    data _____

    people _____

    things _____

    ideas _____

Place a (1) next to your first choice. Place a (2) next to your second choice.

2. Do you want to work in a particular field? Examples would be:

agriculture	recreation	arts/humanities
business	construction	transportation
government	communications	marketing
health	manufacturing	military
education	natural resources	product services
personal services		

List up to three fields that interest you, with (1) being your first choice, (2) your second choice, and (3) your third choice.

(1) _____

(2) _____

(3) _____

3. In which occupational environment would you feel most comfortable? Place a (1) next to your first choice and a (2) next to your second choice.

realistic _____   artistic _____   enterprising _____

investigative _____   social _____   conventional _____

4. In what kind of a setting would you like to work? Would it be in a large city, a suburb, a rural area? Would you like to work inside, outside, or both? Do you want to work in a particular part of the country? In a particular climate? In the following spaces, list up to three of your preferences about the setting in which you would like to work, with (1) being the most important factor.

(1) _____

(2) _____

(3) _____

Now summarize your answers on the following chart.

1. Skill area	First choice _____	Second choice _____
2. Field of interest	First choice _____	Second choice _____
		Third choice _____
3. Occupational environment	First choice _____	Second choice _____
4. Setting	Most important _____	Second most _____ important
		Third most _____ important

You now have choices in each of the four areas that make up the world of work. By yourself or with a few family members or friends, try to brainstorm all of the possible careers that may fulfill each of your first choices in the four areas. Write the suggestions in the following spaces. After you have brainstormed using your first choices, try your second and third choices. Come up with as many possibilities as you can.

_____   _____

_____   _____

_____   _____

_____   _____

_____   _____

SUMMARY—YOUR CAREER OPTIONS LIST

By this time, you have several lists of possible careers. Consider your most important interests, work values, skills, personal values, and lifestyle considerations. Now go back over each list in this chapter, sections A through G. Circle those careers that you would like to investigate, based on your own interests and needs. After you have circled your choices, write them on your career options list.

My Career Options List
1. _____
2. _____
3. _____
4. _____
5. _____
6. _____
7. _____
8. _____
9. _____
10. _____
11. _____
12. _____
13. _____
14. _____
15. _____

With your career options list, you can now begin to explore the world of work. The information on the following pages will help you to investigate the careers on your list.

If you have run out of space to list your career options, you may wish to use the Continuous Career Options Listing in the appendix.

How to Investigate Career Information

You now have several possibilities on your career options list. You have selected these based on your interests, on the suggestions of others who know you, and on your evaluation of your unique self. Before you can begin making a career decision, however, you need something that is very important.

INFORMATION!

Too many people try to make a career decision without first having the information they need. Recall the analogy in the introduction of this book that compares your career search to that of buying a car or a house. You may think that your car or your house is the largest monetary investment in your lifetime. However, when you compare your lifetime earnings to the cost of a car or a house, it is apparent that the earnings you accrue throughout your life are your single largest investment. When other possible benefits that you earn—such as health insurance, life insurance, retirement, social security, vacation, and sick leave—are added, the amount grows even more. You need to find out as much as possible about a career before you prepare to enter it. There are four basic ways to find out about a career. They are:

- **Experience**
- **Printed material**
- **The Internet and the World Wide Web**
- **Talking with people**

It is important to get the best, most direct, most up-to-date information available before making a decision. The information that you obtain can prevent career blunders. Here are some guidelines to follow.

A. EXPERIENCE

Perhaps the best way to learn what a career is like is to experience it. Working in a field can give you valuable insight into whether or not a particular career is for you. Although direct experience in a job is not always possible, there are several ways that you may be able to obtain this experience.

. . . .

**Information is
your best
weapon against
career blunders.**

. . . .

1. Get a **part-time job** in the field.

   You may start at a low level but still get a good deal of exposure to what the career involves. You can find out what the people who work in the field are like and can learn much from talking with them. You can learn about the daily routine and about the advantages and disadvantages of the job.

2. Do **volunteer** work.

   Many organizations, particularly those in public service and health, have opportunities for volunteers. By volunteering, you learn the same things that you would were you actually employed. Volunteer work also gives you the opportunity to ask questions and to get to know as much as possible about the career.

3. Explore the possibility of **cooperative education**.

   This valuable program, which is offered by most colleges, provides an opportunity to receive on-the-job training, college credit, pay, job experience, and future contacts.

4. Volunteer to take on an **internship**.

   You do not normally receive pay for an internship, but you do receive valuable on-the-job experience. If you are very interested in a career, explore the possibility of an internship program with those colleges or other organizations that provide training for that career.

5. Ask to spend a **day or two on the job** with someone who does the work in which you are interested.

    Even in one or two days you will find out a great deal about a career or job. Because people like to talk about their work and like to share their experiences with others, a day or two on the job will be easier to arrange than you might think possible. This technique is often called *job shadowing*.

6. Take a **course**.

    Check out your interests while you develop expertise and gain knowledge about a field. Adult education programs, community colleges, and continuing education courses offer opportunities to get more information at moderate cost. When you take a course in a field you are investigating, you may be able to meet and discuss related careers with others who work in the field.

B. PRINTED MATERIAL

A great deal of printed material is available covering career choice, the job market, and information on specific careers. Some general sources of this information are:

libraries	professional organizations
career resource centers	government agencies
bookstores	periodicals
newspapers	directories
company reports,	employee handbooks
computerized career	in-house newsletters
information services	The World Wide Web

Printed material can be very helpful in obtaining career information, particularly at the beginning of your investigation of the world of work. However, as you read printed material on careers, it is important to ask the following questions.

1. Is the information accurate?

Check more than one source. Keep in mind the relationship between supply and demand. What are the opportunities in a field, and what is the projected growth? How many people are preparing to enter the field?

2. Is the information up to date?

Career trends often change, sometimes very quickly. What is the date of publication of the material you are reading? If it is several years old, you should check another source. Often, the material in newspapers and periodicals is more up to date. Have there been any recent changes in the economy, in government support, or in society that may affect the outlook for the career? Remember the time lapse between the writing of a book and its publication.

3. Is the information biased?

Be alert for any age, sex, or minority biases in the printed material. Many libraries will have screened their materials for apparent sources of bias. In addition, information provided by professional organizations and industries about their own fields may be overly positive, because these organizations and industries naturally want to put their best foot forward.

4. Is the information comprehensive?

Use more than one source of information. Learn as much as you can from a variety of resources. Obtain as many specific details as you can. Look up additional sources of information. Many career resource centers have specialists who are familiar with a wide variety of career information. Work with these people.

5. What other sources of information are available?

As you read any printed material, be constantly aware of sources of additional information. Write down the names and addresses of professional organizations, companies, and individuals. Check with these sources for additional printed materials or for personal contacts with whom you can talk about the career.

6. What conclusions can I make?

If you are very interested in a career, do not make a decision solely on the basis of what you have read. Talk with people and see whether you can do the work as an intern or on a similar basis. Also remember that a poor job outlook does not mean that there will be no jobs available. It simply means that you will have to work much harder at finding a job and will need a backup plan in case you cannot find a job right away.

C. The Internet and the World Wide Web

The rapidly expanding information networks found on the Internet, World Wide Web and on-line services provide new opportunities for career exploration. You can communicate through E-mail with individuals who may have information that is important to you. You can access any one of over 10,000 newsgroups, many of which have career information that may be relevant to your investigation. You can obtain information and share information through mailing lists, which also help you to learn about the leading people in your field. The World Wide Web provides access, complete with graphics, to a wide variety of institutions, businesses and information sites.

In addition to the Internet and the World Wide Web, which provide a wealth of information, various private on-line services also offer excellent career information resources. For example, America Online (www.aol.com) offers its Career Center, which contains items such as a career resource library, employer contacts data base, self employment service, federal employment service, and several others. America Online's Career Center even offers on-line group career counseling sessions. It also provides an interest inventory and a program to match an individual's interests, abilities and work preferences to potential job areas.

CompuServe (www.compuserve.com) provides good opportunities to access business resources, including many business related databases. While CompuServe does provide ConpuServe Classifieds and E Span, two services that offer job listings, it is more useful for access to professional forums and career research.

The Microsoft Network (home.microsoft.com) provides its Career Forum, which offers a variety of career planning services, job search assistance, tutorials, and information.

Prodigy (www.prodigy.com) offers its Career Channel, which provides a variety of information and relevant links to the World Wide Web.

These on-line services all provide Internet access. There are many other providers of this access and you can easily obtain a wealth of information by going directly to the World Wide Web. Most colleges and universities provide students with free Internet access. The possibilities for doing career research using the World Wide Web are virtually limitless. Many organizations provide a variety of free career planning assistance throughout their Web sites. You can access information on corporations and job trends, and obtain information on training requirements and the availability of internships in some fields. In addition, you can access a multitude of job listings. The Internet and the World Wide Web have made it much easier to do career research. To do this research, it is recommended that you use a search engine such as Yahoo! (www.yahoo.com), Hot Bot (www.hotbot.com) AltaVista (www.altavista.digital.com). If you have not had much experience doing research on the Internet, it is recommended that you take a brief workshop or use a reference book, such as:

Dixon, Pam, *Job Searching Online for Dummies.* Foster City, CA:IDG Books Worldwide, Inc., 1998.

Graber, Steven (ed.), *Adams Electronic Job Search Almanac 2000.* Holbrook, MA: Adams Media Corp., 2000.

Wolfinger, Anne, *The Quick Internet Guide to Career and Educational Information.* Indianapolis, IN: JIST Works, Inc., 2000.

For a comprehensive listing of useful sites on the World Wide Web for career exploration and job hunting, go to Chapter Fifteen, The World Wide Web Sites for Career Exploration and Job Hunting. For information on using the Internet for job hunting and for a listing of more resources, turn to Chapter Twenty, Job Hunting in Cyberspace.

D. Talking with People

One of the best ways to find out about a career is to talk with people who are actually working in that career. Such exploration of a career is usually preferable to just reading printed material, because there are distinct advantages in talking directly with people. Some of these advantages are as follows.

1. The information you receive is ***up to date.***

   You are talking with someone who is doing the work now.

2. The information you receive is more ***local.***

   Printed material is often addressed to the entire country. When you talk with someone, you get much better information about the career possibilities in your geographic area.

3. You find out about the *job setting.*

   If you talk with people at their places of work, you can get a sense of what it might be like to work there.

4. You can get information *you wouldn't find in most books.*

   People are often candid about telling you the advantages and disadvantages of their jobs when you talk with them in person. You have the opportunity to interact, ask questions, and get to know the people.

5. You develop a *network of contacts.*

   Every person with whom you talk becomes a potential contact when you begin looking for a job.

How do you find people with whom you can talk? Think of all your contacts and then expand your list. Some possible sources of people who can help are:

- **Friends and family members**
- **Contacts made through family or friends**
- **Officials of unions and professional organizations**
- **Chambers of commerce**
- **Community service agencies**
- **College instructors**
- **Career counselors**
- **Resource center directors and librarians**
- **Company officials**
- **Personnel directors**
- **Public relations officials**

Once you have identified people with whom you wish to talk, you can plan to interview them. This leads into one of the most valuable skills in the career and life planning process: *informational interviewing.*

E. INFORMATIONAL INTERVIEWING

Each day you have the opportunity to talk with people about their jobs or careers. You can do this at work, at social gatherings, with family, with neighbors and friends, and in many other ways. You can formalize this process of finding out about the world of work by selecting people who are in a position to give you firsthand information. The process of talking with people who have jobs that interest you is called *informational interviewing.* While you may hesitate to ask people to take the time to talk with you, the results are definitely worth any risk of refusal or discomfort that you may face.

This is your opportunity to ask those burning questions that you wish you had asked during your last job or career search. When you start getting cold feet about making that first call for an appointment or visiting a worksite, just weigh the benefit of having the information about the career field against your jitters. The importance of obtaining the information that you require for your career and life planning outweighs any hesitancy that you may have about contacting people whom you do not know. Remember that people like to talk about their careers.

You may be turned down for an interview. Don't let a little "no" stop you in your tracks. Move on to the next person whom you would like to interview. Remember, your first priority is to get the information that you need in your career search.

Informational interviewing is merely talking with someone who is presently working in a career that interests you. Gathering information that you need in order to make a decision is your goal. The art of informational interviewing is developed with practice. This valuable career and life planning tool can be incorporated regularly into your work life.

There are four ways to do informational interviewing. Choose one or all of the following approaches, depending on your situation:

1. **Walk-in method**—Drop in on a prospective interviewee whom you have identified. Depending on the type of career you are investigating, this may be an effective method of informational interviewing. For example, if you are researching the auto mechanics field, you probably would be welcome on a drop-in basis. On the other hand, most business people prefer appointments, so use your judgment. This method may be less stressful for you initially, but you may not obtain the information during your visit if your interviewee is not available. However, you can use this technique to uncover names and to make future appointments.

2. **Telephone method**—Call an organization and ask for the name of the person who works in an area that interests you. Tell the person that you are doing career research and need additional information in order to make a career decision. Try to make an appointment to see the person at a mutually convenient time: during working hours, at the lunch hour, during a break, or during off-work hours. Informational interviewing is done best *in person* rather than over the telephone. As an alternative to telephoning, you may wish to send an E-mail message and followup with a telephone call.

3. **Referral method**—Call someone you know or someone who has been referred to you by a friend, and ask the person for an informational interview. This method can be very productive, because you are building on a personal contact. This may be a good way to begin informational interviewing, because there is less stress involved in arranging for the interview.

4. **Letter method**—Obtain the name of the person you wish to interview and write a letter clearly stating your purpose and desire to speak with the person. The following letter is provided as a guide for requesting an informational interview. You will notice that it does the following.

- Names the person to whom you are writing
- Tells the person why you are writing
- Tells the person you are *not looking for a job*
- Keeps the initiative with *you*

Letter Requesting an Informational Interview

Mr. James Smith
Director of Marketing
ABC Corporation
Anywhere, U.S.A.

Dear Mr. Smith:

In my personal career exploration research, your name came to my attention as someone who could provide me with valuable advice and information because of your expertise and experience in the field of marketing.

I am currently (employed full-time, attending school full-time, or some other statement about your current status) and I am not at this time looking for employment. I am, however, giving serious consideration to a career in marketing. I would therefore like to talk with you about marketing as a possible career in order to obtain your valuable advice and perspective about the field.

Realizing the demands on your time, I will telephone you on Monday, April 5, to see if we can arrange a brief meeting at your convenience.

Thank you for your interest and help as I explore a variety of career opportunities.

Sincerely,

Now it is time to think of people who may be able to help you with your informational interviewing. The following diagram illustrates your network of contacts. You are in the center. Work your way around the circle and write on the lines the names of people who might be able to assist you: friends, relatives, friends of friends, spouses of friends, neighbors, acquaintances, classmates, teachers, counselors, professional associates, and any others who can provide contacts or information.

These four methods of information interviewing: walk-in, telephone or E-mail, referral, and letter can be vital to your career investigation. Use one or more methods to achieve your goal. The advantage of informational interviewing is that it *works!* Some of the reasons it works are:

- People like to talk about their work.
- People are usually flattered that you are seeking their advice.
- People are empathetic with others who are going through career transitions because most have experienced the indecision and frustration that go with making a career decision.
- People like to help others because it makes them feel good about themselves.

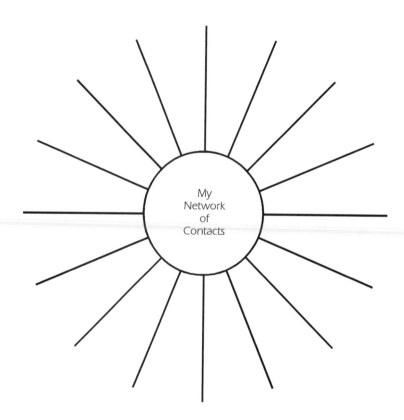

My
Network
of
Contacts

The following are some helpful hints on how to go about informational interviewing. Although interviewing may seem difficult, it is not, and it gets easier with each interview. Follow these simple steps and make informational interviewing work for you.

Know What You Want to Accomplish

The primary objectives of informational interviewing are to:

- Investigate a specific career field
- Uncover areas that may have been unknown to you
- Gain insight into what is happening in a career field and about future trends
- Obtain information that will help you to narrow options
- Obtain advice on where you might fit in
- Learn the jargon and important issues in the field
- Broaden your own network of contacts for future reference

Identifying People to Interview

Here are some sources to use in developing resources of people whom you may wish to interview.

- Personal referrals (friends, friends of friends, family, acquaintances)
- Directories
- Company organizational listings
- Calling organizations and asking for the name of a person in a specific job or finding the name of that person on an organization's web site.
- Professional associations
- Yellow Pages
- Newspapers and periodicals
- College departments

Arranging for the Interview

Here are some guidelines for setting up an informational interview.

- Use the method that is most appropriate for the type of career you are investigating.

  "drop-in"
  telephone
  referral
  letter
  E-mail

- Obtain the person's name.
- Explain your purpose.
- State why you are contacting this particular person.
- Emphasize that you are not looking for a job.
- Call early or late, when you may be able to talk directly with the person.
- Maintain the initiative. Call to follow up after writing a letter or after making an initial inquiry.
- Be prepared for refusals. What is the worst thing that could happen?

Preparing for the Interview

If you do some homework before the interview, you will have a much better chance of conducting a successful interview and acquiring valuable information. You will also make a better impression on the interviewer, which can be helpful when you ask for additional contacts or if, in the future, you ever contact this person about a job.

- Learn as much as you can about the organization. Do your homework through research—look at company literature, annual reports, employee handbooks, and other sources. You absolutely must check out the organization's Web site.
- If possible, learn something about the person whom you will be interviewing.
- Learn about the career in general—nature of the work, major trends, and current issues.
- If the organization has been in the news, review newspaper and magazine articles about the organization.
- Prepare questions about the *person*, the *field*, and the *organization*.
- Ask questions that are based on the research that you have done. Corroborate your information.
- Write down the questions that you wish to ask.
- Develop priorities for the interview. Decide ahead of time which information is most important for you to obtain.
- Make sure that you know how to get to the place where you will conduct the interview and leave plenty of time to get there.

Conducting the Interview

- Restate your purpose and why you are talking with this particular person.
- Remember that this is not a job interview, so you don't have to be nervous.
- Develop rapport. Ask open-ended questions. With your questions, show that you have done your homework.
- Try to get the answers to your most important questions. Take notes.

- Ask about alternative ways to prepare for entering the career field.
- Observe the job setting and general atmosphere. How do they match with your expectations?
- Don't ask for a job.
- Obtain the names of other individuals whom you can contact.

Follow-up

Good follow-up is just as important as good preparation. Here are some suggestions for action after you have conducted an informational interview.

- Send a typed thank-you letter. In many situations, it may be acceptable to send a thank-you note via E-mail. When in doubt, however, send a letter.
- Call later on or send an E-mail message to say how you are progressing.
- Keep the door open to future contacts with the person whom you interviewed.
- Evaluate your style of interviewing. What could you have done better? Use what you have learned when you conduct your next interview.
- Evaluate the information you received. How does it relate to your plans?
- If appropriate, contact the person you interviewed when you begin looking for a job.
- Keep your notes organized, including all dates of contacts, names, addresses, phone numbers, and E-mail addresses.

Informational interviewing is an effective tool and an important resource in your career and life planning. It helps you to discover much of what you need to know in order to make an informed decision. Make the interview a benefit for you.

F. INFORMATIONAL INTERVIEW GUIDE

This guide provides you with an outline for conducting an informational interview. Copy this three-page guide and take it, along with a notebook, to an informational interview. Questions relate to three important areas: the person, the field, and the organization. Of course, not all questions listed here can be used because of time limitations. Go through the list before the interview and choose the most important questions to ask. Use other questions as time permits.

The Interviewee

You can find out about the person you are interviewing, the *interviewee,* by asking some of the following questions.

1. How long have you worked in this field?
2. How did you decide to enter this field?
3. How has your career progressed?
4. How would you describe a typical day on your job?
5. What skills do you use in your job?
6. What kinds of experiences prepared you for this job?
7. What challenges do you face? daily? long term?
8. What are the rewards that you get from your job? What gives you the most satisfaction?
9. What are the frustrations that you experience?
10. What does it take to be successful in your job?
11. How does this job fit into your career plan?
12. What is your major contribution to your profession?
13. Are there opportunities to continue to learn on your job?
14. What expertise have you developed?
15. Looking back, would you have done anything differently in your career?
16. What effect does your career have on your lifestyle and your family?
17. Would you enter this field again if you could start over?

The Field

You can research the *field* you are investigating by asking some of the following questions.

1. What type of preparation, credentialing, and training must one have to enter this field?
2. Is there growth in the field? What is the job potential?
3. What are the current needs in the field?
4. What can I do, if I enter the field, to make myself marketable and competitive?

5. What are the future directions in the field? What changes are expected?
6. Will there be new opportunities for employment as a result of future changes?
7. What kinds of skills and what type of commitments are necessary to be successful in this field?
8. What are the advantages and disadvantages of working in this field?
9. What are the characteristics of people who become successful in this field?
10. What experiences would be helpful for someone entering this field?
11. What are the typical entry-level salary and benefits?
12. What are the opportunities for professional growth?
13. How mobile are people in this career? Are there opportunities in a variety of geographic locations?
14. What technologies are important in this career?
15. What recommendations would you have for an entry-level person considering this field?

The Organization

You should try to do some research on the *organization* that you will be visiting. Never ask the interviewee something that you could easily have learned through reading or the Internet. Do your homework and ask questions that build on your knowledge about the organization. Here are questions that you may wish to ask your interviewee and others whom you may meet. Keep in mind that some interviewees may be reluctant to give candid answers to some of these questions. If you sense reluctance to answer a question, move on to another question. Don't push.

1. How does your position fit into the organization's structure?
2. Who are the organization's leaders? How long have they been with the organization? How are the leaders perceived?
3. Where does the organization's funding come from? Is there stability in this funding?
4. What is the management philosophy of the organization? Do decisions come from the top down or are decisions made by work groups?
5. Are there frequent staff meetings? How do people feel about attending?
6. What are the opportunities for growth? Is there a professional development program? Are people encouraged and promoted from within?
7. What is the style of supervision in the organization?

8. What kind of hours do people work? Are the hours standard for everyone or flexible? Is overtime encouraged? Are vacations encouraged?

You can learn more about the organization by making some of the following observations. Remember that some of these questions can be thoroughly answered only through extended observations. However, your initial impressions are also important if you only have the opportunity for a brief visit.

1. What is the atmosphere of the organization? Do people seem happy to be there?
2. Do people seem willing to communicate and to share ideas and work with their colleagues?
3. Do people enjoy going to meetings?
4. Do the supervisors spend time with the people that they supervise?
5. Is there a group approach to decision making? Do people feel that they are included in the process?
6. Is there a cooperative or a competitive atmosphere in this workplace?
7. What is the physical environment? Is there good lighting, ventilation, workspace allocation, equipment, privacy, and security?
8. Do employees have access to health and fitness services as a part of the job?
9. Does the organization support professional development in terms of providing tuition assistance, encouraging people to develop new skills, and providing time for professional development activities?
10. What is the dress code for the organization? Are employees dressing informally? Notice the details of dress for future employment interviewing.

The World Wide Web Sites for Career Exploration and Job Hunting

The World Wide Web has already changed the way we communicate, shop, and plan for travel, and will continue to change how we conduct our businesses and our lives. The possibilities seem to be limitless. The World Wide Web has certainly made it easier to do career research and to identify possible employment opportunities. This chapter provides a listing of useful Web sites that relate to career planning and job hunting. While many sites provide information in both areas, the sites are listed in two groups: sites that provide mainly career resource information and sites that provide mainly job finding information. While all of these sites have been checked for accuracy as of this writing, be aware that rapid changes occur in this developing field.

For information on using the World Wide Web in exploring career options, see Chapter 14, part C., The Internet and the World Wide Web. For information on using the World Wide Web for job finding, see Chapter 20, part E, Using the World Wide Web in The Job Search. For information on using the World Wide Web to transmit your resume, see Chapter 21, part F, E-Mailing Resumes.

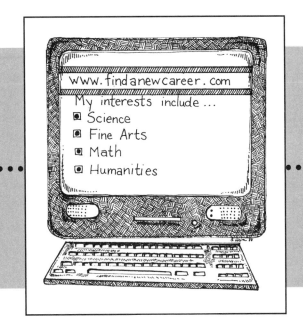

CAREER RESOURCE INFORMATION

America's Career InfoNet (www.acinet.org)
This site is part of the America's Career Kit from the U.S. Department of Labor and provides excellent general information on the U.S. job market and well as valuable resources for career planning.

Association of Computer-Based Systems for Career Information (www.acsi.org/)
This site provides links to career information systems in most states. Membership is necessary to proceed.

Bureau of Labor Statistics (www.bls.gov/)
This is the federal government's primary site for comprehensive information about jobs and careers.

Career and Educational Guidance Library: Career Exploration Links (www.uhs.berkeley.edu/CareerLibrary/links/careerme.htm)
This is a good reference for careers related to programs of study.

Career Paradise: Career Planning Process (www.emory.edu/career)
This comprehensive site developed by Emory University provides a variety of assistance in career planning and good links to other resources.

Career Resource Center (www.careers.org)
This site provides job information resources including many links to employers and reference materials.

Careers On-Line (http://disserve3.stu.umn.edu/col/)
This site provides information on employment opportunities for people with disabilities. There are job listings and recent updates.

Careers: *Wall Street Journal* (www.careers.wsj.com)
This site provides interesting, interactive, up to date information on job hunting and salaries.

Catapult on Job Web (www.jobweb.org/catapult/catapult.htm)
This is a good general resource provided by the National Association of Colleges and Employers, and is especially strong in cyberspace research tools.

Hoover's Online (www.hoovers.com)
Good employer information provided, including financial reports, some free, some for a fee.

Job-Hunt (www.job-hunt.org/)
There are good referrals in this list of site descriptions.

JobHunters Bible (www.jobhuntersbible.com)
This companion website to Richard Bolles, *What Color is Your Parachute* is an extensive selection of well organized links.

JobProfiles.com (www.jobprofiles.com)
This interesting site provides first hand accounts of what it is like to work in different careers.

JobStar California (www.jobstar.org)
This site provides links to 333 salary surveys and career guides.

Occupational Information Network (www.doleta.gov/programs/onet/)
These are products developed by the U.S. Department of Labor with information about occupations, skills, and training.

Occupational Outlook Handbook: (www.bls.gov/ocohome.htm)
This is the on-line version, recently updated, of the book published every two years by the U.S. Department of Labor, which provides succinct information on a variety of careers.

Quintessential Career and Job-Hunting Resources Guide: (www.quintcareers.com)
Very extensive and well organized list of links.

The Riley Guide: Employment Opportunities and Job Resources on the Internet (www.rileyguide.com)
This is a comprehensive, detailed guide to using the internet for job search and other services.

The Salary Calculator (www.homefair.com/calc/salcalc.html)
This compares the cost of living in the U. S. and international cities.

U.S. Chamber of Commerce ChamberMall: (www.uschamber.com/mall/states.html)
This provides links to all state chambers of commerce. May be valuable for information when considering a relocation.

Wage Web (www.wageweb.com)
This site provides information on 150 benchmark positions. National data is free, but there is a fee for local data.

Workindex.com (www.workindex.com)
This is the Cornell University School of Industrial Labor Relations gateway to the best workplace oriented websites and includes good job listings in various fields.

JOB HUNTING INFORMATION

America's Job Bank and America's Talent Bank (www.ajb.dni.us/)
This Department of Labor site links 1800 state employment service offices with over 1000 new listings daily. The applicant must register, but there is no charge.

Best Jobs in the *USA Today* (www.bestjobsusa.com)
This site includes all national regional and local ads from *Employment Review* magazine and the recruitment section in *USA Today*.

Bilingual-Jobs.com (www.bilingual-jobs.com)
This includes a good resume section in a job bank for English-speaking bilingual professionals.

Black Collegian Online (www.black-collegian.com)
This on-line version of this comprehensive magazine provides very good career planning and job search information.

Career City (www.careercity.com)
This up-to-date site provides technical and professional job help with networking, negotiating and good government occupational links. There is an interesting fast search feature.

Career Magazine (www.careermag.com)
There are good search paths, career resource and job bank information here.

Career Mosaic (www.careermosaic.com)
This is very comprehensive and specific.

Career Site (www.careersite.com)
The service is free, but the applicant must register to obtain anonymous profiling.

CareerBuilder.com (www.careerbuilder.com/index.cfm)
This interesting site gives help in the search process covering over 40 career sites.

Careerbuzz.com (www.careerbuzz.com)
This is a good, lively place to access the job bank and also get advice on dress and links to other information.

CareerPath (www.careerpath.com)
This includes help wanted ads from newspapers all over the United States.

CareerWeb (www.cweb.com)
The Employment Guide allows seekers to post a resume for no fee. There are many levels of jobs posted.

College Grad Job Hunter (http://collegegrad.com/home.shtml)
This is a detailed site including a job bank for entry level, internships, employer search and internet job search strategies.

Cool Works (www.coolworks.com/show/me)
This is a very interesting site for seasonal jobs in unusual places.

Dice.com (dice.com)
Specific information is provided for high tech jobs in this lively site.

E.span (www.espan.com)
This is a basic but comprehensive job database.

Federal Jobs Digest (www.jobsfed.com)
This is a private company where the user must subscribe, free to get job specifics. The information is up-to-date.

Headhunter (headhunter.net)
This comprehensive site for professional jobs allows seekers to search jobs, post a resume and apply on-line. Employers keep jobs updated.

HotJobs.com (www.hotjobs.com)
This up-to-date, accessible site offers a job bank and notifies the applicant of openings that meet stated criteria.

Internet Career Connection (http://iccweb.com)
Here are two job banks with good links to the federal government and *Career Magazine.* Job seekers pay to post resumes.

Job Bank USA (www.jobbankusa.com)
This could be useful for employers and job seekers.

Job Direct (www.jobdirect.com)
This site is good for first jobs: entry level and internships.

Job Hunt (www.job-hunt.org)
This is a complete, comprehensive listing of on-line job search resources.

Job Options (www.joboptions.com)
After registering, the job hunter can search more than 6000 companies and recruiters by company name, industry and location and e-mail resumes.

Job Source Network (www.jobsourcenetwork.com)
This is a comprehensive source of links to many job sites.

Job Trak (www.jobtrak.com)
This very good job and resume bank requires registration because access is limited to students and alumni of over 900 colleges and universities that participate in the service.

Job Web (www.jobweb.org)
This well done job and employer database is sponsored by the National Association of Colleges and Employers.

Monster Board (www.monster.com)
This excellent site enables the job seeker to set up a personalized job search center.

Nation Job Network (www.nationjob.com)
There are very general categories and the seeker must sign up for job search.

Online Career Center (www.occ.com/)
This is an excellent online job and resume database.

Online Sports Career Center (www.onlinesports.com/pages/careercenter.html)
This interesting site provides job information for careers in sports other than being a professional athlete. There are also shopping links.

Overseas Jobs (www.overseasjobs.com)
There are thirty categories of international jobs here and interesting sidetracks and ads.

Recruiters Online Network (www.recruitersonline.com)
A no-charge registration is necessary to access this network for employment professionals to search the job database.

Saludos Hispanos (www.saludos.com)
This is an employment service for bilingual Hispanic college graduates including job listings, links to other sites and resume posting.

Search Engines for Job Bank (www.job-search-engine.com)
This searches other job banks in the US and Canada.

TechJobs Supersite (http://supersite.net)
High tech positions only.

US Agency for International Development (www.info.usaid.gov/about/employment)
This is very specific for Foreign Service jobs, but also includes work opportunities in humanitarian efforts worldwide.

USAJobs (www.usajobs.opm.gov)
This is the official site for jobs and employment information provided by OPM.

VaultReports.com (www.vaultreports.com/index.cfm)
This interesting, detailed site requires a no fee membership, and provides industry articles, career advice, and company snapshots.

Yahoo! Classifieds (www.classifieds.yahoo.com/employment.html)
This good site provides specific information.

16

What to Look for When You Investigate a Career

You now have your list of career options that you plan to investigate. You also know how to go about obtaining information through experience, printed material, electronic databases and networks, the World Wide Web, and talking with people. As you seek information from these resources, what is it that you want to find out? What are some of the things that you should look for when you are investigating a career?

A. GENERAL QUESTIONS

Consider the **who**, **what**, **where**, and **when** of career investigation:

1. *Who*

   - Who are your coworkers likely to be? Are you likely to share their interests, values, and personal characteristics?
   - Who is likely to be your supervisor?
   - If you will be dealing with the public, who will you be serving, and in what capacity?

2. *What*

   - What will your duties be?
   - What will a typical workday be like?
   - What skills will you use?
   - What are the education and training requirements?
   - What are the salary and benefits?
   - What are the current job possibilities in this field?
   - What important interests, work values, life values, and lifestyle needs are you likely to fulfill in this career?

3. *Where*

   - Where are you likely to be working? by yourself? in a large office with many others? inside? outside?
   - Where, geographically, are you likely to work? Will your career allow you to work in various parts of the country or will you be limited to certain locations?
   - Where, in terms of the type of organization, are you likely to be working?
   - Where will your skills take you? Can you work with a variety of organizations? Will you be restricted to one type of organization?

4. *When*

   - When can you expect promotions to occur? What lateral and developmental opportunities are available?
   - When can you expect to increase your earning power and your benefits?
   - When you want to do something different, can you move within the organization?
   - When you want to change jobs, how easily will you be able to find another job in a different organization?
   - When a few years pass, what is the job outlook likely to be?

B. EMPLOYMENT PROJECTIONS

Evaluate how many jobs will be available in the career you are investigating and where these jobs will be. Ask yourself the following questions.

1. Exactly *how many jobs* will be available?

   If information you read indicates a 30 percent growth rate in an occupation over the next five years, what is the starting point? If there are 20,000 total jobs in the field, a 30 percent growth rate would mean that 6,000 jobs would be created. If there are 100,000 jobs in a field, the same 30 percent growth rate would create 30,000 jobs. All other things being equal, the second would be a better choice, because five times as many jobs would be available.

2. Will the career be affected by *fluctuations in the economy?*

   Some occupations, such as construction and travel, may be much more dependent on a good economy than others, such as information systems, health, and accounting.

3. *How many people* are preparing for the occupation at the present time?

   If a certain occupation is growing modestly but is also seen as highly desirable, with many people entering the field, the number of job seekers may soon outstrip the demand.

4. Do you wish to work in a *specific geographic area?*

   If your choice is limited by the area in which you plan to live, good employment projections in some fields may be of no value to you.

C. TRAINING REQUIREMENTS

Consider the amount and type of training required for entry into a career. Ask yourself the following questions:

1. *Is a college degree required* for entry, even at a basic level?

   In some fields, there are so many people who want jobs that the entry-level requirements are driven up to a high level. For example, someone who wishes to become a social worker may need a master's degree simply to compete for jobs with others who have master's degrees.

2. Is *certification* required?

People who wish to enter many of the health professions must meet state certification requirements and may have to take qualifying exams. Some software and hardware providers have developed their own certification requirements for specialty areas.

3. How important is *experience* in finding a job in a given field?

The job market for some careers dictates the need for hands-on experience as well as education. Part-time work, cooperative education, or volunteer work can be useful in such situations.

4. Are there *alternative ways to get training* for an occupation?

If so, is one better than the others? For certain occupations, you may have a choice between a public college, a private college, or a proprietary specialty school. It is important to evaluate the costs, the type of training provided, and the merits of each as preparation for the job market.

5. How *long* will the training take?

Some careers require a long-term commitment for entry. Others can be entered in a relatively short time with minimal training. What commitment can you realistically make to training for a particular career?

6. Can a career be entered with the *skills you already have?*

Is additional training really necessary? If you have worked before, you have transferable skills. Does the new career you are considering really require new skills, or can you transfer the same skills you used in your past work, with simply a different focus?

7. Are there *union* or *on-the-job training programs?*

Some unions run apprenticeship programs and some companies have extensive training programs for their employees.

8. If a college degree is required, must it be in a *specific field?*

Some potential employers may require a degree with specific training as a part of the academic program. Other employers may want a more general degree that stresses overall thinking and problem-solving skills.

D. Salary and Benefits

Your informational interviewing, reading, networking, and Internet search should provide you with some information on the general salary range you can expect in a given career. Consider the following questions.

1. How important are salary and benefits to you? If high salary and good benefits are primary values for you, they should be significant factors in choosing a career.
2. What is the salary range? Some careers offer only a low starting salary but have good potential for raises and bonuses. Other careers have relatively fixed maximum salaries and limited chances for advancement.
3. What is the method of payment? Some of the alternatives include:

a. annual salary	b. hourly wage
c. commission	d. wages plus commission
e. wages plus tips	f. payment by the piece
g. payment of a fee for services rendered	h. payment of a retainer for services to be rendered

4. What benefits are provided? Some jobs provide numerous benefits, others very few. Some of these benefits include:

a. health insurance	b. life insurance
c. retirement	d. sick leave
e. paid vacation and holidays	f. expense account
g. profit sharing	h. bonus
i. tax sheltered compensation plans	j. disability insurance
k. credit union	l. company car
m. free parking	n. clothing and equipment
o. tuition assistance	p. discount privileges
q. medical facilities	r. recreational facilities

E. Nonmonetary Rewards and Other Factors

In addition to salary and benefits, there are other, less tangible, rewards that may be important to you. You should consider the following questions.

1. What is the *work environment?* Do people seem to get along well together? What style of supervision is provided? Is it appropriate for you?

2. Do you want to work with *other people around or by yourself?* Do you need an environment free from distractions, or do you like it rather hectic?

3. Are there opportunities for *positive reinforcement?* Do people compliment one another, or is the atmosphere highly competitive?

4. Can you be *independent*, or must you do *someone else's bidding* most of the time? To what extent is the work you do dependent on someone else's work?

5. What kind of *hours* are required? Do people work long hours with no overtime pay? What kind of *flexibility of time* would you have? Are you locked into a fixed schedule or do you have some control over the hours you work?

6. How will the job affect your *family responsibilities?* Will it take a considerable amount of time away from your family? Is this acceptable to you?

7. Is there *variety?* Will you be doing the same thing every day? What opportunity is there for personal and professional growth?

8. Are you *philosophically* in agreement with the job and with the organization? Do you believe in what you would be doing? Is the job consistent with your values?

9. Can you *transfer* your work from one geographic location to another? Once you have settled in a job, are you tied to that area or are you mobile?

10. Are there *visible end products* so that you can see what you have accomplished, or are the results of the work more vague? What kind of payoffs do you need?

11. Does the job allow you to make use of your most important skills and abilities?

12. Some other factors you may want to consider include:

    a. travel requirements
    b. challenge
    c. risk

    d. prestige
    e. physical setting

F. WORKSHEET FOR INVESTIGATING A CAREER

Make several copies of this worksheet. Use it as a guide for summarizing information about each career you investigate.

1. What would I do? How would I spend a typical day at work?

2. Training requirements—how long will it take to get ready to enter the field?

3. Projections—what is the future job market?

4. Salary and benefits—what can be expected?

5. What are the nonmonetary rewards?

6. What are the opportunities for career mobility?

7. With what type of people would I be working?

8. What are the liabilities and limitations of this career

Evaluation of Career Options

After completing the previous chapters, you have now identified at least two or three potential career options that intrigue you. How do you evaluate the information that you have uncovered about yourself and your career options? How do your career options reflect your skills, values, interests, and lifestyle requirements? Compare your unique mixture of needs with the information that you have gathered through research and informational interviewing. Perhaps one or more of these options will fulfill most of your requirements for a satisfying career. This evaluation will assist you in merging the work you have done so far in self-assessment and collection of career information. The evaluation may point to areas that you need to investigate more thoroughly.

Present Options

The career options I am considering now are:

1. _____

2. _____

3. _____

Evaluation of Career Options

· · · · · · · · · · · ·

This is the
moment of truth
when your hard
work pays
dividends!

· · · · · · · · · · · ·

Consider the research that you have completed. In the column on the left side of the following page, fill in the requirements of this career option in each of the six categories. Then fill in *your* requirements in each category. Check (√) the appropriate column after you evaluate whether there is a match, no match, or if you need more information. Complete this process for your first, second, and third career options so that you can accurately assess your next steps.

Career Option 1

Based on my research, this option requires the following.	Match	More Info	No Match	Based on my self-assessment, the following are important to me.
Work Values				My Work Values
Interests				My Interests
Skills and Abilities				My Skills and Abilities
Self-Esteem				My Self-Esteem
Personal Values				My Personal Values
Lifestyle				My Lifestyle
Totals				

Total your check marks in each column for your evaluation of career option one. What additional information do you need? How can you obtain this information?

Career Option 2 _____

Based on my research, this option requires the following.	Match	More Info	No Match	Based on my self-assessment, the following are important to me.
Work Values				My Work Values
Interests				My Interests
Skills and Abilities				My Skills and Abilities
Self-Esteem				My Self-Esteem
Personal Values				My Personal Values
Lifestyle				My Lifestyle
Totals				

Total your check marks in each column for your evaluation of career option two. What additional information do you need? How can you obtain this information?

Career Option 3 _____

	Match	More Info	No Match	
Based on my research, this option requires the following.				Based on my self-assessment, the following are important to me.
Work Values				My Work Values
Interests				My Interests
Skills and Abilities				My Skills and Abilities
Self-Esteem				My Self-Esteem
Personal Values				My Personal Values
Lifestyle				My Lifestyle
Totals				

Total your check marks in each column for your evaluation of career option three. What additional information do you need? How can you obtain this information?

Compare the results from your career options evaluation by recording the following summary of totals.

	Matches	More Information	No Match
Career Option 1			
Career Option 2			
Career Option 3			
Totals			

Based on your assessment of your career options and on the assessments that you completed in Sections I and II, consider completing the following tentative career outline. If you do not feel ready to complete this outline, do not be concerned. Perhaps you need to do more research and to talk with more people. A conference with a career counselor may help. In any case, when you are ready, complete your tentative career outline.

A. TENTATIVE CAREER OUTLINE

1. What are your life and career goals, now that you have summarized your results and weighed your list of career options? Be as specific as you can.

2. What conflicts, if any, exist between your lifestyle needs and your career options? For example, if a top need is money, will your career options provide this for you? What compromises are acceptable to you? What compromises are unacceptable?

3. What interests would you like to use in your career and what interests would you like to reserve for your leisure and noncareer activities?

4. What skills and abilities would you enjoy using in your career? Do you need to build on these skills through continuing education? How do you plan to increase your skills and abilities?

5. How will your self-esteem be enriched by your career options? How will you continue to be challenged in your career?

6. What would you like the *purpose* of your work to be? What accomplishments would you like to look back on ten years from now?

7. Where would you like to live and work? In what setting and geographic area would you be happiest?

8. For whom would you like to work? In what kind of organization—size, purpose, type of work—would you feel most comfortable?

9. What additional information do you need to narrow your options and to make decisions about your career options?

10. Is anything holding you back from accomplishing what it is that you want to accomplish? What barriers and fears do you need to confront?

B. TIMETABLE OF EVENTS

John's career goal is to become a professional accountant. His timetable shows *one* route to achieve this goal

John's Timetable of Events

Career Goal: Professional Accountant—as an entrepreneur or employed by an organization.

Step	Goals (Education and/or Experience)	Time Required
1.	A.S. degree, Business Administration Part-time work as teller in a local bank	2 years
2.	B.S. degree, Accounting Part-time work with some accounts functions	2 years
3.	Full time work with primarily accounts functions Miscellaneous courses toward M.B.A.	3 years
4.	Finishing M.B.A. degree Prepare for and successfully complete C.P.A. exam	about 4 years

Now put your tentative career outline to work by assigning a specific timetable to it. Remember that this is a tentative timetable. You control this plan and you are free to change and review it at any time. Estimate your timetable on the following form, using John's sample as a guide. Think in terms of how long it will take to reach your desired goals. Then consider the steps needed to move toward these goals and plot a timetable for the events.

In the following space, write your tentative career timetable.

Career Goal:

Step	Goals (Education and/or Experience)	Time Required
1.		
2.		
3.		
4.		
5.		
6.		
7.		
8.		

C. CAREER SURPRISES

You are satisfied with your job and have not been actively involved in career planning for some time. Suddenly, your boss, a friend, or a colleague lets you know about an opportunity to make a change. The new job is yours if you want it. But do you want it? Often, career opportunities arise at unexpected times. How do you decide if the time is right for you to seize the opportunity? Common approaches are to make lists of positives and negatives and to talk with friends and family members. While these approaches can be helpful, they may not be sufficient. The following checklist will help you deal with an unexpected career opportunity—a career surprise!

1. Personal values

What are your top five to ten personal values in order of importance? If necessary, go to Chapter 4, Personal Values. Examine your top personal values in light of your career surprise. Does the job support your values or do value conflicts exist? For example, if your family values are most important, will the job require you to spend more time away from home or will it require you to move? In the space below, write your most important values and how they relate to your new job opportunity.

_____

_____

_____

_____

2. Work values

What are your most important work values? Again, you may wish to review Chapter 1, Work Values. Is your new job opportunity in harmony with your work values or are there potential conflicts? For example, some people accept promotions and then find that most of their workday consists of unfulfilling activities. In the space below write your work values and how they relate to your prospective new job.

_____

_____

_____

_____

3. Growth, learning, and challenge

Consider the learning opportunities that your career surprise will provide. Will you be able to expand your repertoire of skills and knowledge by accepting the job? Will this opportunity challenge you to grow personally and professionally? How will this experience position you in relation to achieving your long-range goals? In the space below, write some of the learning and growth opportunities provided by your career surprise.

_____

_____

_____

_____

_____

4. Lifestyle

How would your career surprise affect your lifestyle? Would you have to relocate, alter your commute, travel out of town, or change your working hours? Think about your most important lifestyle considerations and how these relate to your new job opportunity.

_____

_____

_____

_____

_____

5. People

What people would you be working with in your new job? Who will serve as your supervisor? Satisfaction in many jobs is closely linked to the people with whom you work and especially to your supervisor. In the space provided, jot down your impressions of your prospective new boss and colleagues. Do you need to find out more about them before you make a decision?

_____

_____

_____

_____

6. Benefits

Does your career surprise mean a higher salary range? Are the benefits superior to those of your present job? Are there more intrinsic rewards, such as the personal satisfaction of contributing to your community? Do these potential benefits outweigh any potential disadvantages of making the change?

_____

_____

_____

_____

_____

7. Risks

What are the risks involved in accepting the new job? Is the organization stable? Do the funds that will cover your salary come from the organization, or are they dependent on grants or other less predictable sources? Is the job environment preferable to your present job? Does the job reflect your interests and skills, thereby enhancing your chances for success? In the space below, write the risks involved in your career surprise. What are the risks of refusing this job?

_____

_____

_____

_____

_____

8. Future growth

Does your new job opportunity have as much potential for growth as your present job? more? less? Some jobs seem attractive at first but may lead to a dead end. In the space below, write the potential for growth in both your present job and in your career surprise.

_____

_____

_____

_____

_____

9. Pros and cons of your career surprise

Now you can list the positives and negatives of your new job opportunity in relation to your values and preferences. One or two factors may be much more important than all the others combined, so be sure to rank your priorities. This is a good time to ask your mentors and your board of directors for their input on your decision. It may be helpful to talk with a professional career counselor to objectively evaluate your options. In the spaces below, summarize the pros and cons of accepting your career surprise.

Pros _____   **Cons** _____

1. _____   _____

2. _____   _____

3. _____   _____

4. _____   _____

5. _____   _____

6. _____   _____

7. _____   _____

8. _____   _____

10. Intuitive reaction

This section has addressed a logical and sequential process for dealing with your unexpected career opportunity. Now consider your "gut" reaction to your career surprise. What are you saying to yourself? If you are feeling scared or nervous, this is a natural response to change. In the space below, write about what your intuitive sense is telling you about your career surprise.

Summary

This outline for dealing with a career surprise is designed to assist you in making a thoughtful, but rather quick, decision, since these opportunities usually require a quick response. Every career decision requires some risk of the unknown. Make your decision, maintain your confidence, and go with it. Even if you decide not to accept the career surprise, you may feel better about your present job since you will have made a conscious decision to stay.

> By learning to trust your intuition, "miracles" seem to happen
> —*Susan Jeffers,*
> *Feel the Fear and Do It Anyway*

Resources for Career Investigation

There are many sources of information about careers. The following is an annotated bibliography of some of the major career reference books. They are separated into two categories: handbooks and directories. They are included in this chapter to provide a handy reference for a variety of career and job market information.

Handbooks and Job Facts

Adams Jobs Almanac, 2000. Carter Smith. MA: Adams Media Corp, 1999.

Over 10,000 employers are profiled in this guide plus industry forecasts of the hottest industries and companies in each region of the country.

America's 50 Fastest Growing Jobs. Michael Farr. Indianapolis, IN: Jist Works, 1995.

Contains detailed information on the jobs with the fastest growth rates including projected growth rates, working conditions, salary, and many other details on each job described.

American Almanac of Jobs and Salaries. John W. Wright. New York: Avon Books, 1996.

A valuable guide for students, employees, managers, and professionals. Covers hundreds of occupations and professions and includes job descriptions, salaries, requirements, benefits, and evaluations of career prospects for each field.

Book of U.S. Government Jobs: Where They Are, What's Available and How to Get One. Dennis Damp. Moon Township, Pa: Brook Haven Press, 1996.

Provides up-to-date information on all of the changes in the federal hiring process and what federal job seekers must know to take advantage of these changes.

Career Advisor Series. Michigan: Gale Research, 1993.

A five-volume set includes career directories for health care, magazines, newspapers, public relations, and radio and television. Designed to give job seekers a competitive edge, these how-to-get-started career directories offer inside advice from the experts. Includes tips on interviewing, resume preparation, entry-level opportunities, career resources, and internship information.

Career Atlas–How to Find a Good Job When Good Jobs Are Hard to Find. Gail Kuenstler. Franklin Lakes, NJ: The Career Press, 1996.

Categorizes career opportunities in the context of four general areas: the sciences, solving practical problems, selling and managing, and arts and communications

Career Choices Series. Career Associates. New York: Walker and Company, 1992.

A twelve-volume series that lists the career choices available for students of art, business, communications and journalism, computer science, economics, English, history, law, mathematics, the MBA, political science and government, and psychology. Includes information on the job outlook, industries seeking qualified applicants, and interviews with people actually in the field.

Career Finder. Lester Schwartz and Irv Brechner. New York: Ballantine Books, 1990.

Unique directory that matches individual interests and abilities to hundreds of job descriptions.

Career Information Center Directories. New York: Macmillan Publishing Company, 1992.

A thirteen-volume series of job facts arranged by specific career clusters. Similar in format to the *Occupational Outlook Handbook.*

Careers in Mental Health: A Guide to the Helping Professions. Maryland: Garrett Park Press, 1986.

Ten mental health fields are described, from art therapy and rehabilitation therapy to clinical psychology and psychiatry. Book tells where the jobs are, how to prepare for them, what hiring requirements and salary levels are, and what composes a typical work day in each field.

Chronicle Guidance Educational Briefs. New York: Chronicle Guidance.

Updated on a four-year cycle. More than 500 individual occupational briefs. Similar in format to the *Occupational Outlook Handbook* but more specific.

College Majors and Careers. Paul Phifer. Maryland: Garrett Park Press, 1999.

Describes 60 of the most popular college majors and cites occupations closely related to them.

College Majors Handbook. Indiana: JIST Works, 1999.

Actual jobs, earnings and trends for those considering a college major and for graduates of 60 college majors.

Complete Guide to Public Employment. Ron Krannich and Caryl Krannich. Virginia: Impact PBN, 1995.

Describes opportunities with federal, state, and local governments; trade and professional associations; contracting and consulting firms; foundations; research organizations; political support groups; and international institutions.

Educator's Guide to Alternative Jobs & Careers. Ronald C. Krannich. Manassas, VA: Impact Publications, 1991.

Provides information on career alternatives for those in education who wish to use their skills in different work areas.

Encyclopedia of Careers and Vocational Guidance. Illinois: J.G. Ferguson Publishing, 1993. Volume I includes articles describing major career fields. Volume II gives specific facts about hundreds of occupations based on the DOT occupational group arrangement. Volume III focuses specifically on technical careers.

Good Works: A Guide to Careers in Social Change. New York: Dembner Books, 1991.

Contains detailed information on 600 social change organizations in the United States involved in consumer protection, ecology and the environment, civil rights, corporate accountability, and other social change concerns.

Harvard Guide to Careers. Martha P. Leape. Massachusetts: Harvard University Press, 1991.

Annotated bibliographies, useful directories, and trade periodicals are listed to help you locate sources of career advice and identify potential employers.

International Jobs: Where They Are, How to Get Them. Eric Kocher. Massachusetts: Addison-Wesley, 1993.

Describes opportunities in the international marketplace, especially in the fields of business, banking, and consulting. A valuable resource for those interested in working abroad.

Job Bank Series. Robert L. Adams. Massachusetts: Bob Adams, Inc. 1999.

Potential employers, locations, contact persons, phone numbers, and descriptive information are supplied for the following major United States job markets: Atlanta, Boston, Chicago, Dallas, Denver, Detroit, Florida, Houston, Los Angeles, Minneapolis, New York, Ohio, Philadelphia, San Francisco, Seattle, St. Louis, and the Washington, D.C. metropolitan area.

Job Opportunities for Business and Liberal Arts Graduates 1993. New Jersey: Peterson's Guides, 1992.

Employer profiles detail key facts such as products and services provided, majors sought, starting locations by city and state, and contact information.

Job Opportunities for Engineering, Science and Computer Graduates 1993. New Jersey: Peterson's Guides, 1992.

A look at professional opportunities in high technology including new career frontiers in aerospace, biotechnology, computers, telecommunications, and advanced materials. Summarizes educational requirements, salary ranges, duties, and outlook for specific jobs in each area.

Job Seeker's Almanac. New Jersey: Peterson's Guide, 1999. Concise information about thousands of companies.

Job Strategies for People with Disabilities. Melanie Astaire Witt. Princeton, NJ: Peterson's Guides, 1992.

Shows people with disabilities how to locate resources, how to uncover the best career possibilities and determine job accommodations for various positions.

Jobs 1996. Ross Petras and Kathryn Petras. New Jersey: Prentice-Hall, 1995.

Identifies the fastest growing companies, regional job trends, occupational outlooks, names, addresses, and more.

Jobs for English Majors and Other Smart People. John Munschauer. New Jersey: Peterson's Guides, 1991.

Offers practical suggestions to the job seeker who is inexperienced, who is interested in changing careers, or whose qualifications do not easily fit into a predetermined employment slot.

Jobs! What They Are, Where They Are . . . What They Pay. Robert Snelling. New York: Simon and Schuster, 1993.

Highlights the current top seven entry-level job areas. Includes up-to-date information on what jobs are available, the duties and responsibilities involved, how much various jobs pay, the education and skills you need to qualify for them, and the possibilities for advancement and future growth.

Network Your Way to Your Next Job . . . Fast. Clyde C. Lowstuter. New York: McGraw-Hill, 1995.
Provides a comprehensive guide to the process of networking including general guidelines and specific actions that can be taken to enhance job market exploration.

Occupational Outlook Handbook. Updated every two years. Washington D.C.: Government Printing Office.
This book, published by the Department of Labor, sketches thousands of different occupations, including nature of the work, places of employment, qualifications needed, earnings, and working conditions, and even future employment outlook. A must for every career hunter!

Occupational Projections and Training Data. Washington, D.C.: Government Printing Office, 1998. An indispensable aid for those interested in job trends and job outlooks. A statistical supplement to the *Occupational Outlook Handbook.*

Salary Survey Reports. Pennsylvania: College Placement Council, 1993.
Gives the monthly beginning salary offers to college graduates organized by curriculum and type of employer.

Where the Jobs Are: A Comprehensive Directory of 1200 Journals Listing Career Opportunities. S. Norman Feingold. Maryland: Garrett Park Press, 1990.
Replaces the highly successful *900,000 Plus Jobs.* This new volume lists more than 1,200 periodicals that run ads for open positions in each issue.

Directories/Referral Sources

100 Best Companies to Work for in America. Robert Levering. New York: Doubleday, 1994.
Using a five-point system, the author rates each company on pay, benefits, job security, opportunities for advancement, and ambience. The 100 companies listed received the best ratings from among 350 candidates.

100 Best Non-Profits to Work For. Hamilton, Leslie. IDG Books Worldwide 1998

Academic Job Digest. Michigan: Taylor Pub. MI, 1990.

The first directory to finding jobs with universities. Both academic and administrative. Includes publications for more than 100 universities.

Adams Electronic Job Search Almanac 2000. Graber, Steven MA: Adams Media Corp., 1999
Comprehensive and authoritative career directory with 16,000 entires including 2,000 new listings.

Almanac of American Employers. Jack W. Plunkett. Texas: Corporate Jobs, 1998.
A guide to America's 500 most successful large corporations, profiled and ranked by salaries, benefits, financial stability, and advancement opportunities.

The Big Book of Minority Opportunities: The Directory of Special Programs for Minority Group Members. Willis L. Johnson, ed. Maryland: Garrett Park Press, 1995.
A comprehensive listing of career information services, employment skills banks, and financial aid sources.

Business Organizations, Agencies, and Publications Directory. Michigan: Gale Research Company, 1991.
A listing of trade, business, and commercial organizations, government agencies, labor unions, stock exchanges, chambers of commerce, trade and convention centers, trade fairs, publishers, data banks and computerized services, educational institutions, business libraries, information centers, and research centers.

Career Guide: Dun's Employment Opportunities Directory. Pennsylvania: Dun and Bradstreet, 1993.
This reference offers comprehensive, accurate coverage of the more than 5,000 major U.S. companies that have indicated that they plan to recruit during the year. Information is easy to access and is cross-referenced by company, geography, industry classification, and educational discipline sought.

Career XRoads. Crispin, Gary and Mehler, Mark. Kendall Park, NJ: MMC Group, 1999.
Directory to the 500 best jobs, resume and career management sites in the world wide web.

College Placement Annual. Pennsylvania: The College Placement Council, 1992–1993.

Lists the principal employers who recruit college graduates. Includes name and address of the organization, name of the parent firm or subsidiary, name and title of the recruitment representative, the region in which the organization recruits, and the occupational openings for which the organization will recruit. Separate volumes for business and nontechnical majors and for engineering, science, computer science, and other technical majors.

Consultants and Consulting Organizations Directory. Michigan: Gale Research Company, 1993.

A reference guide to concerns and individuals engaged in consultation for business, industry, and government.

Directory of Career Resources for Women: A Comprehensive Guide to Career Resources and Opportunities for Women. California: Ready Reference Press, 1989.

Covers virtually every type of career resource, including career development seminars, job referral services, talent banks, special training, resume preparation, career counseling, fellowships, continuing education courses, and reentry programs.

Directory of Career Training and Development Programs. California: Ready Reference Press.

Describes in detail training programs available from business, government, and professional organizations. Includes program title, qualifications, length of training, type of training, benefits, and contact person.

Directory of Directories. Cecelia Marlow, ed. Michigan: Gale Research Company, 1988.

Describes major directories complete with addresses, prices, and frequency of publication.

Encyclopedia of Associations. Katherine Gruber, ed. Michigan: Gale Research Company, 1999.

A guide to national and international organizations that includes addresses, membership tallies, publications, and conference schedules.

Federal Yellow Book. Washington, D.C.: Monitor Publishing Company, 1993.

A must for those seeking contact with people in federal government agencies. Gives the telephone numbers of top people in government. Includes departments, independent agencies, and regional offices.

Fourth of July Resources Guide. Devon Smith. Maryland: Garrett Park Press, 1990.

Highlights careers in such fields as human services, consumer advocacy, volunteering, civil rights, mental health, and others. For each field, this book lists books, directories, concerned organizations and potential employers, and public service groups.

Hoover's Handbook of American Business. Texas: Reference Press, 1999.

An overview of major U.S. corporations with financial information, histories, product lists, executive names, and contact information.

International Jobs Directory. Krannich, Ronald and Caryl. Manassas, VA: Impact Publications, 1999.

A guide to employers in the international arena. Offers specialized advice and information for the international job seeker.

Internships, 2000. Princeton, New Jersey: Peterson's Guides, 1999.

Over 35,000 opportunities to get an edge in today's competitive job market through on the job experience.

Jobs Almanac 2000. MA: Adams Media Corp., 1999.

Over 10,000 major employers are profiled in this guide, with information on jobs commonly filled, experience required, and even benefits packages offered. Forecast of 21st century careers and long-range trends.

Job Opps 1994. New Jersey: Peterson's Guides, 1994.

Four-volume set covers health care, business, engineering and technology, and the environment. Each volume highlights up to 2,500 companies noting the number of employees and expertise needed in new hires, an industry outlook, proven job search strategies tailored to each industry, and details on the top ten employers in each industry.

Job Seeker's Guide to Private and Public Companies. Michigan: Gale Research, 1992.

Four regional editions profile nearly 15,000 companies. Includes company names, addresses, and phone numbers; business descriptions; personnel contacts; application procedures; company history; parent company and branch offices; and benefits offered.

National Business Employment Weekly Jobs Rated Almanac. Les Krantz. New York: John Wiley & Sons, 1999.

Detailed publication that rates jobs according to many factors including salary, availability and benefits.

National Directory of Internships. Sally Migliore, ed. North Carolina: The National Society for Internships, 1996.

A complete description of more than 26,000 internship opportunities across the country from high school through graduate school and beyond. Contains indexes by field of interest, location, and name of organization.

National Trade and Professional Associations of the U.S. Washington, D.C.: Columbia Books, 1999.

A great directory for finding the association that has information related to a variety of career areas. More than 7,500 national organizations are listed.

Places Rated Almanac. David Savageau. Foster City, CA: IDG Books Worldwide, Inc., 2000.

Rates and ranks 333 metropolitan areas on factors including climate, cost of living, jobs, arts, recreation, health care and environment, education, transportation, and crime.

Summer Employment Directory of the United States. New Jersey: Peterson's Guides, 1999.

Job openings are clearly defined; instructions are precise.

Washington 93. Washington, D.C.: Columbia Books, 1993.

A comprehensive directory of the key institutions and leaders in the national capital area.

Work, Study, Travel Abroad: The Whole World Handbook. New York: St. Martin's Press, 1992.

Introduces the essentials of working, studying, and traveling abroad. Includes regional maps of twelve global regions on six continents.

SECTION FOUR

Conduct an Effective
Job Campaign

You have evaluated your unique self, considered how to deal with changes and life transitions, and have investigated the job market. In this section you will learn some traditional and nontraditional ways of looking for a job. You will consider methods that can give you more control over a job search than you might think possible. The section includes an outline on conducting a job campaign, making the best use of your time, and protecting your ego. It continues with a chapter on résumé writing, including samples of different kinds of résumés. It will show how you can use some of the same principles for résumé writing when you fill out employment application forms. It will provide information about using the Internet, World Wide Web, and other on-line services in conducting a job campaign. Finally, it will provide advice and information on how to prepare for and conduct an employment interview.

The Job Campaign

The process of looking for a job can be a difficult experience. It is stressful and it is easy to feel that you do not have much control over what is happening. You may even find yourself stalling or denying that you need to start the process of job hunting. It is natural to avoid something that you think is going to be painful. This is particularly true if you are unemployed. It is important to remember, however, that you *do* have more control than you might think. You have specific actions that you can take and there is specific information that you need to uncover. By developing a goal and a plan to reach that goal, you can assume more power over the job-finding process. You can develop a strategy in which you *act* on events and opportunities rather than react to the wishes of others. To begin, however, you should be aware of some of the cold, hard facts of job hunting. You can then begin to develop a plan to attack and reduce these negative aspects of the job-hunting process.

A. JOB HUNTING—THE COLD, HARD FACTS

1. Job hunting can be very stressful. The process creates fear and anxiety for most people and can damage a person's ego.
2. People who are job hunting often feel that they have little control over the process and outcome. This feeling of powerlessness can undermine a person's self-confidence.
3. People often take the path of least resistance by approaching the job hunt in a very passive way. For example, staying home, cutting out want ads, and sending out letters and résumés is not very stressful in the short term, but can lead to a great deal of stress in the long run when rejections come rolling in. This is passive job hunting.
4. People sometimes put more energy into buying a car than into choosing a job. Some will take almost any job, just to get the process over with. The uncertainty in job hunting can be painful.
5. Even very secure people have trouble taking action when it comes to job hunting. Every job interview becomes a potential rejection. Every telephone call holds the possibility of a turn-down.
6. Active job hunting requires a significant investment of time, money, energy, and ego. Job hunting demands hard work.
7. Rejection is an unavoidable part of the job-seeking process. The following can be expected to be part of any job campaign.

obstacles	missed opportunities
barriers	self-doubt
turn-downs	unfulfilled expectations
rejections	unresponsiveness
disappointments	disinterest
fear	ambiguity

All of these can be damaging to the ego if they are not balanced with positive approaches and activities.

8. Looking for a job without defined career goals can lead to uncertainty and discouragement. It is important to make self-assessment the first part of the job-hunting process.
9. It is important to use time effectively by investing the most time in the job-hunting methods that will produce results and by having a clear idea of what types of jobs to pursue.
10. The job-hunting process involves positioning one's self to be in the right place at the right time. Planning, assessment, and actively pursuing goals can help you do exactly that.

Rejection Shock

• • • • • • • • • •

Take care of
yourself during
your job hunt.
Your ego is your
most precious
resource.

• • • • • • • • • •

Before considering how to deal with the realities of a job campaign, there is a significant problem to be aware of. This problem is *rejection shock*. This is a term used to describe a withdrawal from the job hunting process after someone receives one or more rejections. Rejection shock can become severe if you allow it to hurt your ego. People protect themselves from further rejection by simply not initiating any new contacts. They develop elaborate rationalizations for not making contacts and for not continuing to actively look for a job. They wait for something to happen. They are afraid to continue their job search for fear that they may again be rejected. Some people remain unemployed for years as a result of rejection shock. The longer they go without taking action, the more difficult it becomes for them to overcome rejection shock. Your primary responsibility as a job hunter is to protect your ego and avoid rejection shock.

How can you guard against rejection shock? Here are some suggestions.

The Ten-point Rejection Shock Avoidance System

1. After you have been rejected for a job, *immediately* begin initiating other contacts.
2. Try not to take a rejection personally. Many other factors, such as quotas and preselection, can skew the results.
3. Use your support system of family and friends to serve as a buffer and to lighten your spirit.
4. Join or form a job club with one or more job hunters. Get together at least once a week to share your feelings, exchange ideas, and swap job leads.
5. Develop a plan for your job campaign. Expect rejections as a normal part of the campaign.
6. Beware of investing too much time in activities that may bring a large number of rejections, such as blanket mailings of résumés or applying for jobs for which you are minimally qualified.
7. Make use of community support services, such as courses, groups, and mental health centers. Find a career counselor who can help you to clarify goals and to develop your job-hunting strategies.
8. Avoid the temptation to engage in long-term career planning instead of looking for a job. If you are not working, invest your energy in finding a job.
9. Instead of looking for your ideal job, be willing to compromise. This is especially true if you are not working. Use state employment agencies and other services that can be of help in your job search.

10. Set goals for yourself each day. Get out and do something. Make a special attempt to arrange personal contacts with others, including those in your network of contacts and those in professional organizations.

B. WHAT IS AN EFFECTIVE JOB CAMPAIGN?

An effective job campaign involves:

1. Having a specific plan of action and a career goal that you want to attain
2. Using your time effectively. Plan to spend a great deal of time on your job campaign and schedule daily activities. Balance difficult and rewarding tasks
3. Developing a system to protect your ego and to avoid procrastination and rejection shock
4. Doing job market research using:

   - Experience
   - Printed material
   - The World Wide Web and the Internet
   - Talking with people

5. Expanding your network of personal contacts and using informational interviewing
6. Spending the most time on the methods that hold the most promise for finding a job
7. Writing a good résumé, and knowing how to accurately complete employment applications
8. Rehearsing your interviewing techniques and being prepared for job interviews
9. Following up on contacts, interviews, and referrals, including timely thank-you letters, phone calls, and E-mail messages
10. Rewarding yourself periodically for sticking to your job campaign

Remember that the person who finally is hired for a given job may not be the most qualified for the job. It's the person who knows how to get hired that most often gets hired.

C. ORGANIZING YOUR JOB CAMPAIGN

Planning, preparation, and follow-through are essential in the job-hunting process. The following information will help you to organize your job campaign.

1. **Have a specific plan of action and a goal that you want to attain.**

    a. Analyze your unique self and determine what jobs will best fulfill your needs. You can probably find *a* job, but you want a job that is more than just *a* job.
    b. Concentrate your search in areas that hold potential for future growth and expanded opportunities.
    c. Define the specific type of job that you want. Target your efforts to the type of job that is on your career path. Expand the places where you might find this type of job.
    d. Develop a plan that incorporates several short-term goals to help you reach your major goal. Set a time schedule for the achievement of these short-term goals.

2. **Use your time effectively.**

    a. A job campaign is demanding. Expect to spend many hours thinking, planning, and assessing your alternatives.
    b. Plan to call prospective employers and write follow-up letters every day. Job hunting may require a full-time commitment, especially if you are unemployed.
    c. Plan a variety of activities each week, including:

    - Planning
    - Self-research
    - Job market research
    - Telephone calls
    - Nonjob trips (to library, to meet friends)
    - Writing letters and E-mail messages
    - Letters
    - Informational interviews
    - Job interviews
    - Third-party meetings
    - Thinking and processing

    d. Plan some rewards for yourself for using your time effectively.
    e. Remember how much time you spend at work every day. It's worth it to spend a great deal of time finding a job that you will enjoy.
    f. Distribute your time among different job-hunting activities.

3. **Develop a system to protect your ego and avoid rejection shock.**

    a. Make regular commitments to yourself and to others and keep them.
    b. Maintain your support systems with family and friends.
    c. Keep active. Stay with your plans.
    d. Become familiar with time management techniques.
    e. Regularly get together with other job hunters or career changers to share feelings and information.

f. Seek out institutional support: community colleges, churches, local clubs, and professional organizations.

g. Acknowledge your needs and seek out support. Affirm your skills and abilities, use self-esteem-building exercises, and develop positive approaches to your everyday activities.

h. Take care of yourself every day.

4. **Do job market research, using experience, print material, the World Wide Web and the Internet, and talking with people.**

Experience

a. Consider cooperative education programs and internships at area colleges as a means to obtain a job, experience, and contacts.

b. Do temporary work in order to make money, to get experience, and to make contacts for a full-time job.

c. In your spare time, do volunteer work to obtain experience and be well situated when a job opening occurs.

d. Write a proposal or develop an idea that solves a problem for a company or organization.

Printed material

a. Newspapers and want ads are usually not good sources of specific job openings, since only about 15 percent to 20 percent of all job vacancies are listed in newspapers. You need to be aware of ads that are come-ons. These ads may feature positions that sound much better than the jobs that are actually available. However, newspapers can be a good source of general information. Pay particular attention to:

- Articles on future trends
- Grand openings
- Contracts awarded
- Promotions
- New businesses
- Companies that are hiring
- Articles on careers
- Potential informational interviewees

b. The Yellow Pages can provide useful information. You can identify companies and organizations where you can inquire about available positions or about future job openings. This is particularly useful if you are looking in a new geographic area.

c. Professional journals, newsletters, and trade magazines often have listings of available jobs, but are also useful in other ways. You can identify key people to contact; you can find out what is going on in the field; you can obtain information on new jobs that are likely to appear; and you can learn the jargon of the profession. All of this can be particularly helpful when you go for an interview.

• • • • • • • • • • •

Remember that the person who gets hired may not be the most qualified. It is the person who knows how to get hired that gets the job.

• • • • • • • • • • •

d. Company literature, employer handouts, and in-house newsletters can provide useful information on the organization and often have sections on available positions. These may give you a chance to learn about openings before they are advertised on the outside. Call the specific organization for these materials.

e. Directories of organizations, associations, and businesses can be used as sources of names and addresses of individuals who can give you information. These individuals may also be prospective employers. Check at your local library or career resource center for directories, journals, and other print material that might be helpful in your job search. Ask the reference librarians for assistance and to verify that you have not overlooked an important source of information.

f. The World Wide Web, the Internet, electronic databases and networks. This rapidly growing source of job information deserves special attention and is described in chapter 20.

Talking with people

a. Friends, family members, and contacts made through friends and family can be good sources of information. Don't be reluctant to let others know that you are looking for a job. Most people want to help.

b. Through newspapers, journals, contacts, and other sources, identify the names of individuals who might have jobs available or know where or when jobs might become available. Contact these individuals and ask for informational interviews.

c. State employment agencies provide some assistance in finding jobs and often have a data bank of available jobs. Most colleges and high schools also have job search information and job listings available for students.

d. Human resource offices in private and public organizations can be sources of job information. It is important to remember, however, that these offices primarily screen candidates. They do not usually hire. If you are interested in an organization, it is important that you meet people who are in a position to hire you. Human resource offices often want to screen you "out" rather than screen you "in."

e. Private employment agencies can help you to find a job at a cost to you or to the employer. Some companies prefer that agencies do their recruiting for them, and thus the primary loyalty of many agencies is to the employer. They will attempt to match you to whatever jobs they have available at the time, which may not be in line with your career goals. *The best person to help you find you a job is you!*

5. **Expand your network of personal contacts and use informational interviewing.**

    a. Almost 80 percent of all jobs are obtained through personal contacts of one kind or another. Therefore, it is essential that you expand your personal contacts.

    b. Use friends, family, associates, and all of the resources described previously. Expand your contacts and identify people who may be in a position to hire you or to know where jobs are available.

    c. Make your skills and abilities known to as many people as possible. Ask for referrals. Form a job-finding group. Encourage suggestions. Use the telephone and the Internet to make contacts. Arrange face-to-face meetings with as many people as possible.

    d. Make use of *informational interviewing*. The basic techniques are the same as those described in Section III. However, you will now use informational interviewing as a means of meeting people who may have a job available or who may know of a job that would interest you. Recall the job hunter's number one responsibility, which is to protect the ego and avoid rejection shock. If this is number one, then the process of informational interviewing becomes an invaluable, nontraditional technique in job hunting. Informational interviewing can help you to:

- Decide on the job
- Decide whom to interview
- Decide what organizations to explore
- Decide whether you are interested
- Decide whether the combination of job, people, and organization matches with your goals, skills, interests, values, lifestyle, and self-esteem

What other method offers so much valuable information that can help you make decisions about jobs? The procedures for informational interviewing remain the same, so check back in Section III. However, make the following changes in the informational interviewing techniques, since you are now looking for a job.

- Use the process of informational interviewing wisely and honestly. How do you really know that you want to work for an organization if you do not know the details that would help you make a quality decision about a job?
- Interview for the information that will help you to make an employment decision that blends with your goals, skills, values, lifestyle, and self-esteem needs.

- Keep the information part of the informational interview flowing with questions about available positions, required qualifications, and potential contacts.
- Do not ask for a job either on the telephone or during the interview. You will probably be referred to human resources. Your goal is to obtain information; then you will make a decision about the organization.
- Do not produce a résumé or a completed application form. The focus of the interview shifts from the interviewee, who offers the information to you, the interviewer. This "bait and switch" approach weakens the potential benefits derived from informational interviewing. Keep the ball in your court.
- Ask the person whom you are interviewing for other sources of information or about jobs that may soon be available.
- Arrange informational interviews with people who might be in a position to hire you.
- Remember that potential employers may like to have the opportunity for a preliminary interview with you before an actual job interview is arranged.
- Write a letter requesting an informational interview that clearly states your purpose. This can be somewhat different from the letter you would write if you were not looking for a job. It is best not to use E-mail in this situation. If you are interested in an organization, send a follow-up letter and a copy of your résumé. Notice that the following points are made:

  1. It is addressed to a specific person.
  2. It tells the person why you are writing.
  3. It tells the person your situation.
  4. It keeps the initiative with you.

  Samples of both types of letter are on the following pages.

- Send your résumé or completed application form with your typed letter of appreciation for the informational interview.

6. **Spend the most time on the methods that hold the most promise for finding a job.**

   a. Since 80 percent of all jobs are obtained through personal contacts, spend the most time pursuing and increasing these contacts.

b. Be aware of new developments that may create jobs, such as:

- Emerging problems
- Unreleased plans
- Impending retirements
- Expansions
- Reorganizations
- Jobs that will be advertised in a few weeks

c. Organize and maintain a diversified, active job campaign.
d. Less effective methods include:

- Shotgun letters and résumés
- Relying heavily on newspaper want ads
- Relying heavily on employment agencies
- Relying solely on human resource offices
- Relying solely on the World Wide Web and the Internet

You may wish to use these methods, but don't depend solely on them. Your job campaign strategy can be summarized by looking at the following diagram. You can then move to the next important steps in an effective job campaign.

- Résumé writing
- Completing applications
- Employment interviewing

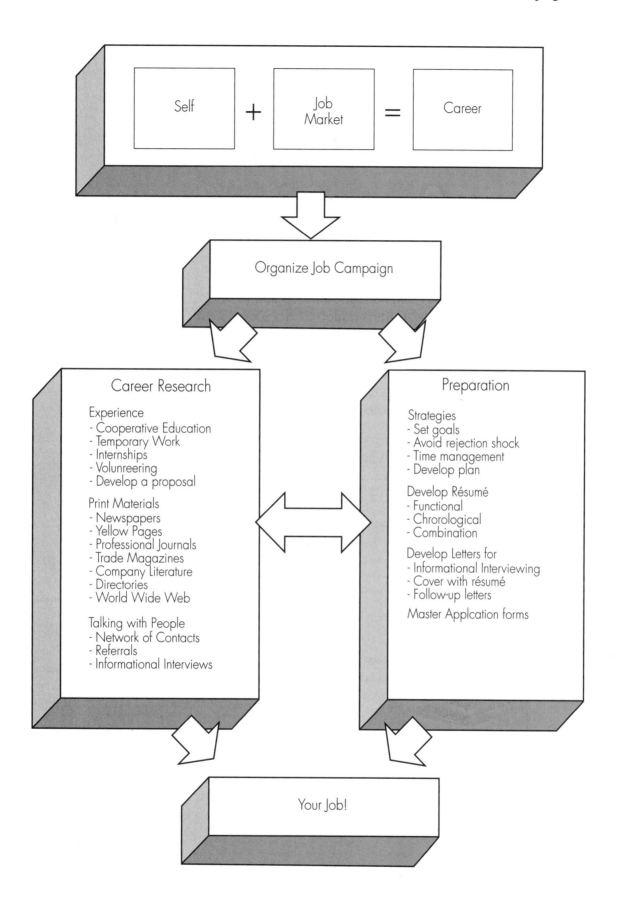

Self + Job Market = Career

Organize Job Campaign

Career Research

Experience
- Cooperative Education
- Temporary Work
- Internships
- Volunreering
- Develop a proposal

Print Materials
- Newspapers
- Yellow Pages
- Professional Journals
- Trade Magazines
- Company Literature
- Directories
- World Wide Web

Talking with People
- Network of Contacts
- Referrals
- Informational Interviews

Preparation

Strategies
- Set goals
- Avoid rejection shock
- Time management
- Develop plan

Develop Résumé
- Functional
- Chrorological
- Combination

Develop Letters for
- Informational Interviewing
- Cover with résumé
- Follow-up letters

Master Applcation forms

Your Job!

**Letter for requesting an informational interview—
written by someone who is looking for a job**

Mr. James Smith
Director of Institutional Research
XYZ Corporation
Anywhere, U.S.A.

Dear Mr. Smith:

In my personal career exploration research, your name came to my attention as someone who could provide me with some valuable advice and information because of your experience in the field of institutional research.

I am currently considering a career transition. I have experience in managing research projects on a small scale and I am very interested in the technological advancements in the area of institutional research. I have investigated the field and have some specific questions related to current trends, technical developments, and skills that may be needed in the future. I would like to talk with you to learn more about these and other issues from your very valuable perspective.

Realizing the demands on your time, I will telephone you on Monday, April 6, to see whether we can arrange a brief meeting at your convenience.

Thank you for your interest and help as I explore a variety of career opportunities.

Sincerely,

Follow-up letter from someone who is looking for a job, has conducted an informational interview, and is interested in a job with the organization.

Mr. James Smith
Director of Institutional Research
XYZ Corporation
Anywhere, U.S.A.

Dear Mr. Smith:

I would like to thank you for meeting with me on April 14 to discuss career possibilities in the field of institutional research. The information and insight you provided were most helpful. I appreciated your sharing your expertise and time with me. I especially enjoyed hearing about the recent advances in technological applications in institutional research.

I was pleased to discover from our discussion that I seem to have the skills and qualifications necessary to enter the field of institutional research. I would appreciate your considering me for a position when a vacancy does occur. Your organization and your personal approach are very appealing to me, and I feel that I could make some significant contributions to your program.

I am enclosing a copy of my résumé for your reference. I will be contacting you in the near future to discuss future employment possibilities with you. Thank you very much for your consideration and for the information and assistance you have given me.

Sincerely,

D. Job Campaign Analysis

If you are presently in the process of looking for a job or you can recall the last time you engaged in a job campaign, this section will be helpful. You will have the opportunity to

- Consider the four stages of job hunting
- Review the expenditure of your most valuable personal resources
- Analyze the results of your job campaign

This chapter has presented the hard, cold facts of job hunting and the organization of an effective job campaign. The challenge now is for you to evaluate the specific components of your job campaign. The process of job hunting has the potential of making you feel out of control and powerless. This analysis will help you to regain some of the control that you perceived was lost. Remember that looking for a job produces stress. Use this stress to your advantage by turning it into energy and action.

1. Evaluate the Job-hunting Stages

Consider the following four stages of job hunting. Identify the stage that you are presently going through and consider how you can move to a new stage by upgrading the techniques in your job hunt.

The four stages of job hunting are:

Stage 1 Flip-flop
Stage 2 Fledgling
Stage 3 Focused
Stage 4 Flight

The following chart outlines the characteristics of these stages.

Four Stages of Job Hunting				
	Stage 1	Stage 2	Stage 3	Stage 4
	Flip-flop "Trying-on"	Fledgling "Testing"	Focused "Committed"	Flight "Action"
Risk	None–Low	Minimal	Significant	High
Personal Visibility	None	Minimal	Significant	High
Confidence Level	Tentative	Testing	Less ambivalent and clearer	Purposeful Determined
Decison Making	Unsure	Clarifying	Commitment	Commitment to action
Action Taken	Reading want ads Preliminary investigation	Résumé ready Initial contacts Talk with counselor Convenient discussions	Writing letters Sending résumés Informational interviewing Articulating decision	Active job hunting Letting go of old job Interviews Poised for movement
Internal Talk	I could do this.	I think I can do this.	I am going for it.	I am going to make it happen.

Description of the Job-hunting Stages

Stage 1—Flip-flop

Stage 1 is named "flip-flop" because you are trying to figure out where you fit into the world of work. Reading the want ads is a low-stress, low-risk job-hunting method. It is also not very effective. It is one task to define your career and quite another to locate a job that supports your goals. The answers to your questions in this stage are critical to your moving to the next stage. If you have a "can do" attitude, movement to the next stage will be assured.

Evaluating the appropriateness of jobs based solely on the information found in a $1'' \times 1''$ want ad or in a listing on a web site limits your possibilities. Want ads and job descriptions often present jobs in jargon and technical terms. Each person molds a job description to fit individual skills, personality, goals, expertise, and style. Don't be daunted by words that describe a job.

The trying-on of different jobs is characterized by your internal talk of, "I could do this job or I could do that job." Indecision, frustration, and a feeling of uncertainty about fitting into a job may cloud your thoughts. This internal debate is a natural part of the process. This stage may take a long time. The low risk and low commitment may be attractive, but it is important to set a deadline for moving into the next stage. Calculate the risks of going forward to the next stage of job hunting versus the price of not moving forward. The risks of movement to the next stage may be worth taking when compared with doing nothing, especially when you consider your career goals, self-esteem, and professional growth.

Stage 2—Fledgling

Stage 2 is named "fledgling" because you begin to take small, comfortable risks related to your job hunt. You start to branch out by engaging in convenient conversations about your objectives, digging out your résumé, and consulting with those closest to you or with a counselor. This period of testing is again critical to your movement to the next stage. The information you discover in this stage may propel you forward into a job commitment or you could remain in this stage in order to avoid a job commitment. Only you can judge. There is minimal risk associated with this stage and stage 1. The leap to the next stage requires courage and trust in your decision-making abilities. To help make this leap, ask yourself the following questions.

- Will this job provide me with learning opportunities?
- Will the learning opportunities provide me with necessary skills?
- Does the job fit into my career and life plan?
- Am I excited about what I would learn?

If you have answered "yes" to most of the questions, you are ready to move to stage 3. Remember, you do not have to possess all the expertise *before* you apply for a job. It is quite acceptable to be in process, that is, to be gaining the expertise through course work, apprenticeship, or self-directed learning. Your in-process status demonstrates commitment to potential employers, builds self-confidence, and serves to verify that this is the job area for you. Remember, the commitment that you make in moving to stage 3 is not permanent. It means that right now in your career and life plan, this is the way you choose to direct your job-hunting energies. By making a decision, you save valuable human resources—yours.

Stage 3—Focused

The leap to stage 3 is no small task. This stage is named "focused" because you have made a decision, you are ready to risk more of your personal resources, and you are occupied with the tasks ahead. The résumé or sample application has been revised and cover letters written. You are sending your package (résumé or application plus letter) to selected employers. You are actively involved in informational interviewing with peers in other organizations or in your organization. As your visibility increases, the knowledge about your interest in other areas is spreading. As you articulate your career and life goals, you are clarifying them for yourself and for others.

The decision is in clearer focus and there is relief in knowing that you are moving toward a goal. The exact picture may not yet be in full view, but the movement is a goal in itself. The variables of job market, geographic area, economy, and personal limitations you have placed on your job hunt may encourage or thwart the process at this stage. The only variable that you have control over is the personal limitations that you have placed on your job hunt. If you are in this stage for a long time—and only you can be the judge of time—then reexamine the lifestyle considerations and work values in Section I. You may have placed too many restrictions on your job hunt. Examples of some restrictions include the person who restricts the job hunt to a 5-mile radius from home or one who will only apply for a job that is part-time. Negotiation is a part of the process. Consider breaking your own barriers to employment.

Stage 4—Flight

Stage 4 is named "flight" because you are ready to take off into another job. You have listened to your inner voice that said it was time to leave your present job and are in the process of letting go on an emotional level. The risk is high because your visibility is high. Active job hunting requires confidence and direction. In this stage you feel purposeful and clear about your direction. You do not second-guess yourself. You are poised for employment interviews or are already engaged in employment interviews with several organizations. Flight to the next job is just a matter of time. The goal in this stage is to work toward a job offer.

Many variables must come together before you are offered a job. Some of these variables involve matches between:

- Job requirements and your skills and abilities
- Salary and benefits package and your financial needs
- Demands of the job and your lifestyle considerations
- Culture of the organization and your personality
- Supervision style and your work values
- Potential for learning and your career and life plan

In stage 4, you may have one foot in and one foot out of your present job. Look before you leap into another job by considering these variables and by returning to Section I if you need further clarification of your personal goals.

2. Review the Expenditure of Your Personal Resources

Recognize that job hunting is one of life's most stressful challenges. Since you may feel somewhat out of control during your job hunt, it will be helpful for you to regain some of your control by quantifying those factors over which you do have control—your valuable personal resources. Guard them vigilantly and expend them wisely. Your personal resources can be divided into five categories.

a. **Energy**—Do you seem to spend a great deal of time lost in thought and strategizing the "what ifs" in your job hunt? Visualizing, daydreaming, and emotional energy necessarily are used up during the job hunt. How much energy do you spend on thinking, processing, and planning in each job-hunting method?

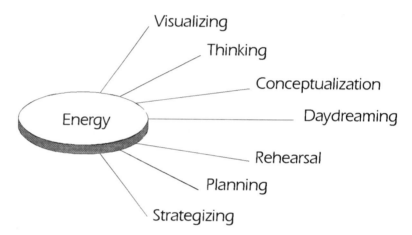

b. **Action**—Do you seem to be overwhelmed with all the details that are involved in job hunting? Follow-up calls, thank-you letters, informational interview letters, and organizational research require action on your part. Action in your job hunt requires effort. Approximately how much action are you devoting to writing, calling, travel, research, and reading in your job hunt?

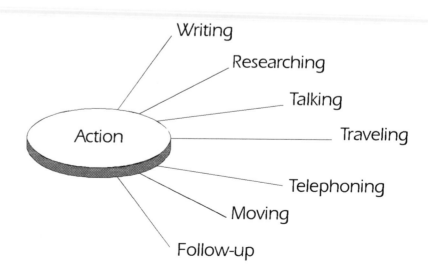

c. **Money**—What financial resources are you expending on your job hunt? Have you invested in additional training, newspaper subscriptions, interview clothing, and professional development to market yourself effectively? These expenses are a part of the overall cost of job hunting. How much money have you spent on your job hunt?

d. **Ego**—How are you feeling about yourself during your job hunt? Your self-esteem is your most precious resource during these times of uncertainty. In every interview, in every phone call, and in every contact you initiate, your ego is on the line. Your motivation, your creativity, and your enthusiasm are interwoven with your ego. In the job hunt all of these resources are needed to make an impact and get the job. How much ego do you risk on each job-hunting method?

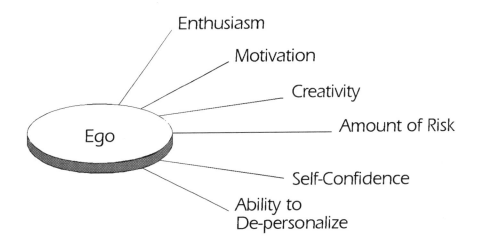

e. **Time**—Do you question the time you spend on your job hunt and feel guilty if you do not spend every waking moment on an activity related to finding a job? Rather than feeling guilty, analyze and decide how much time you are willing to allocate to each job-hunting method. Your time is the sum total of your expenditures of all the other personal resources. In the list below, consider the approximate amount of time you spend on each method of job hunting.

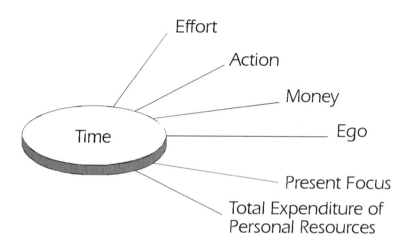

3. Analyze the Expenditure of Your Personal Resources

Several job-hunting methods are listed in the left column of the following chart. Fill in any additional methods that you are currently using in the space marked "other." Mark something in each box. Identify the amount of energy, action, money, ego, and time that you expend on each of the job-hunting methods listed. Your personal investment in job hunting is significant, and these five personal resources are critical to your success. Since you possess a finite amount of each resource, you need to use them wisely. Assign the following values to each of the job-hunting methods listed.

0 = No expenditure of resources in the method
1 = Low expenditure of resources in this method
2 = Medium expenditure of resources in this method
3 = High expenditure of resources in this method

Expenditure of Your Personal Resources					
Job-hunting Methods	Energy	Action	Money	Ego	Time
1. Newspaper ads, other want ads, research					
2. Contacts with personnel or human resources offices					
3. Contacts with employment agencies					
4. Sending résumés, letters, applications					
5. Using federal, state, local employment commissions					
6. Utilizing college career centers or local agency assistance					
7. Networking in professional organizations					
8. Informational interviewing in person					
9. Telephoning for appointments and follow-up					
10. Researching library work, general company investigation					
11. Other method:					
12. Other method:					

4. Analyze the Results of Your Job Campaign

If you have only so much effort, action, ego, money, and time to spend on your job hunt, it makes sense to allocate these resources carefully and weigh them in terms of present and probable results. By evaluating your job-hunting efforts you can save valuable personal resources. What job-hunting methods are working for you, and what job-hunting methods are draining your valuable resources? The same listing of job-hunting methods is provided for you to evaluate the results of your labor.

With some approximation, analyze the results of your job hunt thus far by counting how many

- contacts made in each method
- responses you have received by telephone, letter, or fax
- employment interviews you have gotten through each method
- job offers or negotiating sessions you have experienced using the methods listed

Analysis of Your Job Campaign				
Job-hunting Methods	**Number of Contacts Made**	**Responses Letter/Phone**	**Employment Interviews**	**Job Offers**
1. Newspaper ads, other want ads, research				
2. Contacts with personnel or human resources offices				
3. Contacts with employment agencies				
4. Sending résumés, letters, applications				
5. Using federal, state or local employment commissions				
6. Utilizing college career centers or local agency assistance				
7. Networking in professional organizations				
8. Informational interviewing in person				
9. Telephoning for appointments and follow-up				
10. Researching library work, general company investigation				
11. Other method:				
12. Other method:				

Your present job campaign may be ineffective. Continue to evaluate your job campaign by answering the following questions.

1. Does your job campaign have balance? Does it allow you the time and energy to process information and consider alternatives, or are you always running from place to place?
2. Are your present job-hunting methods getting results?
3. Are there some methods that are not worth the investment of your energy, action, time, money, and ego? Should you continue to use them?
4. If the expenditures of your resources are not yielding the results that you desire, then how can you strive to improve the efficiency of your job campaign?

When your cart reaches the foot of the mountain, a path will appear.

—*Chinese Proverb*

Job Hunting in Cyberspace

The Internet and World Wide Web and on-line services such as CompuServe and America Online provide the most rapidly growing resources for job hunters. There is an explosion of information available to anyone who can access these networks. This information is updated constantly and therefore represents a source of career information and work opportunities that should be considered by anyone who is conducting a job campaign.

In addition to information on jobs, it is possible to gain access to a wealth of information on organizations and to communicate with other people through interest groups and networks, and even send résumés and applications electronically. The potential of the Internet and other on-line services for job hunting and career exploration is unlimited and there will continue to be constant changes. This chapter will outline the possible uses of the Internet and on-line services and provide resources for further investigation.

A. The Internet

The Internet was developed by the U. S. Department of Defense in the 1960's as a means of linking the Pentagon, military bases, contractors, and universities in a communications network. Over the years, a rapidly expanding number of organizations connected themselves to the Internet and with the end of the Cold War, the Internet became open to the general public.

The Internet simply is the combination of millions of individual computers and the many computer networks all over the world that are connected electronically. The speed of the communications potential is quite remarkable, providing users the opportunity to communicate throughout the world. The Internet is an ever-changing combination of individual users and organizations. There is no Internet headquarters or Internet coordinating staff, except for a registration requirement for domain names administered by the National Science Foundation. Therefore, it is necessary to use a software system that will provide some type of organized access to the wealth of information available in the Internet.

Some operating systems, such as Windows 98, have Internet access built in. A variety of Internet/World Wide Web "browser" programs provide access as well as the on-line systems described later in this chapter. There are many indexes that can help you to find career and job information. Here are a few examples, with addresses. Because of the constant change and growth in the Internet, always check the latest sources for up to date information. The Career Resource Center provides a multitude of links to job resources on the Web.

www.careers.org

Purdue University's placement service provides a comprehensive collection of links to job information on the Internet.

http:/www.cs.purdue.edu/homes/swlodin/jobs.htm/

www.cco.purdue.edu/

Job Hunt provides a wide variety of links into several categories of job information, newspaper listings, recruiting agencies, companies, and a wide variety of other sources of information.

www.job-hunt.org

Riley Guide is an index to employment opportunities and job resources on the Internet. It provides information on links in a variety of categories and to job resources in each state and Canada.

www.dbm.com/jobguide

B. ON-LINE SYSTEMS

There are commercial systems that charge a fee for the use of their services and provide a variety of information and related resources as well as Internet access. Four of the leading commercial systems are America Online, CompuServe, Prodigy and Microsoft Network. The advantage of these systems is that the information and services available are better organized than the Internet since they are run as profit-making businesses and someone is in charge of providing the service. For example, America Online offers its Career Center, which provides a wide variety of information and services such as:

- A talent bank that, for a fee, will put your résumé in its worldwide data base
- A self-employment service designed to help you start a home-based business
- A service providing information on federal employment opportunities
- A career resource library of career related information
- Employment agency and employer databases for potential job contacts
- A job listing database which includes several job listing services. You can even list a job that you have available through this service.
- A career counseling service in which you can participate in an on-line group career counseling session, participate in career assessment exercises, and help you match your interests, abilities, and work preferences to potential careers
- An occupational profiles database

Other on-line systems provide different services: CompuServe has a comprehensive database from which one can obtain a wealth of career information, an excellent opportunity for career research. Prodigy provides a classifieds listing and a career bulletin board which consolidates career information and messages. Additional services will probably be available from these on-line systems and others by the time you read this book. The growth in on-line information is tremendous.

C. Accessing the Internet, World Wide Web, and On-line Systems

You need a computer, a modem, a telephone outlet, and a communications program. You may already have these in your home. If you are a student, you can probably gain access through computers on campus. You may have access through your work. New systems that provide Internet and on-line access are being developed constantly and large communications organizations such as A.T.&T., MCI-Worldcom, and Sprint are getting involved. New access software will improve everyone's ability to use the Internet and on-line systems effectively. If you are planning to purchase a system to provide access, there are many resources that provide extremely helpful information as well as practical assistance on using the Internet and on-line services. Some of these resources are listed later in this chapter.

D. Usenet Newsgroups

The Internet provides opportunities to correspond with others who work in areas that interest you. Internet newsgroups can be an excellent resource for obtaining information and for communicating with people who may be able to assist you. Through newsgroup mailing lists you can receive information on a variety of topics related to your career interests. These groups are offered through commercial systems such as America Online, or you can access Usenet through a direct Internet connection. You can post messages in these newsgroups, which are sent to interconnected computer systems.

In addition to providing information, Usenet newsgroups can be good sources of job listings. They can be a particularly good source of local, as well as national, job listings, and can be a good resource for people who are relocating to a specific geographical area. Newsgroup job listings usually contain more information on the positions listed that typical classified advertisements. Some Websites such as CareerMosaic (www.careermosaic.com), JobHunt (www.job-hunt.org), and Deja News (www.dejanews.com) make it possible for you to search many employment-related newsgroups. While newsgroups can be a good source of information and job listings, think carefully before you post your resume with a newsgroup, since there is no way that you can keep your resume confidential. Anyone has access to your resume, including your current employer.

For a good resource on using Newsgroups, try Graber, Steven (ed.), *Adams Electronic Job Search Almanac 2000*. Holbrook, MA: Adams Media Corp., 2000.

E. USING THE WORLD WIDE WEB IN THE JOB SEARCH

The World Wide Web provides organizations and individuals with the opportunity to develop "home pages," usually with graphics, that allow you to access all kinds of information about an organization. These home pages can be linked so that you can jump from a topic on one home page to the same topic on another home page. The potential for organized access to information is tremendous, limited only by the programming of the information on the organizations' home pages and the speed of the available communications links. Organizations can place all kinds of data, including employment opportunities, on-line with easy access through the organization's home page. To obtain access to the World Wide Web, you should have "web browser" software available through a commercial on-line service or elsewhere. See item H in this chapter for a listing of helpful resources for accessing the Internet and the World Wide Web.

For a listing of useful sites on the World Wide Web for career exploration and job hunting, go to Chapter 15, The World Wide Web-sites for Career Exploration and Job Hunting.

F. BE CAREFUL!

The explosion of information available through the Internet and the World Wide Web can be an extremely useful resource in career planning and job hunting. But it can be captivating and can easily distract you from the important work-finding activities that have been described in this chapter. You can access the information using your (or someone else's) computer. You can even interact with others on-line and send your résumé on-line. There is even a possibility that you may be able to find work on-line.

However, there is no substitute for the face-to-face meetings, the interpersonal contacts that are essential to the job campaign. You can easily allow yourself to spend hours in front of the computer accessing all of this wonderful information. Remember that you must get out and around and talk with people in order to conduct an effective job campaign. The computer can be an extremely useful tool in the career exploration and job hunting process. Use it as a tool, but don't let it overwhelm you by taking your energy and time away from the other techniques that will help you to find the work of your choice.

G. THE MOST IMPORTANT CYBERSPACE APPLICATION TO CAREER PLANNING AND JOB HUNTING

While the use of the Internet and the World Wide Web can be helpful in the job search, as described in this chapter, there is a more important application of the new technology to your career planning. The developments in technology are becoming pervasive throughout the workforce in the 21st century. Most planners maintain that we have just begun to see the effects of the technological and information revolution. No matter what career field you enter, you will gain an advantage by taking every opportunity to learn how to use new technologies. Learn about new developments. Try out new software applications to your work. Volunteer to be a part of work groups exploring new technological applications. Take courses and workshops whenever they are given. Be open to change and to the new technologies that will come with change. By welcoming new technologies and learning how to use them, you will open yourself to new career opportunities.

H. ADDITIONAL RESOURCES FOR JOB HUNTING IN CYPERSPACE

Bolles, Richard Nelson, *Job Hunting on the Internet*. Berkeley, CA: Ten Speed Press, 1999.

Cochran, Chuck and Peerce, Donna, *Heart and Soul Internet Job Search*. Palo Alto, CA: Davis Black Publishing Co., 1999.

Dikel, Margaret, Roehm, Francis, and Oserman, S. *The Guide to Internet Job Searching*. Illinoiw: VGM, 1998

Dixon, Pam, *Job Searching Online for Dummies*. Foster City, CA: IDG Books Worldwide, Inc., 1998.

Knox, Deborah L. and Butzel, Sandra S., *Life Work Transitions.com. Putting Your Spirit Online*. Woburn, MA: Butterworth-Heinemann, 2000.

Nemnich, Mary B. and Jandt, Fred E., *Cyberspace Job Search Kit*. Indianapolis, IN: JIST Works, Inc., 1998.

Oakes, Elizabeth (ed.), *Career Exploration on the Internet*. Chicago: Ferguson Publishing Co., 1998.

WetFeet.com's *Industry Insider Guide - The Inside Scoop on the Job You Want*. San Francisco: Jossey-Bass Publishing Co., 2000.

Wolfinger, Anne, *The Quick Internet Guide to Career and Educational Information*. Indianapolis, IN: JIST Works Inc., 2000.

Résumé Writing

Your résumé is an important part of your job campaign. It presents in writing the skills, accomplishments, and qualifications that you bring to a potential employer. The process of writing your résumé is an efficient way of organizing your qualifications so that *you* know what you have to offer an employer. For this reason, it is very important that you spend a good deal of time writing and rewriting your résumé. It is not a good idea to have someone else write your résumé for you.

Think of the skills and abilities that you have developed that would contribute to your career goals. No one can write these attributes better than you because no one knows you better than you do. Your résumé should be neat, clearly written, and positive. The process of writing your own résumé will help you to focus on your skills and abilities, communicate your strengths, and interview effectively.

A. Characteristics of a Good Résumé.

What do you want your résumé to do for you? Here are some characteristics of a good résumé.

1. A résumé presents your *accomplishments*. It should show how *well* you perform, rather than just presenting descriptions of previous jobs that you have held.
2. A résumé demonstrates how your qualifications will *meet the needs of employers*. It should focus not on what you want but on what you have to *offer* the employer.
3. A résumé describes your major strengths and potential without being too long.
4. A résumé shows your own unique personality and experiences and should make an employer want to talk with you.
5. A résumé is interesting to read rather than challenging to read.

B. Questions to Ask Before You Write Your Résumé

1. What is your purpose in writing a résumé? Are you changing jobs in the same career area or are you changing careers? It will make a difference in how you organize your résumé.
2. What type of job are you seeking? It can help to have a specific objective.
3. What type of person and experience are required for the job? You can find this information through research, informational interviewing, and networking.
4. What skills and abilities do you have to offer an employer?
5. Which skills, abilities, and accomplishments do you want to stress? Focus on those that support your career objective.

C. Organization of Your Résumé

There is no specific résumé format that is best for everyone. Choose the style that is best for you. Although there are many variations in format, most résumés can be categorized in three types.

- **Chronological**
- **Functional**
- **Combination chronological and functional**

1. The chronological résumé is the most traditional format and is appropriate if you are looking for a position that is a logical step in your career. Your work history is given in chronological order, with the most recent experience first. Dates of employment are included, and the résumé is presented as an exact account of your time and experience.

2. The functional résumé emphasizes skills and accomplishments. Dates of employment and specific jobs are deemphasized. Particular skill areas such as writing, managing, research, communication, and others are highlighted. Examples are given to show how well you perform, but these examples can come from several different jobs. This format may be particularly useful if you are changing careers.

3. The combination chronological and functional résumé gives an orderly account of your employment history, but it also focuses on areas of skills and accomplishments that you wish to highlight. The format helps you to clearly show how well you perform, while giving an account of the progression of your career.

D. CONTENTS OF CHRONOLOGICAL, FUNCTIONAL, AND COMBINATION RÉSUMÉS

1. Heading

Start with your name, address, and telephone numbers (work and home) where you can be reached or where a message can be taken. Include your E-mail address, if you have one.

2. Objective

State the type of position that you wish to obtain and give some indication of what you have to offer a potential employer. Do not write the objective in terms of what you want from a job. Indicate how you would be able to meet the employer's needs. Although it is important to give a sense of purpose, it may not be necessary to give a specific job title in your objective. Identify the function and the general level of the type of job you want. You may need to tailor your objective for each position that you seek. Be sure to include terminology relevant to the type of position that you are seeking in case your résumé is scanned by a potential employer.

3. Experience and Accomplishments

This is the most important part of your résumé. Remember that it is *not* a series of job descriptions. Show what you have achieved, the special contributions you have made, the responsibilities you have assumed, and the recognition you have received. If you can quantify what you did, by all means do so.

Example: Developed a new inventory system that resulted in annual savings of $25,000.

Include any awards and indicate how proficient you are in specific terms. Avoid general grandiose statements that are self-serving. In describing your experience and accomplishments, use action verbs such as:

• Sold	• Developed
• Planned	• Promoted
• Trained	• Established
• Supervised	• Negotiated
• Designed	• Managed
• Initiated	• Performed
• Implemented	• Created
• Coordinated	• Researched

Remember to demonstrate what you have done and what you are capable of doing in the future.

For chronological résumés

Show your best experience first. Generally start with your most recent experience (unless it does not support your objective) and work backward. Give the name and location of each employer and the dates of your employment. Include part-time or summer work if it was moderately recent and if it relates to your objective. Show the sequence of your career and present your career as a series of progressive accomplishments.

For functional résumés

List three or four areas of expertise you possess and then document that expertise with your work or volunteer experiences. Examples of areas of expertise are:

• Organization	• Budgeting
• Purchasing	• Supervision
• Communication skills	• Programming
• Teaching	• Coordination
• Repairing	• Writing
• Marketing	• Installing

Give as many specific examples of your expertise as you can for each area. Write in a manner that illustrates results and accomplishments. Use a variety of strong action verbs. Draw on every aspect of your life, including any volunteer work as well as paid employment. You may not want to use dates or give specific job titles if you wish to follow a functional format.

For combination résumés

Follow the guidelines for both chronological and functional résumés and have two sections; one for accomplishments and one for specific experience.

Special instructions for this section

- Define abilities rather than duties
- Stress your accomplishments
- Use correct dates

- Use brief and direct descriptions
- Write clearly and simply
- Use strong action verbs

4. **Education**

Put education before your experience if it is the major qualifying factor for the position you are seeking. List your highest degree first and work backward. If high school or vocational school is your highest level, include it. Otherwise, high school education is usually not included. Supply names of schools attended, dates (for chronological format), academic honors, grade point average if outstanding, class standing if in the upper third, and major subject areas. Be sure to include special workshops, training, and certifications if they relate to your objective. If you are writing a functional résumé, you may not wish to include dates in this section if you have not done so in other sections of your résumé. Include recent on-the-job training in the education category of your résumé, depending on what you see as your main selling points.

5. **Special Skills, Memberships, Military Service, and Awards**

Include any special technical skills that relate to your objective. You may also wish to include memberships in professional organizations, and particularly any awards received, offices held, or professional presentations you offered. If you wish to include military service, describe it in civilian terms. Remember to sell yourself. Present this information in a positive manner. Include any special information that demonstrates how well you perform and in turn emphasizes your professional objective. Distinguish yourself from other job applicants by allowing your unique combination of skills to shine through your résumé.

6. **Interests, Community Contributions**

Include special interests, travel, skills, licenses, certifications, community activities, or any other information that:

- Relates to your objective
- Puts you in a positive position so that a potential employer may want to meet you

7. **References**

Never list your references on your résumé. Indicate that they will be furnished on request. You will want to select particular references depending on the position you are considering. Choose people who can attest to your work-related skills and work habits.

E. ELECTRONIC SCANNING OR TRANSMISSION OF RÉSUMÉS

With increasing capabilities to scan materials and put them in an organization's data base, more and more résumés will be scanned electronically or will be sent to an organization via E-mail. Many companies in the United States sell résumé scanning software and automated applicant tracking systems. People in organizations can review résumés and applications on their computer screens, making this process much more efficient.

In addition to scanning résumés so that they can be entered in a database, the new software allows an organization to search résumés for certain experiences, skills, or training that is deemed important for a particular position. Résumés can also be scanned for certain factors and routed to appropriate offices within an organization. The new applicant tracking software can also generate letters of rejection or letters offering interviews and can also store résumés or selected applicant information for potential future openings.

What does this new approach to the review of résumés and applications mean to the job hunter? It is more important than ever to construct a good, well-organized résumé. However, since scanning programs will be used much more frequently in the future, here are some factors to consider.

1. Since scanning programs will search out key words, use more nouns in your résumé in addition to action verbs. Specific experience, training, and skills should be described using accepted names and the jargon appropriate to the field. Here are some examples.

Certified Public Accountant
Microsoft Office 2000 Suite Trainer
Certified Novell Engineer (CNE)
Training in A.D.A. compliance
Experienced in conflict resolution techniques
Certified A.S.E. mechanic
Experience in contract management and acquisitions

Check position descriptions on the websites, classified ads, and organizational newsletters as a source of these words. Include them in your objective, which can also incorporate a summary of your skills, experience, and education.

2. Use common fonts no smaller than a 10 and no larger than a 14. Scanners can more easily deal with your résumé if your document is not too fancy.
3. Use plain white or ivory paper and don't use borders. When mailing your résumé, use a large enough envelope so that you do not have to fold your résumé. All of these make scanning your résumé easier.

Make sure to continue to send a cover letter with each résumé and keep up to date with the latest technology.

F. E-Mailing Résumés

As an important part of your job search, you must have your résumé ready to e-mail to a potential employer. In preparing your résumé, use the guidelines provided in this chapter, with the following adjustments:

1. Set the margins in your word processing program for no more than 65 characters. Select a simple font with 10 point or 12 point type.
2. Use all caps for your name and major headings. Use parentheses around your phone number area code. Use a left-justified format. Use your spacebar to indent items, not tabs.
3. Save your résumé as text only or ASCII, making sure that you double check all of the information and run a spell check. Close the file, reopen it, and fix spacing problems with your spacebar.
4. E-mail your résumé to a friend so that you can see how it transmits. It is usually best to send the résumé as text in your e-mail message, not as an attachment.

5. Follow up with your printed résumé and a cover letter.
6. Important note: If you send out your résumé to be posted on one of the job search sites, be careful. Your current employer can easily see your résumé unless you keep your search confidential by blocking your name, contact information, and current employer. Some sites, such as CareerSite.com and Monster.com allow you to do this.

Since sending résumés via e-mail will be an increasingly important part of your job search, consider the use of additional resources. Here are some that are available:

Criscito, Pat, *Résumés in Cyberspace*. Hauppauge, NY: Barron's. 1997.

Dixon, Pam, *Job Searching Online for Dummies*. Foster City, CA: IDG Books Worldwide, Inc., 1998.

Gonyea, James C. and Gonyea, Wayne M., *Electronic Résumés—A Complete Guide to Putting Your Résumé Online*. New York: McGraw-Hill, 1996.

Graber, Steven (ed.), *Adams Electronic Job Search Almanac 2000*. Holbrook, MA: Adams Media Corp., 2000.

Jandt, Fred E. and Nemnich, Mary, *How to Make a Snazzy Online Résumé*. Indianapolis, IN: JIST Works, Inc., 1999.

Weddle, Peter D. *Internet Résumés*. Manassas Park, VA: Impact Publications, 1998.

Whitcomb, Susan Britton, *Résumé Magic*. Indianapolis, IN: JIST Works, Inc., 1999.

Check the references in Chapter 20, Job Hunting in Cyberspace, for additional information. Also go to Chapter 15, The World Wide Web—Sites for Career Exploration and Job Hunting.

G. DEVELOP YOUR OWN HOME PAGE

The ease of developing a home page provides you with another opportunity to showcase your work. If you have examples of your accomplishments that can be clearly provided on a home page, consider this option. If you do create a home page and plan to use it in your job search, make sure that it is very professional. Remove any information and links that are not related to your goal of finding a job. While this opportunity may be very attractive to some job hunters, especially those who have graphic examples of their work, it is not essential. It is much more important to have both a good electronic résumé and a good print résumé. If you wish to create a home page, there are many workshops and study guides available to help you.

H. General Tips on Writing Your Résumé

- Use your own language. You are the best person to write your résumé.
- Use this formula for length: one page for ten years' experience, two pages for more than ten years.
- Write it, edit it, show it to others, and rewrite it.
- Type it neatly and organize it logically.
- Never have a misspelled word.
- Use a word processor to prepare your résumé. It then can be easily adapted to display qualifications that match specific job descriptions. Use the best printer available to you. Typesetting your résumé is good but expensive and allows less flexibility for last-minute changes.
- Place the most significant and powerful information in the beginning of your résumé and in the beginning of each heading. Don't hide the information that packs a punch.
- Use correct dates and correct information throughout.
- Organize the résumé to highlight your strongest skills and accomplishments.
- Don't make paragraphs too long. Double space between paragraphs. Make your résumé readable. Most employers only scan.
- Stress your abilities and accomplishments.
- Sell yourself.
- Increasingly, organizations will ask that résumés be sent using the Internet. In addition, many résumés will be scanned into an organization's communication network. These developments only serve to increase the importance of good résumé preparation.

I. Sample Résumés

On the following pages, sample résumés are provided in three different formats.

- **Chronological**
- **Functional**
- **Combination**

Remember, the best person to compose your résumé is YOU!

There is no one right way to write a résumé. Use the format that most favorably presents your experience, your background, and your career goal. Once you have written a résumé, you will need to update it frequently. The best time to revise your résumé is when you do not feel pressured to do so. Try to keep an accurate résumé on file at all times. You never know when opportunity will knock. Résumé writing is usually considered a difficult task because it is hard to write about yourself. However, writing a comprehensive, positive résumé is a worthwhile process, because it can reinforce your self-worth and can increase your self-confidence.

A note of caution: relying too heavily on your résumé in the jobseeking process can be discouraging as well as counterproductive. How you use your résumé in your job search is as important as developing your résumé. A survey of human resource executives reported that they spent less than one minute scanning the average résumé they received and that only 5 percent of all résumés sent resulted in an interview. The résumé is merely a tool. It will never replace the value of informational interviewing and other job search techniques. You may wish to review the job-seeking techniques described earlier in this chapter to enhance your job campaign.

Chronological Résumé

Antoine Jackson
1000 Main Street
Chicago, Illinois 60673
Telephone: Home (312) 555-5555
Office (312) 555-9000
E-mail: AJackson@msn.com

Professional Objective	Regional sales manager for an organization that will utilize my experience in creating new sales promotions and in developing efficient delivery of sales services to customers
Education	B.S., University of Illinois. 1982. Major: Marketing. Top third of graduating class. Special emphasis on retail sales and merchandising. Considerable work in accounting and information systems.
Experience	XYZ Men's Shop, Chicago, Illinois.
1989 to present	*Manager, Assistant Manager.* Responsible for all advertising and copy layout for this large department store. Worked closely with all buyers in planning sales campaigns. Coordinated and completed modernization plans for basement floor. Assisted in selection of men's suits and shoes. Trained new sales personnel and implemented new training program.
1985 to 1989	J.C. Company, Peoria, Illinois. *Retail Shoe Sales.* Started as clerk. After six months, promoted to new outlet as assistant manager. Responsible for all display work, newspaper advertising, and sales promotion. The store had an annual volume of $250,000.
Summer Work	Earned half of total college expenses selling cookware on commission for four summers.
Military Service	United States Army, 1982–1985. *Communications Specialist.* Served in Germany and at the Pentagon.
Background	Brought up in Chicago area. Active in community affairs, such as Illinois Junior Chamber of Commerce and active alumnus of University of Illinois. Member of social fraternity. Have traveled extensively throughout the western part of the United States.
Interests	Primarily interested in hiking—outdoor activities and conservation societies, such as Sierra Club and Save the Animals Foundation.
References	References will be furnished upon request.

Chronological Résumé

Sarah Kozlowski
100 Main Street
Minneapolis, Minnesota 67854
Telephone: Home (612) 555-0032
Work (612) 555-1111
E-mail: sarahk@aol.com

Professional Objective

Database management with an organization that can benefit from problem-solving skills, knowledge of six programming languages, and ability to adapt to organizational needs and challenges.

Education

A.A.S. 1995, Minneapolis Community College. Majored in computer information systems. Completed cooperative education in computer information systems and took additional course work in accounting and business management. Elected to Phi Theta Kappa academic honor society. Graduated magna cum laude.

Experience and Accomplishments

Computer programmer, ABC Corporation, St. Paul, Minnesota, 1997–present. Began as a trainee and was moved into a programmer position within six months. Wrote programs and became familiar with most aspects of the information systems of the company. Used COBOL, JAVA, and C++ extensively. Promoted to assistant manager of the data system.

Secretary to the human resources director, BCD Corporation, Minneapolis, Minnesota, 1989–1994. Supervised two clerk typists. Developed and administered a new records system. Wrote letters and reports for the director. Monitored the office budget and initiated all work orders and purchase requisitions.

Bank teller, Second National Bank, Minneapolis, Minnesota, 1987–1989. Dealt with customers and monitored money flow. After one year, promoted to supervisor of the evening shift.

Special Skills

Have a working knowledge of four computer languages including COBOL, JAVA, C++, and EVENT-DRIVEN BASIC. Took extra courses in mathematics to develop good analytical skills. Have worked with ORACLE and ACCESS database programs.

Background

Have interests in bridge, tennis, and archery. Work as a volunteer at Community Hospital twice each week. Sing in church choir and teach religious education.

References

Excellent references furnished on request.

Chronological Résumé

RICHARD E. MOSSER
123 South Taylor Street
Lima, Virginia 22204
E-mail: RMosser@compuserve.com

Home: (804) 111-1111   Office: (804) 555-5555

OBJECTIVE: Electrician with full range of responsibilities from maintenance to installation with a medium-sized company that encourages professional growth.

SUMMARY: More than 12 years experience in all phases of the electrical field. Expertise Expertise in troubleshooting electrical circuits and providing necessary maintenance. Effective supervisor of tradespeople.

EXPERIENCE:

1994–PRESENT   Lima City Government, Lima, Virginia
ELECTRICIAN
- Repaired, installed, adjusted, modified, and tested electrical systems and devices for 300,000 square feet of office and classroom space; including:

—Electrical panels	—Fluorescent	—Magnetic starters
—Conduit	—Computer	—Switches, receptacles
—Motors	—Breakers	—Incandescent lights
—Ballasts	—Wire	—Telephone lines

- Purchased material for more than 1,000 electrical items
- Trained two apprentices on electrical maintenance procedures
- Supervised 1–4 tradespeople
- Read blueprints and schematics for wiring of new equipment, new additions, and new buildings
- Worked with voltages up to 480-volt 3-phase systems

1987–1994   XYZ Management Company, Lima, Virginia
ELECTRICIAN
Total electrical renovation of apartments for new tenants. Replaced fixtures, switches, receptacles and wiring

1986–1987   ABC Electric Company, Lima, Virginia
ELECTRICIAN HELPER
New wiring of single-family homes, townhouses, commercial work on high-rise office buildings in the Central Virginia area

EDUCATION

1995–1998   Best Community College, Lima, Virginia
Courses focused on technical mathematics
Dean's List with G.P.A. 3.68

1983–1986   Training Community College, Highland, New York
Electrical Construction, 1,920 hours of study, certificate awarded 1986.

SPECIAL LICENSE
April 6, 1987   Virginia Journeyman's License # 5678-JK

REFERENCES   Excellent references available on request

Functional Résumé
For Someone Who is Returning to Paid Employment

AMY LYNN CHAN
605 Pearl Street
Rockville, Maryland 21210
Telephone: (301) 524-2263
E-mail: alchan@hotmail.com

PROFESSIONAL OBJECTIVE

Administrative assistant position where my coordinating, analyzing, planning, and budgeting skills would benefit a small to medium-sized organization

COORDINATING SKILLS

Coordinated fund-raising activities of twenty members of the local Parent Teachers Association, successfully raising $10,000 for playground facilities. As member of the Women's League of Rockville Methodist Church, initiated a relief center to meet clothing needs of the community. Also developed a schedule to meet demands of five busy family members, including carpools, cleaning, cooking, and general household management

BUDGETING SKILLS

As treasurer of our local civic association, managed $12,000 budget for two years.

Organized and managed family budget for 17 years. During this period, have accumulated savings necessary for four years of college for daughter. In addition to financial matters, have learned to budget time through well-organized scheduling of community activities and family responsibilities

COMMUNICATION SKILLS

Developed interpersonal skills during ten years' experience with PTA and church members. Have learned the subtleties of persuading adults to contribute time and money to community projects. Have invested considerable time and effort in developing open communication among family members. Retain a sense of humor in tense situations

INTERESTS

Traveling, reading, and sewing

MEMBERSHIPS

Elected treasurer of local civic association—three-year term. Voted to board of directors for Rockville Methodist Church—one-year term. President of PTA two years consecutively

REFERENCES

References furnished on request

Functional Résumé
For Someone Who Is Moving from a Clerical Position to a Different Career Objective

TERESA MUÑOZ
100 S. Main Street
St. Petersburg, Florida
H—(555) 413-3000 W—(555) 111-1111
E-mail: Teresamunoz@rocketmail.com

CAREER OBJECTIVE: Position as assistant to Director of Public Relations, where my skills in design, management, analysis, writing, and interpersonal relations would contribute to the overall goals of a growing organization

ART/DESIGN/ PRODUCTION SKILLS: Edited, organized, prepared, proofed, designed layout and artwork, and ordered printing for brochures, fliers, and booklets for information-centered placement office of a large college. Served as contact person for outside printers. Prepared designs and camera-ready art for a variety of clients on a freelance basis.

PUBLIC RELATIONS SKILLS: Assisted staff in placement office by helping employers with job listings, answering inquiries about placement office functions and services; assisted with planning and setting up of annual job fair—greeted employers, lettered name tags, helped employers set up, and acted as troubleshooter for last-minute needs

MANAGEMENT/ LEADERSHIP SKILLS: Supervised a secretarial staff of five. Coordinated work schedules, organized work flow, trained new personnel, and served as office manager

WRITING SKILLS: Answered general information correspondence. Wrote memos and letters of request. Composed justifications for new equipment and tuition assistance requests. Took notes and prepared minutes for staff and committee meetings. Edited and proofread all copy.

COMPUTER SKILLS: Experience with Microsoft Office, Powerpoint, McIntosh operating system, QuarkXPress, Adobe Photoshop and Adobe Illustrator

STRENGTHS: Ability to coordinate activities logically, find creative solutions to problems, work out satisfying compromises, and establish priorities so that deadlines are met. Ability to see the big picture—to understand how all the pieces fit together. Responsible and dependable. Wide variety of interests and abilities. Willing to try new things

EMPLOYMENT HISTORY: Administrative Assistant and Secretary to Director of Placement, XYZ College, St. Petersburg, Florida (7 years). Administrative Assistant and Bookkeeper, First National Bank, St. Petersburg, Florida (2 years). Various freelance assignments, designs for brochures, fliers, advertisements, booklets, and so on (7 years).

EDUCATION: B.A. Degree, XYZ College, 1988. Major in public relations and communications
A.A.S. Degree, ABC Community College, 1989. Majored in commercial art with emphasis in advertising design and illustration

REFERENCES: Will be furnished on request

Combination Chronological-Functional Résumé

THOMAS DIVINCENZO
100 Exeter Street
Sacramento, California
Telephone: Home (916) 555-0321
Office (916) 555-1111
E-mail: TDivincenzo@mailexcite.com

Professional Objective

To make a contribution in a position in social services that requires good interpersonal and organizational skills, in an organization that can benefit from my experience in budgeting, leadership, and training

Competencies

Interpersonal Skills
- Maintained a caseload of 50 young and middle-aged adults and helped them to establish personal goals and action plans
- Initiated and led a series of support groups for young adults
- Provided interest and psychological testing and interpretation to a wide variety of adults
- Developed a community counseling program that has served more than 2,000 adults per year

Leadership and Training
- Supervised a staff of twelve social workers. Staff has one of the lowest turnover rates in the state
- Initiated training programs for staff that have been adopted in six other agencies
- Led numerous training workshops in effective leadership, assertiveness, developing potential, administering human services programs, and others

Budgeting and Organization
- Administered an office with a total staff of 25 and a budget of $500,000
- Developed new systems of record keeping that have reduced errors in reimbursement rolls by 75 percent
- Organized an on-line system that has decreased record-keeping costs by 50 percent
- Served as a consultant to several organizations on budget and program organization

Professional Experience
- Director of Social Service Agency, Sacramento, California. 1994 to present
- Social Worker, Department of Social Services, Los Angeles, California, 1986–1994
- Department Manager, XYZ Drug Stores, Los Angeles, California, 1984–1987

Education
- M.S.W., U.C.L.A., 1986. Graduated in top quarter of class, completed practicum experiences in group leadership, counseling, and organization of social services
- B.A., U.S.C., 1983. Majored in psychology, minored in sociology. Elected vice-president of student government association

Community Service, Professional Organizations
- President of civic association
- Vice-president of state social service association
- Published four articles on social service programs
- Received fellowship for study at a summer institute on the developmental needs of adults
- Member, Chamber of Commerce in Sacramento

References

Available upon request

Combination Chronological-Functional Résumé
For Someone Who Is Changing Careers

ZAIDAN SYED
1000 Main Street
Washington, D.C.
Telephone: Home (202) 555-0032
Office (202) 555-1111
E-mail: Zaidansyed@aol.com

Professional Objective

To work as a convention and program coordinator for an association that will benefit from my skills in organization and teaching

Professional Accomplishments

Organization and

- Developed a comprehensive program for teaching college-level English to high school seniors
- Supervised up to ten workers at various convention assignments
- Organized and led overseas educational trips for high school students
- Initiated and followed through on more than twenty educational trips for high school seniors to various cities and theater programs
- Assisted the director of the New Orleans Convention and Visitors Bureau in the staffing of convention sites throughout the city
- Coordinated the work of a team of English teachers
- Developed skills in use of Microsoft Office, Powerpoint and other presentation software, Web page design

Teaching

- Developed instructional programs for students at all grade levels (9–12) in high school English
- Completed 20 years of successful teaching at the high school level
- Supervised various student organizations, directed plays, served as advisor for a variety of activities
- Elected as faculty representative to local educational association

Professional Experience

Convention Work

Assistant administrator, program coordinator, New Orleans Convention and Visitors Bureau, 1984–1988. Organized the staffing of conventions, worked with various associations in the planning of conventions, provided direct assistance at convention sites

Teaching

High school English teacher, Alpha High School, Washington, D.C. 1988–present. Developed advanced placement programs High School English Teacher, Beta High School, New York, New York, 1979–1984

Education

M.S., Guidance and personnel administration, George Washington University, Washington, D.C., 1994 B.A., English, New York University, 1979

Memberships

National Council of Teachers of English, 1989–present
American Association of Convention Planners, 1997–present
Junior League of America, 1991–present

References

Provided on request.

Résumé Worksheet

Use this worksheet to record as much information as you can think of that you might want to include in a résumé. Then take the information and organize it according to the format that you prefer.

Professional Objective

Education

Experience

Special Skills

Awards, Honors

Interests

Memberships

J. Cover Letters

When you apply for a position, you should send a cover letter along with your résumé. Your cover letter gives you the opportunity to focus your qualifications on the specific position for which you are applying. As a general principle, draw attention to what you can do for the organization, not what you expect to get from the organization. Here are some guidelines for writing cover letters.

Guidelines for Writing a Good Cover Letter

1. Indicate the position for which you are applying.
2. Address your letter to the appropriate person. Do some research to find the person's name. Avoid the use of: Dear Sir or Madam, Gentlemen, or To Whom It May Concern.
3. State why you are interested in the position.
4. Demonstrate how your skills and experience would be appropriate for the position.
5. Select one or two specific accomplishments in your experience that are particularly relevant to the position, and draw attention to them in your letter.
6. Maintain the initiative by stating that you will call to see whether an interview can be arranged.
7. Try to keep the length of the letter to one page.
8. Use good quality stationery and, by all means, do not handwrite the letter. The following is a sample cover letter. It is very brief in order to give a concise example of a format. Yours could be longer to allow you to focus more on appropriate accomplishments.

K. Applications

Applications are generally disliked by employers and applicants alike, but knowing how to complete application forms is a necessary part of your job campaign. Your application should reflect your best skills, abilities, and accomplishments. An application is different from a résumé. Where résumés can be tailored to disguise unemployment, job hopping, or underemployment, an application usually tells all in chronological sequence. Some general application hints will be offered in this section as well as some do's and don'ts.

Employment interviewing is difficult enough without having to complete a long application form while you wait. Request that the employment application be sent to you ahead of time so you can type it and work through it at your own pace. Some organizations may be able to provide a disk for use in entering application data into the organization's information network or may provide access to their applications

Date

Mr. James Smith
Director of Marketing
ABC Corporation
Anywhere, U.S.A. 50000

Dear Mr. Smith:

It has come to my attention that you have a position available in your office as Assistant Director of Marketing. I am very much interested in being considered for this position.

I have several years of appropriate experience in marketing as described in my résumé, a copy of which is enclosed. I would especially like to draw your attention to my work in marketing with XYC Corporation, in which I formulated a new marketing program for the company which resulted in a 25 percent increase in sales. I feel that I can offer you and your organization my experience and skills in program development and my administrative skills, which I have used in marketing for more than five years.

I would appreciate your consideration of my application for this position. Realizing the demands on your time, I will call you on Monday, April 6, to see whether we can arrange for an interview. I look forward to meeting with you in the near future.

Sincerely yours,

through their home pages. In other cases, you will have to enter information at the work site.

1. Some General Application Do's

- Communicate your background clearly with action verbs.
- Type your application or use a word processing program, if possible, and proofread it twice.
- Include all dates of employment and verify those dates.
- Complete all blocks on the form. If an item is not applicable, put N/A.
- Always attach a well-written résumé.
- Include a cover letter if you are mailing your application.
- If possible, customize your application by cutting and pasting additional lines in the "Description of Work" area to accommodate

your experience. The use of a word processing program makes this much easier. Unlike a résumé, in which you narrow your employment description to a few lines, on an application you may be called on to explain and list your duties, responsibilities, and, especially, your accomplishments. You might list them as follows, expanding each as fully as possible

—My responsibilities were . . .
—The skills used were . . .
—My accomplishments were . . .

- Include all experience—paid and volunteer.
- Make your application interesting—use action verbs.
- Consider applying for temporary or part-time work. This may give you the opportunity to get your foot in the door.
- Use references who can attest to your work ability and can remember you. Ask for their permission first.
- Make sure that your references will give you a *good* reference.

2. Some General Application Don'ts

- Don't misspell words.
- Don't omit your signature and the date that you completed the application.
- Don't attach former job descriptions, transcripts, or letters of recommendation unless specifically requested.
- Don't omit church, community, civic, or club work.
- Don't overlook special sections such as honors and awards. Think of some honor you've received or some other special qualifications distinctions or experiences that would set you apart from other applicants.
- Don't be negative.
- Don't make your application a challenge to read. If it is hard to read, people will ignore it.

3. How You Can Compensate for Gaps, Job-Hopping, and Underemployment

a. *Unemployment gaps:* If your employment gaps are three months or more, you should normally state the amount of time. Rather than putting "unemployed" on the form, which is negative, state what you were doing—traveling, researching a career, job search, consultant, home improvements, self-employed.

b. *Job hopping:* Lump a few jobs in the same space, especially if they were for three months or less, and give a general description of what you accomplished during that period. You may decide not to list some jobs that lasted less than a few months.

c. *Underemployment:* Underemployment is a term used to describe an employee whose skills and abilities are not being fully used in a job. If this is your situation, you may wish to change or upgrade your job title and description to better reflect what you are doing in your job. You can always list your accomplishments and the skills you used in the experience section of the application, thus helping to clarify the expertise you use on the job. If you have few accomplishments thus far, then get going and start thinking of some creative projects you could initiate, design, and implement in your job.

Employment Interviewing

It is rare that someone is hired for a job without an employment interview. Interviews are a necessary and critical component of your job campaign strategy because:

- An interview gives the employer the opportunity to meet you in person and to evaluate your attitude, appearance, personality, confidence, and knowledge about yourself.
- An interview gives you the opportunity to meet the employer, to look over the organization in person, and to evaluate the specific job for which you are applying.

This two-way appraisal includes the employer asking, "Will this applicant fit into our organization?" and you asking, "Will this position fit in with my career goals?" Both are equally important. Employment interviewing can be stressful if you give all the decision power to the employer. Recall the cold, hard facts used to describe job hunting in the beginning of this section. These facts can certainly apply to interviewing as well. How can you maintain as much control as possible over

employment interviewing? Here are some strategies that you can use to develop effective job interviewing techniques.

A. KNOW WHAT YOU WANT TO ACCOMPLISH

Keep your purpose in mind. Why are you at this interview? According to Richard Lathrop,* there are three primary objectives of a job interview.

1. To convince the employer to hire you because you have the appropriate skills, abilities, personality, and interests for that job.
2. To evaluate the job, setting, employer, coworkers, and company. Do you want to work here?
3. To demonstrate how the employer would benefit if you were hired. Discuss the employer's needs—not yours.

B. BE PREPARED—USE THE 4 R'S

Preparation is vital. Planning ensures performance, especially in employment interviewing. Reducing the discomfort that usually accompanies employment interviewing is possible, but only in the preparation stage. This is the one aspect of the job-hunting process where you have complete control. Candidates who are uncomfortable with employment interviewing report feelings of powerlessness and fear of the unknown. Preparation is one action that you can take to allay the negative feelings that can interfere with employment interviewing. The 4 R's present ways that you can retain some control and feel more positive about the process of employment interviewing.

Reflect

- Reaffirm your skills and abilities.
- Review your self-assessment in section I.
- Determine what aspects of your experience relate to the job and the employer's needs.
- Consider your potential contribution to the organization.
- Compare your values to the organization's philosophy.
- Know the points that you want to make.
- Think through your career goals in relationship to this job.

---

*Lathrop, Richard. *Who's Hiring Who.* Berkeley, Calif.: Ten Speed Press, 1989, p. 194.

Research

- Obtain the organization's information through human resources, public relations offices, and the World Wide Web:

  —annual reports
  —employee handbooks
  —policy statements
  —employee newsletters

- Use libraries and the World Wide Web for company literature and recent newspaper articles about the organization.
- Develop appropriate questions that reflect your research.
- Obtain a copy of the job description.
- Visit before interview day so that you are sure of the location and to get a feel for the atmosphere.
- Talk with employees about the organization.
- Seek out the individuals who will be interviewing you.
- Use the technique of informational interviewing, if appropriate.

Rehearse

- Practice your interviewing technique in front of a mirror, with an audio or videotape recorder, and do a mock interview with a friend.
- Review your body language, especially under pressure.
- Use gestures that emphasize your points rather than detract from your interview.
- Be yourself—allow your uniqueness to show through.
- Remember to smile in practice sessions and during the interview. It relaxes the facial muscles and communicates positive feelings to the employer.

Remember

- Pack your tailored résumé, sample application, a good pen, questions that you have developed, references' names and addresses, and data on the organization.
- Select work samples, portfolios, brochures, letters, and reports that display your skills.
- Choose clothing that corresponds with the work environment and the position that you are seeking. When in doubt, overdress.
- Reduce all unnecessary stress on the actual day.
- Allow extra time to arrive early.
- Never go to an interview without first checking the organization's web site.

C. Use Nontraditional Methods of Getting Interviews

Be creative in arranging for interviews. This can be particularly important if you are changing careers. Some possible approaches include:

1. Uncover the informal hiring system by talking with employees. The formal hiring system usually involves the human resources office, and you want to have other options available to you.
2. Be referred by an employee. By developing a comfortable relationship through informational interviewing, you could be recommended for a particular job. Most people get their jobs through people they know. Employers usually prefer to hire people who are known quantities.
3. Develop your referral network as explained in the last chapter. Talk with people who do what you would like to do. Some clever ways of meeting contacts are in elevators, the company cafeteria, a local restaurant, the ladies' or men's rooms, or local night spots where employees gather. You may choose their offices also, but sometimes the clever ways pay off.
4. Informational interviewing is the most effective way of uncovering unadvertised job openings. Calling a potential employer for information is less threatening than asking for a job interview. Informational interviewing is one of the best ways of finding out about possible job openings and how your qualifications may relate to those openings.

D. Conduct Your Employment Interview with Style

There is no one right way to interview. Relax and be yourself. Remember that this process is a two-way appraisal that requires active listening and active participation. Passivity is not an effective strategy in employment interviewing or in job hunting and ultimately leads you in the direction of rejection. Your primary responsibility to yourself is to prevent rejection and preserve your ego in the job-hunting process. Remember the following guidelines for job interviewing.

1. Use the 8 E's of interviewing.

Enthusiasm	for the position and the organization shows you at your best.
Energy	is demonstrated through your attitude and in your résumé. Show that you can take action.
Eye contact	between you and the interviewer is essential in interviewing.
Elaborate	on the questions but be succinct. Don't use one-word answers.

Exchange	ideas because the interview is a two-way appraisal. Don't forget to do your evaluation of the organization.
Equality	exists in the interviewing relationship. Retain your personal power.
Ease	in interviewing comes from practice. Breathe deeply and smile to aid relaxation.
Etiquette	is also important in interviewing. Shake hands, thank your interviewer, and write a follow-up letter about the interview.

2. The person interviewing you may not be a good interviewer because he may not know how to guide the interview to bring out your skills. If the interview gets sidetracked, take the initiative in getting back on track.

3. Explain how you could meet the needs of the organization by contributing your expertise.

4. Demonstrate your experience and refer to your résumé. Offer suggestions or ideas that may help the organization.

5. Do not bring up questions regarding pay, vacations, and benefits. Wait until the employer mentions them.

6. Don't volunteer negative information about yourself and don't criticize former employers or coworkers.

7. Don't accept or reject a job offer on the spot. Allow yourself some time to discuss it with others and think about it yourself.

8. Do not misrepresent yourself. Faking skills or experience can backfire.

9. Have some solid questions about the organization, upward mobility, or the leadership style. Research your questions through the use of company information.

10. Take the initiative and suggest that you would like to follow up with a telephone call the next week to see how the selection process is coming along.

11. If the employer indicates that you will not be selected, ask for other referrals or advice.

12. The interview practices of organizations vary. You may need to clarify the type of interview that will be used so that you can prepare effectively for the event:

- *Small group interview* with two or three interviewers
- *Large group interview* with four or more interviewers
- *Simulation interview* with problems and conflicts to solve in a specified amount of time, either written or orally
- *Social interview* that involves dinner, lunch, or both
- *Presentation interview* that requires an extemporaneous talk, discussion of an issue, or a prepared presentation
- *Multiple interview* where several candidates are interviewed at the same time and compete to answer questions

- *Stress interview* that poses discomfort, like one leg of the chair shorter than the others
- *Video interview,* in which candidates are taped
- *Electronic Interview* using the Internet or another network

E. Sample Interview Questions

The following questions are representative of those that you might be asked during an interview. Think of how you would answer them. It will help you to be better prepared. Avoid memorized or "canned" answers because they may show through in your interview. Be honest, be yourself, be natural, and be responsive. Listen carefully to each question asked.

- What has brought you to this point in your career?
- What did you like and dislike about your previous jobs?
- Why do you want this job?
- How does this position fit into your future plans?
- What do you want to be doing five years from now? ten years?
- What are your weaknesses?
- What could you have done better on your last job?
- What can you do for this company?
- What interests you about our service or product?
- What are your salary requirements?
- What do you like to do with your leisure time?
- How do you respond to pressure?
- What would you like to accomplish during your lifetime?
- How do you plan to achieve your goals?
- How important is job satisfaction in your life?
- What kind of people do you enjoy working with? dislike working with?
- What have you done recently that shows your initiative and willingness to work?
- How would you describe yourself to others?
- How do you feel about overtime?
- What was the last book you read?
- What type of supervision do you prefer?
- Are you able to list some character and employer references?
- How do you feel about our organization so far?
- What is your ideal job?
- Describe your concept of success.

F. Ten Key Considerations for Effective Interviewing*

According to Richard Lathrop, the following are the ten most important factors that employers consider when evaluating an interviewee.

1. Appropriate clothing
2. Good grooming
3. A firm handshake
4. The appearance of controlled energy
5. Pertinent humor and a readiness to smile
6. A genuine interest in the employer's operations and alert attention when the interviewer speaks
7. Pride in past performance
8. An understanding of the employer's needs and a desire to serve them
9. The display of sound ideas
10. Ability to take control when employers fall down on the interviewing job

G. Follow-Up

After the interview, it is important for you to follow up with your contacts. Perseverance pays off.

- Review what happened in your interview. What could you have done to make it better? What else could you have emphasized?
- Send a typed thank-you letter to the employer.
- Call the following week to see how the selection process is coming along. If you can go in person, do so.
- If you are not offered the job, leave the door open for future contact. Another job may open up. Ask for other suggestions and alternatives.
- Keep in contact with the employer.

---

*Lathrop, Richard. *Who's Hiring Who.* Berkeley, Calif.: Ten Speed Press, 1989, p. 197.

H. INTERVIEW CHECKLIST

Preparation

_____ Know your skills and abilities—what you have to offer.

_____ Know your career goal(s).

_____ Research the company or organization through print and electronic resources.

_____ Have a résumé with which you feel satisfied.

_____ If the organization has a standard application, complete it before you come for the interview.

_____ Know about your field of interest—openings, salary ranges, possible jobs.

Filling Out the Application

_____ Bring your résumé.

_____ Know your social security number.

_____ Take a pen with you.

_____ Read the instructions carefully.

_____ Use your correct name, not a nickname.

_____ Answer every question that applies to you, or use N/A if not applicable.

_____ Have available the correct names and addresses of people that you can use as professional and personal references.

_____ Employers expect you to state the kind of work in which you are interested. Therefore, state clearly your particular interest. Do not write the word "anything" in answer to this question.

_____ If there is a blank for "Salary Desired" only give a salary range if you have an accurate idea of what can be expected of this position.

_____ Check the application fully upon completion for possible errors.

For the Big Day

Frame your previous experiences positively!

_____ Dress appropriately.

_____ Make arrangements for transportation necessary to get you to the interview on time.

_____ Arrive ten minutes early for the interview.

_____ Know the interviewer's name.

_____ Do not take friends, parents, or children with you to the interview.

_____ Be prepared to state your qualifications briefly and intelligently.

The Interview Itself

_____ Introduce yourself, shake hands, and state the purpose of your visit.

_____ Smile and look directly at your interviewer(s).

_____ Be a good listener; don't dominate the interview.

_____ Answer all questions briefly and intelligently.

_____ Ask questions about the job to show your interest—and your willingness to contribute.

_____ Make sure that you present your skills and accomplishments that relate to the job.

_____ Be sincere and honest.

_____ Salary questions are tricky. Know your range and keep fringe benefits in mind.

_____ Leave family or personal problems at home.

_____ Do not be critical of former employers or coworkers.

_____ Once the interview is over thank the person for her time and consideration.

Afterwards (Phew!)

_____ Make each interview a learning experience.

_____ How could you improve your next interview?

_____ What points could you stress more strongly?

_____ Practice will help you with your next interview.

_____ Send a thank-you letter.

I. ELECTRONIC INTERVIEWS

Computerized Job Interviews

Computer assisted job interviews are becoming more common, especially for screening large numbers of candidates. These "interviews" provide an opportunity for employers to obtain responses that are structured and can be easily quantified and analyzed. You will most likely encounter computer assisted job interviews when you apply for entry level jobs in fields that require a large number of workers. The process is normally used to screen out unqualified applicants.

You usually complete a computer assisted interview at an employer's human resources office and it will probably consist of a number of short answer or multiple choice questions on your work experience, education, training, attitudes toward work, skills, and other related topics. Remember that this process will be used for screening and you will usually be interviewed in person if you survive the initial screening.

You should prepare for a computer-assisted interview as you would for an in-person interview. You need to articulate your experience and training, your goals, and what you can contribute to the organization. It is extremely important that you learn all that you can about the organization and the field before beginning any interview, but especially a computer-assisted interview.

Internet Job Interviews

This type of interview is very similar to a computer -assisted interview, except that you can answer a series of questions via E-mail rather than traveling to the organization's human resource office.

Telephone Job Interviews

If you apply for a position that is some distance away, you may be asked to participate in a telephone interview. The general guidelines for telephone interviews are the same as for in-person interviews, except that you must demonstrate your enthusiasm about the position and engage your interviewer(s) in a dialogue during the telephone interview. Avoid giving one sentence answers simply because of the impersonality of the telephone conference. Take a very active role in structuring the interview so that you can showcase your skills, experience, and personality. If you are given a choice between a telephone and an in-person interview, you generally should opt for the in-person, even if it is inconvenient. Remember, you may be very interested in the job and an effective job campaign involves expense of both time and money.

J. NEGOTIATING A SALARY

Congratulations! You have received a job offer. Now you must consider the proposed salary and related benefits. It is generally not a good idea to accept or reject a job offer on the spot. Express your appreciation to the employer, ask for any additional information that you might use in making your decision, and tell the employer specifically when you will respond, usually within a day or two. Remember that you now have an opportunity to negotiate, since the employer has made a decision that you are the person for the job. This is the point in the job finding process when you have the most power, and this is especially true if your field is one with a shortage of qualified personnel.

While you have a good deal of power, it is important to avoid being arrogant. You may be working with these people. You may wish to negotiate salary and benefits, but must do so in a positive way. It also helps if you have some idea about the flexibility that the employer has in the offer of salary and benefits.

The research that you have done during the job campaign should help you to know the salary range for this and comparable positions and also if the employer has flexibility in determining your salary and benefits. While many organizations leave room for negotiations, others, especially public organizations such as school systems, may have a rigid salary scale which offers little room for negotiations.

By all means wait until you have a job offer before you attempt to negotiate a salary. When you do make a counter offer, try to do it in person. Avoid negotiating just for salary. Consider other benefits such as an earlier merit increase, tuition, flexible hours, telecommuting, relocation expenses, paid memberships, and additional vacation time. Often, an employer may have more flexibility in providing these benefits than with the salary that can be offered. This is not the time to haggle. Your negotiations need to be very deliberate and professional.

SUMMARY

Conduct an Effective Job Campaign

· ·

 This chapter has provided practical information on planning a job campaign. One important factor to remember is to keep active and maintain control over the situation. You need to protect yourself from rejection shock and have support systems built into your job campaign. You should be thoroughly prepared for each step in your campaign. This is not an easy process, but you greatly increase your chances of success by organizing and controlling your job campaign. Once you have a job or change jobs, your decisions do not stop. Issues of career and life transitions, job revitalization, and lifestyle planning are always part of your life.

ADDITIONAL RESOURCES

Adams Almanac Series. Holbrook, MA: Adams Media Corp.
Adams Cover Letter Almanac, 1995
Adams Resume Almanac, 1996
Adams Job Interview Almanac, 1997

Armstrong, Howard. *High Impact Telephone Networking for Job Hunters*. Holbrook, MA.: Bob Adams, Inc. 1992.

Asher, Donald. *The Foolproof Job-Search Workbook*. Berkeley, CA: Ten Speed Press, 1995.

Baldwin, Eleanor. *300 New Ways to get a Better Job*. Holbrook, MA: Bob Adams, Inc. 1991.

Beatty, Richard. *Job Search Networking*. Holbrook, MA: Bob Adams Inc. 1994.

Bisner, E. Patricia. *The 40+ Job Hunting Guide*. New York: Facts on File, 1990.

Bixler, Susan. *Professional Presence*. New York: Putnam, 1991.

Bolles, Richard. *Job Hunting on the Internet*. California: Ten Speed Press, 1999.

Bolles, Richard N. *What Color Is Your Parachute?* Berkeley, California: Ten Speed Press, 1999.

Bounds, Shannon, and Karl, Arthur. *How to Get Your Dream Job Using the Internet*. Scottsdale, AZ: Coriolis Group, 1996.

Damp, Dennis. *The Book of U.S. Government Jobs: Where They Are, What's Available, and How to Get One*. Moon Township, PA: Brookhaven Press, 1996.

Deluka, Matthew J. *Best Answers to the 201 Most Frequently Asked Interview Questions*. New York: McGraw-Hill, 1997.

Dikel, Margaret, Roehm. Francis, and Oserman, Steve. *The Guide to Internet Job Searching*. Illinois: VGM, 1998.

Farr, J. Michael. *Why Should I Hire You?* California: JIST Works, 1992.

Farr, Michael. *Best Jobs for College Graduates for the 21st Century*. Indiana: JIST Works, 2000.

Faux, Marian. *The Complete Résumé Guide*. New York: Prentice Hall, 1995.

Figler, Howard. *The Complete Job Search Handbook*. Henry Holt, 1999.

Fisher, Donna and Vilas, Sandy. *Power Networking: 55 Secrets for Personal and Professional Success*. Austin, Texas: Mountain Harbour Publications, 1992.

Godin, Seth. *Point & Click Job Finder.* Chicago: Dearborn Financial Publishing Co., 1996.

Gonyea, James C. *The On-Line Job Search Companion*. New York: McGraw-Hill, 1995.

Good, C. Edward. *Does Your Résumé Wear Blue Jeans?* Virginia: Blue Jeans Press, 1985.

———. *Résumés for Re-Entry: A Handbook for Women*. Illinois: Planning Communications, 1993.

Goodwin, Mary; Cohn, Deborah; and Spivey, Donna. *Net Jobs—Use the Internet to Land Your Dream Job*. New York: Michael Wolff & Co., 1996.

Jacobson, Deborah. *Survival Jobs—118 Ways to Make Money While Pursuing Your Dreams*. Los Angeles: Windtree Publishing, 1996.

Job Search Guide—Your Action Plan to Finding the Right Job in Today's Market. Berkeley, CA: Ten Speed Press, 1996.

Job Search—The Total System. New York: John Wiley & Sons, 1996.

Job Hotlines USA—National Directory of Employee Joblines. Harleysville, PA: Career Communications, Inc., 1996.

Kaplan, Robbie. *Sure-Hire Résumés*. New York: Amacom, 1998.

Kennedy, Joyce Cain, and Morrow, Thomas J. *Electronic Job Search Revolution*. New York: John Wiley & Sons., 1995.

———. *Electronic Résumé Revolution*. New York: John Wiley & Sons, 1995.

Kimeldorf, Martin. *Pathways to Work*. Meridian, 1989.

King, Julie Adair. *The Smart Woman's Guide to Interviewing and Salary Negotiations*. Franklin Lakes, NJ: Career Press, 1995.

Kissane, Sharon F. *Career Success for People with Physical Disabilities*. Illinois: VGM, 1997.

Krannich, Ronald L., and Krannich, Caryl Rae. *Dynamite Tele-Search. 101 Telephone Techniques and Tips for Getting Job Leads and Interviews*. Manassas, Va: Impact Publications, 1995.

———. *Dynamite Networking for Dynamite Jobs*. Manassas, VA: Impact Publications, 1996.

———. *Job Search Letters That Get Results*. Manassas, VA: Impact Publications, 1995.

Krannich, Ronald. *The New Network Your Way to Job and Career Success*. Virginia: Impact, 1993.

Additional titles for: (all published in Virginia: Impact)

Krannich, Ron
Dynamite Cover Letters, 1999
Dynamite Resumes, 1999
Interview for Success: A Practical Guide to Increasing Job Interviews, 1998

Larson, Jackie, and Comstock, Cheri. *The New Rules of the Job Search Game.* Holbrook, Mass: Bob Adams, Inc. 1994.

Lathrop, Richard. *Who's Hiring Who?* Berkeley, California: Ten Speed Press, 1989.

Lauber, Daniel. *Government Job Finder.* River Forest, Il: Planning Communications, 1997.

Lauber, Daniel. *Professional's Job Finder.* Illinois: Planning Communications, 1997.

Marcus, John J. *The Complete Job Interview Handbook.* New York: Harper Collins Publishers, Inc. 1994.

McDaniels, Carl. *Developing a Professional Vita or Résumé.* Maryland: Garrett Park Press, 1990.

Medley, H. Anthony. *Sweaty Palms—The Neglected Art of Being Interviewed.* Berkeley, CA: Ten Speed Press, 1993.

Messmer, Max. *Fifty Ways to Get Hired.* New York: William Morrow & Co., Inc. 1994.

Nadler, Burton. *Liberal Arts Power: How to Sell it on Your Résumé.* New Jersey: Peterson's Guides, 1989.

O'Brien, Jack. *The Complete Job Search Organizer: How to Get a Great Job . . . Fast.* Washington, DC: The Kiplinger Washington Editors, Inc. 1996.

Petras, Kathryn and Ross. *The Only Job Hunting Guide You'll Ever Need.* Old Tappan, NJ: S&S Trade, 1995.

———. *Planning Your Career Path Through America's Leading Industries.* Washington, DC: U.S. Dept. of Labor, Bureau of Labor Statistics. Conway Greene Publishing Co., 1996.

———. *Résumés for Government Careers.* Illinois: VGM Career Horizons, 1996.

Potter, Ray. *100 Best Resumes for the 21st Century.* California: IDG Books Worldwide, 1998.

Riley, Margaret; Roehm, Francis; and Oserman, Steve. *The Guide to Internet Job Searching.* Lincolnwood, IL: VGM Career Books, 1996.

Shelly, Susan. *Networking for Novices.* New York, Learning Express, 1998

Smith, Russ. *Federal Applications That Get Results.* Manassas Park, VA: Impact Publications, 1996.

Stoodley, Martha. *Informational Interviewing.* Maryland: Garrett Park Press, 1990.

Stran, Pamela. *Dressing Smart.* New York: Doubleday, 1990.

Studner, Peter. *Super Job Search: Complete Manual for Job Seekers and Career Changers.* California: Jamenair, Ltd., 1987.

Veruki Peter. *250 Job Interview Questions You'll Most Likely be Asked.* MA: Adams Media Corp, 1999.

Walker, Donald. *The Job Seeker's Sourcebook.* Illinois: Planning Communications, 1993.

Washington, Tom. *The Hunt—Complete Guide To Effective Job Finding.* Bellevue, Washington: Mount Vernon Press, 1992.

Washington, Tom. *Interview Power—Selling Yourself Face to Face.* Bellevue WA: Mt. Vernon Press, 1995.

Weddle, Peter. *Internet Resumes.* Virginia: Impact Publications, 1998.

Wegmann, Robert. *The Right Place at the Right Time.* California: Ten Speed Press, 1990.

Wendleton, Kate. *Job Search Secrets That Have Helped Thousands of Members.* New York: Five O'Clock Books, 1996.

Wendleton, Kate. *Through the Brick Wall: How to Job-Hunt in a Tight Market.* New York: McKay Publishers, 1992.

Wilson, Robert F., and Rambusch, Erik. *Conquer Interview Objections.* New York: John Wiley & Sons, Inc. 1994.

Witt, Melanie. *Job Strategies for People with Disabilities.* Illinois: Planning Communications, 1993.

Wood, Patricia B. *Applying For Federal Jobs.* Moon Township, PA: Brookhaven Press, 1995.

Yate, Martin. *Knock 'em Dead: Great Answers to Tough Interview Questions.* Massachusetts: Bob Adams, Inc., 1999.

———. *Career Smarts: Jobs With A Future.* New York: Ballantine Books, 1997.

———. *Cover Letters That Knock 'em Dead.* MA: Adams Media, 1998.

SECTION FIVE

Enhance Work Performance
and Satisfaction

When you make a work commitment, it is important to do your best and to seek opportunities for growth. Because success breeds other successes, you can create new opportunities and increase your work satisfaction by concentrating on doing the best possible job. You will increase your opportunities for promotions and for assuming new responsibilities. You will also decrease the possibility of losing your work or of becoming dissatisfied with your work.

It is helpful to review your work periodically so that you can make necessary changes. This review will help you to maintain your effectiveness on the job. It will help you to seek new challenges and opportunities without having to look for a new job. You may be able to avoid that "locked in" feeling that comes when you think that you have no place to go with your work.

Is it worthwhile to take time once in a while to review your work? Certainly! Few things are more important than your own career and life satisfaction. Various studies of human behavior have shown that work satisfaction is a possible predictor of longevity, while dissatisfaction with one's job can produce stress, which can lead to physical or mental illness. It is important to take charge of your career and your life by periodically evaluating where you have been, where you are, and where you are going. This section will help you to make the most of your work.

How to Be an Effective Worker

A. WORK SUCCESS SKILLS

What action can you take to improve your overall work status? Prepare, plan, and develop yourself to meet the challenge of keeping your job. There are certain skills that will help you to hold on to your job and assist you in reaching your career goals. Think about what skills would be most important to success in your work.

If you were the boss, what skills would you want your employees to have?

1. _____   6. _____

2. _____   7. _____

3. _____   8. _____

4. _____   9. _____

5. _____   10. _____

Now compare your list with some top job-keeping skills employers would like their employees to have. The following list of skills rated most important by employers was developed by the Virginia Employment Commission.

- Ability to do the job well—develop your know-how and competence
- Initiative—work on your own without constant direction
- Dependability—being there when you are needed
- Reliability—getting the job done
- Efficiency—being accurate and capable
- Loyalty—being faithful
- Maturity—handling challenges
- Cheerfulness—being pleasant to be with
- Helpfulness—willing to pitch in and help out
- Unselfishness—helping in a bind even though it is not your responsibility
- Perseverance—carrying on with a tedious project
- Responsible—taking care of your duties
- Creative—looking for new ways to solve your employer's problems

These are very worthwhile skills to develop, because they are highly valued by employers. If you enhance these skills, you are more likely to open new opportunities in your work. It is also much less likely that you will lose your job if you take the time and effort to develop these skills. Remember that these are primarily self-management skills. You have control over them and they transfer from one job to another.

What work success skills would you like to develop or improve? Try to list at least five.

1. _____

2. _____

3. _____

4. _____

5. _____

In the following spaces, give one specific example of how you can take action to develop or improve each of these five work success skills.

1. _____

2. _____

3. _____

4. _____

5. _____

B. FIFTEEN TACTICS FOR CAREER GROWTH

Although job survival may be a major reason for taking the following actions, they can also help you to develop your skills, to expand your network of contacts, to feel better about yourself, and to enjoy your work. In addition to the work success skills that you identified, consider the following career growth tactics. They can help you to keep your job *and* to grow in your career.

1. **Learn to read the management signs.**

   Be aware of the organization's policies and look for danger signals of potential cutbacks, layoffs, and firings *before* they happen. In a time of retrenchment, you may be able to save your job or move to another one rather than hiding your head in the sand and saying "That would *never* happen to me!" Also, be aware of new developments in your organization that may present opportunities for you.

2. **Document your achievements.**

   A record of your accomplishments can be valuable for raises, promotions, and, in extreme cases, to help you to keep your job. Make significant contributions to the organization through your creative or efficient problem solving and keep a log of these contributions.

3. **Get out of your box.**

   • • • • • • • • • • •

   Get out of your box!

   • • • • • • • • • • •

   Become knowledgeable about other areas within your organization and develop skills that would transfer from one job to another. If someone is sick for the day, ask to fill in for that person so that you can broaden your base of knowledge about the organization. Whenever possible, visit someone in person rather than sending an E-mail message or telephoning. The more skills you possess and the more people you know, the harder you are to lose.

4. Think like management.

If you have to make a decision or solve a problem, try to assess how the management of your organization would like you to act. Ask yourself how your supervisor or your supervisor's supervisor would want you to respond, given their orientation and the goals of the organization. Take this, and your own creativity and goals, into consideration before taking action.

5. Concentrate on the things over which you have control.

Use your time at work effectively. Invest your effort in the activities and projects over which you have a considerable amount of control. You, and others, will be able to see the direct result of your work. Avoid spending too much of your time and effort on general issues where there is little that you can do to affect the outcome.

6. Prepare for your next job.

The emphasis on lifelong learning is here to stay. You will need more education and training, given the rapid changes in the world of work. Here are some ways to keep learning.

- On-the-job professional development programs
- Adult education programs
- Apprenticeships and cooperative education
- Community college programs
- Weekend college and other specialized course offerings
- Private, trade, or technical schools
- Home study through correspondence courses
- Industrial training programs
- Government and military training programs
- Four-year college or university programs

7. Promote yourself.

This may be uncomfortable for you, but think of it as taking the initiative to inform others in your company about your projects. Talk about your accomplishments with coworkers and supervisors to keep them up to date with your projects. Inform, don't boast.

8. Find a mentor.

A mentor or sponsor can help you obtain information and to gain access to the inner structure of your organization. Select someone you admire, and attempt to establish a positive professional relationship. Ideally, your mentor should be in a position to help you to grow and to provide you with valuable advice and support.

9. **Continue informational interviewing.**

By continuing to develop your informational interviewing techniques, you can enlarge and enrich your circle of professional contacts, keep up to date in your field, and discover potential career growth opportunities. Remember that people generally enjoy discussing their work and how they got there.

10. **Think success.**

What are your motivating skills? Certain things you do give you a thrill of success. It could be organizing a baseball game or raising funds for your PTA. Identify these skills and use them in your everyday life. If organizing is your motivating skill, use it at work to reorganize outdated systems. If raising funds really interests you, build this into your work or community service.

11. **Show a genuine interest in others.**

Do your best to work cooperatively with others. Show an interest in their work and value what they do. Form support systems and be supportive of others.

12. **Always be willing to learn.**

Learn as much as possible about your job and the organization in which you work. Take any opportunity to attend in-service seminars, classes, skill-building workshops, and other training programs. Many organizations highly value their training programs and the employees who choose to participate.

13. **Be willing to take on new challenges.**

Seize opportunities to meet new challenges in your work. There may be some risk involved, but usually the risk is worth taking.

14. **Maintain a positive attitude.**

Be willing to help others and be nice to others. People will stay away from someone who is always depressed or negative. A positive attitude will help you to feel better about your work and will cause others to be positive toward you.

15. **Be open to change.**

Be willing to accept suggestions from others. Avoid being defensive if you are criticized. Encourage comments from others and show that you are open to new ideas and procedures.

• • • • • • • • • • •

"The greatest discovery in our generation is that human beings, by changing the inner attitudes of their minds, can change the outer aspects of their lives."
—William James

• • • • • • • • • • •

These tactics will help you to:

- grow in your work
- keep your job

- learn new skills
- be in position for promotions

- enjoy your work and your life

- position yourself favorably for organizational changes

Remember that you have a great deal of control over your work because *you control* your attitude, your skills, and, to a certain extent, how others respond to you.

C. PROFESSIONAL DEVELOPMENT

Professional development should be a part of everyone's work. Some organizations provide regular opportunities for professional development by encouraging training in new technologies, continuing education, attendance at conferences, and other activities designed to enhance an employee's career. Other organizations provide few or no incentives for professional growth. An organization's commitment to professional development should be a factor in making a decision whether to work for the organization.

Remember that, whatever the organizational commitment is to professional development, you have the primary responsibility for your professional growth. Just as you must take charge of the direction of your life and career, you must take charge of your own professional development. Your coworkers may complain about the lack of promotion opportunities or professional development and use this as an excuse to do nothing about advancement or learning valuable skills. Even if your present employer does not support or encourage your professional development, there are many challenging and rewarding professional development activities that you can create. The following is a listing of the steps you can take to enhance your professional growth both on and off your job.

Professional Development Opportunities in the Workplace

1. Volunteer to take on new assignments, especially those in which you will be required to learn a new skill.
2. Challenge yourself by accepting new responsibilities for short or extended periods. Expand your outlook by taking on selected aspects of a colleague's job.
3. Train on the job in new technologies, new procedures, and new techniques. Take advantage of in-house training opportunities.

4. Create opportunities to solve old problems or to develop new systems with a team of colleagues. Professionally develop yourself by discovering new approaches to the organization's concerns.

5. Wage a campaign for self-improvement by participating in workshops that deal with topics such as stress and time management, communication skills, relaxation techniques, and health and exercise. Personal growth leads to professional enhancement by increasing creativity, energy, and productivity. Integrate health and balance into your daily routine.

6. Read professional literature that may be available through your human resources office, library, mail system and the World Wide Web. Look for and attend seminars that offer new ideas and attend them.

7. Serve on committees or task forces charged with critical issues such as planning and evaluation.

8. Continue informational interviewing by meeting with colleagues and sharing ideas. Learn about your career and how your skills would be integrated into other organizations. Discuss new approaches to work responsibilities and to fulfilling the goals of your organization. Listen to how others have dealt with challenges similar to those that you face.

9. Represent your organization at local, state, and national conferences or conventions. Offer to present your unique ideas or to serve on planning committees.

10. Investigate tuition assistance opportunities, educational or professional leave, purchase of materials, or any other support for professional growth that your organization makes available to you.

11. Write articles or promotion pieces for journals or newsletters. Contribute to your career and your organization by sharing personal research, innovative ideas, and your opinions.

12. Study with experts in your field. Identify individuals who have achieved distinction and read what they have written. Arrange to hear them speak. Take any opportunity to study with them.

13. Mentor students or interns of any age and at any educational level. Offering your expertise to students learning your profession can help you to clarify your own goals, to learn about new developments in your field, and to give a piece of yourself back to your career.

Professional Development Opportunities Outside of Your Work

1. Register for courses and seminars. Work toward certificates and degrees that will give you credentials and enhance your professional growth.

2. Join professional associations, attend meetings, and volunteer to be an active member.

3. Become an officer or board member of a civic, neighborhood, religious, or professional organization.

4. Develop informal networks of colleagues. Arrange for regular meetings to discuss issues. Find a mentor.

5. Actively work to stay current in the developments in your field. Read professional literature. Write an article, book review, or commentary for a professional journal. Teach a course in which you share your knowledge and experience.

6. Consider all forms of enrichment opportunities sponsored by adult education programs, clubs, churches, community colleges, universities, and community agencies.

7. Give yourself time to reflect, relax, and renew. Some of your best, most creative, and most effective work may be sparked while you are taking a walk, sitting by the side of a stream, climbing a mountain, or traveling in the country. Listen to yourself.

8. Expand your interests. Too much time spent on work issues can negatively influence your ability to grow, to remain enthusiastic, and to be productive on the job. Develop a range of outlets for all seasons that you can enjoy alone or with family and friends. One of the best ways to develop professionally is to be able to concentrate completely on activities that have nothing to do with your career.

9. Maintain good eating habits and have a regular exercise program. Taking care of your body can have a profound influence on your work effectiveness, on your family relationships, and on your mental attitude.

10. Learn, learn, learn all that you can in as many ways as you can as quickly as you can.

D. Evolving Into A Person of Influence

While it is important to think about the influence of others in our lives, your own personal influence is also a consideration. When you think of persons of influence, what characteristics do they possess? Think expansively of those you admire most. Think about people who are related to you, people in your neighborhood, people you work with, people you have read about, and people who have achieved local, national, or world significance. What qualities do you admire in them?

Name at least five characteristics that you believe are critical attributes for a person of influence. Then, prioritize them from one, the most important, to five, least important.

1. _____

2. _____

3. _____

4. _____

5. _____

After you have listed and prioritized your characteristics of a person of influence, analyze your own growth related to each of the characteristics. In column one, self-rate your development in each characteristic, providing your perspective on where you are in relationship to where you want to be. In column two, identify your satisfaction with your development. A five-point scale is provided to assist you in rating. After circling each scale, check the three characteristics you would most like to improve.

Characteristics	My Development	My Satisfaction
	low high	low high
1. _____	1 2 3 4 5	1 2 3 4 5
2. _____	1 2 3 4 5	1 2 3 4 5
3. _____	1 2 3 4 5	1 2 3 4 5
4. _____	1 2 3 4 5	1 2 3 4 5
5. _____	1 2 3 4 5	1 2 3 4 5

Focusing on your own rating and satisfaction, what patterns do you observe? Is there something that you can do to enhance your own sphere of influence? If so, what characteristics can you integrate into your life and demonstrate to yourself and others? How can you maximize your influence to contribute to the world? These are questions for you to consider as you evolve and become a person of influence.

Make Time Your Friend

Time is a finite and precious resource, yet often taken for granted. Without conscious decision making, we allow busyness to take over while events swirl around us. Time can be either a treasure or a curse. Describe your relationship with time in one word.

My relationship with time is _____ .

This section may assist you to analyze your relationship with time by helping you to look at the broader picture of time and values. It will help you focus on the guiding principles directing the expenditure of your time. Traditional time management, which considers your commitments and schedule and offers concrete tips for streamlining work and personal habits, may be important for you to consider in addition to the focus in this chapter. A section on time management can be found in Chapter 26.

Everyone, regardless of income, social status, background, or profession has 24 hours in a day. How you choose to allocate this most precious resource is your very personal decision.

What challenges you about the allocation of time in your work and home life? Do you feel trapped or overwhelmed by time? Do you . . .

- have competing demands for your time?
- feel conflicted about how to allocate time?
- feel pressured with not enough time?
- see the solution as packing more responsibilities into smaller amounts of time?
- feel guilty about time allocation decisions?
- feel out of balance with the time in your life?
- feel anxiety and stress due to tremendous time pressures?
- allow responding to crisis after crisis to shape your days?
- become satisfied with short term solutions rather than long term adjustments that would be necessary to address bigger issues?

If you have answered "yes" to three or more of these questions, it is now TIME to examine your decisions and consider alternatives.

A. Your Time Analysis

If time is a thorn in your side rather than a blessing, complete the following time analysis adapted from *First Things First* by Steven Covey (N.Y.: Simon and Schuster, 1995, pp.32 - 102). It is strongly recommended that you read this resource for additional assistance and for clarification of time and values

Time Analysis

Read through the following four categories and think about how you allocate your time in a typical week. In what category do you spend most of your time? Write a percentage of time for each category so that the numbers add up to 100%, and describe the major activities within each category. Be patient with yourself as you think through a typical week's responsibilities and activities.

Category I: Crisis - Time with the Important and Urgent

Examples: Immediate problems, imminent deadlines, overwhelming projects, anything with immediate response time required

Percentage of time spent in a typical week _____

Describe your weekly activities and responsibilities in this category.

_____

_____

_____

Category II: Planning - Time with the Important and Not Urgent

Examples: Preparation, relationships, thinking, reading, developing strategies

Percentage of time spent in a typical week _____

Describe your weekly activities and responsibilities in this category.

_____

_____

_____

Category III: Interruptions - Time with the Not Important and Urgent

Examples: Some mail, some phone calls, many activities, some reports

Percentage of time spent in a typical week _____

Describe your weekly activities and responsibilities in this category.

_____

_____

_____

Category IV: Time Wasters

Examples: Trivia/minutia, irrelevant mail and calls, daydreaming, extensive personal involvement

Percentage of time spent in a typical week _____

Describe your weekly activities and responsibilities in this category

_____

_____

_____

Now that you have completed the Time Analysis, which category occupies most of your week in your work and home life? Most of your month?

What have you learned from your Time Analysis about how you allocate your most precious resource? How might you better spend your time?

If most of your activities and responsibilities are located in *Category I: Crisis*

If most of your time is taken up by activities and responsibilities that are important and urgent, you may wear out, maybe not today, but tomorrow. You most likely will not have time to complete this workbook or take stock of your situation because you are in perpetual motion. You know that you operate from a place of exhaustion and pain due to fear and a sense of lack of control. Maybe you have never experienced life outside of Category I. If so, the critical question for you is: **will you still be important if what you do is not always urgent and important?** Basing your self-esteem and value on what you do rather than who you are is one of the issues that you will need to address before you attempt to move from one category to another. A balance of activities and responsibilities throughout the Time Analysis is desirable. Only you can decide what is the right balance for you.

If most of your activities and responsibilities are located in *Category II: Planning*

If you are like many adults, the activities and responsibilities characterized as important and not urgent seem to represent time spent with meaning and significance. The lower stress and anxiety means you have the luxury to be creative, thoughtful, and deliberate in your expenditure of time. Why should this time be a luxury rather than an important part of every day, or at the very least, every week? Assessing your own performance, identifying the learning gaps, and taking steps to fill them is critical to your own professional development. This is the category that allows for that type of activity. It is your responsibility in any position to build your expertise and increase your skills. If you are not allocating any time to this category, you will not keep up with others who tend to these critical self-growth areas. Make an appointment with yourself and log it in as you would any other appointment with a dignitary! Taking time to complete the exercises in this workbook is a Category II activity since it is an investment in you and your career. It empowers you to move forward with confidence and some measure of assurance that you are on the "right" track. Allocate the time you need to plan, organize, learn, and create your own future!

If most of your activities and responsibilities are located in *Category III: Interruptions*

Most work involves responsibilities that are considered urgent by someone, but often not by you. It is easy to feel at the mercy of the urgent and not important! Telephone calls, Email, faxes, and office interlopers find you wherever you are and when you least expect them. What a colleague defines as important and urgent may not be as important and urgent to you. Try to expeditiously negotiate the interruptions in your life with grace and respect. Every position has some responsibilities that are routine and urgent, but unimportant in the grand scheme of things. What can you do to affect the system and change the culture so that most of your responsibilities are considered important? Shuffling job responsibilities among co-workers is a way to bring everyone's expertise level up to a certain standard and is helpful when change of personnel becomes inevitable. Another way to view this category is to handle the "not important", detail tasks as though each one were very important and urgent. This may earn you respect and help you build expertise for career mobility. Ignoring urgent tasks, no matter how unimportant, may prove to be counterproductive to your career and the welfare of your organization. Accomplish these tasks with dispatch so you have time to spend in the planning category.

If most of your activities and responsibilities are located in *Category IV: Time Wasters*

What are you afraid of? Pick yourself up and get yourself going. Your unfulfilled potential as a human being, a worker, a citizen, and contributing member of society is a loss to the entire universe. You are not challenging yourself to grow and bloom because of perceived obstacles that stand in your way. Address obstacles by acknowledging that they exist and distinguish between the ones that are outside of your control and those that are a product of your own thinking. Obstacles are 99% of your own making. Work with someone you admire and respect to help you overcome your fear of evolving into a person of influence. Continue your self-growth routine with this book and stretch a little bit at a time by taking on small challenges.

B. YOUR TIME ACTION PLAN

If you are now occupying a category that is not fulfilling and satisfying to you, make a conscious commitment to the important by moving part of your day to the category that would be more beneficial to you. How do you accomplish this when you have conflicting demands imposed upon you by colleagues and supervisors? You move from a less desirable category to a more desirable one by choice and design, not by remaining subject to other people's schedules. You accomplish this by changing your thinking and possibly by changing your life. Your time is your most precious resource.

Ponder the Possibilities:

If you were to choose one personal characteristic that would assist you in fulfilling your *job* responsibilities more effectively and efficiently, what would that characteristic be?

If you were to choose one personal characteristic that would assist you in fulfilling your *personal* responsibilities more effectively and efficiently, what would that characteristic be?

How will you learn, acquire, and/or develop the personal characteristic that will help you to fulfill your job and personal responsibilities more effectively and efficiently?

How will these characteristics assist you in balancing the results from the Time Analysis?

Changing your life is an option you may choose to accept once you analyze and acknowledge the realities of your own life. Try to take hold and consider the overarching issue of the value of time in your life. You have your 24 hours each day to make a difference, create your contribution, and leave a legacy. No one has more hours than that. Make each day count toward what is important to you. Decide on how you want to live your life and do not acquiesce to the factors that you may think are outside of your control. How do **you** choose to allocate your most precious resource?

Don't Be Your Own Worst Enemy

Some people have problems with their work because of situations over which they have little or no control. However, in many cases of work dissatisfaction, the problems come from within the individual. In this section, you will learn how to avoid causing problems for yourself. Are you creating blocks to your work satisfaction? What can you do to overcome blocks that are put there by others or by situations? Internal blocks to work satisfaction originate from your own feelings, perceptions, and actions. External blocks to work satisfaction originate from outside factors.

A. INTERNAL BLOCKS TO WORK SATISFACTION

Many people tend to cause problems for themselves in their work environment. Unreasonable expectations, a negative attitude, an unwillingness to compromise, and work habits inconsistent with the requirements of the specific job are all internal blocks to job satisfaction and job success. These internal blocks can result in the loss of a job or in a very negative work situation. The following are examples of internal blocks to success.

- Frequent absences
- Frequently coming to work late
- Too much attention to outside interests
- Being negative, making trouble
- Misrepresenting the facts of a situation
- Not being adaptable

- Carelessness
- Lack of initiative
- Disloyalty
- Being irresponsible
- Unwillingness to follow rules
- Laziness
- Fear of change
- Unwillingness to take a risk, to try something new

There are many more internal blocks to work success. The most important thing to remember about these internal blocks is that **they are within your control.** You can change them if you choose to. In any work that you have or are considering, it is important to analyze your own work style and to determine how it fits with the expectations of the job. For example, if you do not work well under pressure, you may wish to avoid taking a job in which you would constantly be faced with deadlines. If you have family responsibilities that often take you away from work, you may want to find an employer who is willing to give you some flexibility with your work hours. One way to avoid internal blocks to work success is to match your work style with the organization. This matching works both ways, but when you begin a job, it is unreasonable to expect the organization to bend significantly to meet your needs. You have the control, however, of the initial choice of where you work, the specific job you take, and of adjusting your work style accordingly.

Assessment of Your Internal Blocks to Work Satisfaction

If you are currently employed or can think back to a previous job, list five *internal* blocks that have interfered with your work satisfaction.

Internal blocks

1. _____
2. _____
3. _____
4. _____
5. _____

What can you do to overcome these blocks? Remember that they come from within you, so you do have a good deal of control. Some examples might be to take a course in time management, concentrate on the things you enjoy at work, consciously develop a more positive attitude, and look at change as an opportunity rather than as a threat. Try to think of at least one possible way of dealing with each of the internal blocks that you listed and write your ideas in the spaces below. Be creative!

How to deal with my internal blocks

1. _____
2. _____
3. _____
4. _____
5. _____

DON'T
LET
THE
BLOCKS
GET
YOU
DOWN!

B. External Blocks to Work Satisfaction

At some point in your work life you may be faced with an organizational shift that results in the loss of your job or in your arbitrary reassignment to other work. This could be called an external block, because you have little or no control over the situation. You may work with an organization that has inflexible rules about salary, vacation time, promotion, hours, or your daily tasks. You *may* find that the factors over which you have no control create an unacceptable situation, and you will have to look for other work. However, before you give up on a job, concentrate on those things over which you *do* have control. You may be able to improve your work satisfaction simply by concentrating on the things you *can* change rather than feeling hopeless about the things you cannot change. Some examples of external blocks are:

- Office politics
- No upward mobility
- Financial limits
- No opportunity to try new things

- Lack of education or training
- Geographic location
- Organizational inconsistencies

Assessment of Your External Blocks to Work Satisfaction

Now try to think of five *external* blocks to work satisfaction that you face on your job or have faced in the past, and write them in the following spaces.

External blocks

1. _____
2. _____
3. _____
4. _____
5. _____

What can you do to overcome these blocks? These are blocks over which you may have little or no control, but try to think how you might be able to deal with them, perhaps in one small way. A few examples are to take an assertiveness training course to help you deal with office politics, to start an exercise program to relieve tension and stress, or to research another career to evaluate the amount of risk involved if you were to change careers. Try to think of at least one thing that you could do to deal with each of the external blocks that you listed. Use your imagination. Write your ideas in the following spaces.

How to deal with my external blocks

1. _____
2. _____
3. _____
4. _____
5. _____

C. GETTING STUCK ON A CAREER PLATEAU

At some point in your work life, you may encounter a career plateau. This term refers to a situation in which you find little or no opportunity for growth or advancement within your work environment. Instead of facing another mountain to climb, such as a new set of responsibilities or a promotion, you find that your career has leveled off. Many people face career plateaus at some point during their work lives. If you find yourself on a career plateau, ask yourself the following questions:

1. Do I like my plateau?

Even though you may have limited opportunity for change, you may like it where you are. Do an assessment of your job satisfaction. You may be on a plateau, but it could be an enjoyable place to spend some time.

2. Can I make changes?

You may feel blocked by limited opportunities for growth in your work. However, look carefully at the changes that you can make. Too often we measure career change in terms of major transitions, including promotions, new jobs, and totally new responsibilities. Are there smaller changes that will enhance your work? Consider volunteering to help others, serving as a mentor to new employees, changing procedures, sharing your expertise with new colleagues, catching up on new developments in your field, adjusting the amount of time spent on certain activities, creating new approaches to work responsibilities, and other ways of enhancing your work.

3.   Can I enhance my lifestyle?

Sometimes a career plateau will give you time to relax and consider all aspects of your life. Perhaps too much of your time has been consumed by work. Reduced pressure from your career can provide an opportunity to spend time on interests and hobbies, to make new friendships, to spend more time with family, and to pursue other life-enriching experiences.

4.   Will the plateau change?

You may be at a plateau now, but what about the future? Are new opportunities likely to open up in a year or more? Is it worth waiting in order to assess new developments on your plateau? Perhaps patience will reap greater rewards.

5.   Is there unexplored territory on my plateau?

Have you investigated all aspects of your career? Perhaps there are opportunities that you have not yet considered. Through informational interviewing, creatively exploring options, and keeping an open mind toward your job, you may find that there is a way to move on from your plateau to new heights.

6.   Am I too limited by my plateau?

After answering the preceding questions, if you feel frustrated and limited by your plateau, you may wish to go on to chapter 26, Routine Maintenance—Your Two-year Job Checkup. Complete the activities in that section. If you still feel that you have few options with your current job, it may be time to start the career and life planning process. Go back to Section I and begin the self-assessment that is so essential to the reevaluation of your career and life goals.

D. THE ULTIMATE BLOCK—LOSS OF YOUR WORK

Try to think of the worst external block to achieving job satisfaction and career success. Would it be the sudden loss of your work? As the world of work changes rapidly in the years to come, new jobs will arise and other jobs will be eliminated. Layoffs, reductions in force, organizational consolidations, and forced early retirements are to be expected. You may have some control if you keep aware of the trends and avoid taking a job in a declining field. However, if you do lose your work, here are some points to consider.

1. Expect to feel angry, sad, depressed, and lost for a while. These emotions are normal after a loss.

2. Don't expect to solve this problem right away. Relax and be good to yourself.

3. Be constructive. You have options available. The job loss could even turn out to be positive in the long run.

4. Involve your family and friends. Build a support system for yourself where you can "be yourself." Talk, cry, rant and rave, let it all out.

5. Complete the exercises in this book along with someone else in transition. Compare your results, brainstorm alternatives, and support one another.

6. Seek professional assistance, both in conducting a job campaign and in dealing with your personal concerns.

7. Develop a daily and weekly schedule of activities so that you do not procrastinate.

8. Maintain daily contact with people. Don't allow yourself to feel cut off from others. Use informational interviewing to expand your network.

9. Avoid searching for the ideal job. If you are not working, your primary goal should be to return to work in an acceptable job.

10. Use the job-hunting methods that work best. Keep actively involved in the process. Don't use the passive approach of just sitting at home and sending out résumés.

11. Although this is probably not the best time to do career and life planning, you may use this as an opportunity to change the direction of your career and perhaps to get some training to enhance your options.

12. Join or start a job-hunting support group through professional organizations, churches, agencies, or other contacts in order to share job leads, improve interviewing skills, and build confidence. Encouraging and helping others can have a positive effect on your self-esteem.

26

Take Care of Yourself

Many factors influence your work satisfaction and success. Some have been addressed in the first two chapters of section five. Others may not be as directly related to your work but can have a major impact on how effective you are on the job. Consider carefully the following ways to take care of yourself so that you can be more effective in your work.

A. Avoid Major Value Conflicts

If your work conflicts with your life priorities, as expressed by your values, you may need to make some changes. For example, if your work requires you to be away from your family more than you would like, it is very important to see whether you can change this. If your work requires you to engage in activities that you find distasteful or even dishonest, this can be a real problem that needs action. If you can be committed to the overall purpose of the organization for which you work, you will probably experience less conflict. On the other hand, if the organization's philosophy conflicts with your personal values in significant ways, you can expect to have problems with job satisfaction. In the following spaces, list any value conflicts that you experience in your work.

Value conflicts

_____

_____

_____

_____

Can you tolerate these conflicts or are they serious enough to require action? Remember that to do nothing about a serious value conflict can cause stress and other problems over time.

B. DEAL EFFECTIVELY WITH STRESS

Stress is a by-product of some event or combination of events in your life. It is your body's reaction to what you see as a challenge or threat. You cannot escape stress because it is a part of your life that helps you to grow and to meet certain life demands. Most jobs and certainly everyday life pose stressful situations to you, such as these.

- You had to work overtime and you are late picking up your daughter from preschool when you get a flat tire.
- You have three projects that are due for the boss and your son develops the chicken pox.
- You have three sales appointments and your car develops transmission problems after your first appointment.
- You are getting ready for work and, in the middle of your shower, your hot water is runs out.
- Your in-laws have just arrived for an extended stay. Meanwhile, your daughter announces that she is quitting high school to join a religious cult.

What are some stressful situations you've faced within the past week?

1. _____ 4. _____

2. _____ 5. _____

3. _____ 6. _____

How do you normally react to stresses in your life? Circle those that apply to you.

chronic anxiety   depression
headache   worrying
nervousness   short attention span
backache   not eating
insomnia   hyperactivity
perspiration   increased heartbeat
irritability   drinking
smoking   withdrawing from others
aggressive behavior   need for pills
hives   tenseness

Your perception of life's events can radically alter your reaction. For example, if you view standing before a group of colleagues as a threat, you may break out in a sweat, develop wobbly knees, and feel your heart race. Another person may consider this an opportunity for attention and may not have any stress symptoms whatsoever. How you react to life's events varies according to the amount of stress placed on you at one time.

Stress Management Analysis

Analyze your own stress patterns by completing the following sentences.

1. When I feel anxious or stressful, I usually _____

   _____

   _____

2. I can generally tell when I am under stress. When I am stressed . . .

   a. I think _____

   _____

   b. I feel _____

   _____

c. I act _____

_____

3. Presently, I am spending _____ percent of each day in stressful situations.

4. Although I realize *I am responsible for my own feelings,* the following people and situations contribute to my stress.

Names	*Situations*
a. _____	a. _____
b. _____	b. _____
c. _____	c. _____

5. I usually use the following strategies for coping (thoughts, feelings, and behaviors)

_____

_____

_____

_____

_____

_____

6. The most effective strategies are:

a. _____

b. _____

c. _____

7. The least effective strategies are:

a. _____

b. _____

c. _____

Stress Reduction Program

Your stress-reducing program might include all or some of the following techniques. Use those techniques that work for you and integrate them into your life now.

1. *Get physical.* Work off your tension by playing tennis or just walking. Exercise regularly. Play to relax.
2. *Share the load.* Develop an empathetic support system, including family and friends. Blow off steam and ask for suggestions.
3. *Set priorities.* Make lists and prioritize your tasks. Some things are not worth doing at all. You don't have to do everything. Delegate dinner or pay for house cleaning or painting.
4. *Attitude adjustment.* Accept what you cannot change. Take control of your reaction.
5. *Smell the roses.* Enjoy life's small pleasures. Treat yourself to something. Develop your talents.
6. *Eat right.* Take care of your body by eating properly. A balanced diet can help you feel better.
7. *Rest and sleep.* Leave your worries out of the bedroom. Lack of rest can impair your ability to deal with stress.
8. *Go slow.* Adjusting and adapting takes time. Making too many changes all at once is not healthy. Don't initiate more changes when you are stressed.
9. *Trial and error.* Evaluate how you managed during stressful situations in the past and use your most successful strategies the next time you are under stress.
10. *Ask for help.* Consult professionals if you are withdrawing from life, depressed, overly anxious, or suffer from many stress-related symptoms.

C. MANAGE YOUR TIME EFFECTIVELY

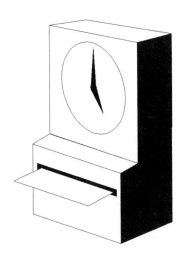

One way that you can take care of yourself is to maintain control of your time. Effective time management helps you to excel at your job and to be better able to devote time to your other life priorities. You can feel much more in control and much less stressed if you can manage your time effectively. The following are some suggestions for improving your time management skills.

1. Establish priorities.

Think about what parts of your job and your life are most important. Make sure that you allow time for the things that mean the most to you.

2. Set goals.

Establish goals at work and outside your work. Evaluate the time that you spend in relation to your goals.

3. Make a schedule.

Plan ahead how you will spend your time. Make sure that your schedule reflects time spent on your goals and priorities.

4. Know what time of day is best for you.

Some people do their best work early in the morning; others are most productive or creative late at night. Try to schedule your most important activities during the time of day that is best for you.

5. Leave time each day for planning.

Spend a few minutes each day thinking about what you have to do. Consider your goals and priorities. Make plans for what you want to do rather than just responding to others' demands.

6. Have a daily "to do" list.

Make a list of things to do and then do them. Cross things off when you complete them. You will be more organized, less likely to forget things, and more satisfied with your accomplishments when you can cross off several things on your list.

7. Use waiting time.

Everyone ends up waiting at some point during the day. Have something to read or something you can do while you are waiting. You may be surprised at how much you can do with this "found time."

8. Don't try to do everything at once.

Break down major projects into smaller tasks that you can accomplish in specific time segments. Avoid putting off major tasks until you have a large block of time to work on them, because it may be quite a while before you can devote a large block of time.

9. Handle paperwork efficiently.

Keep your paperwork organized. Try to handle each piece of paper just once.

10. Eliminate time wasters.

Avoid being drawn into activities that take up your time with little to show for it in the end. Cut out unnecessary functions. Look for ways to streamline procedures to save time.

Now think about how you are spending your time. What are three things that you can do in the next week to manage your time better?

1. _____

2. _____

3. _____

This is just a brief outline of some time management techniques. You may wish to consider taking a course or workshop in time management. It could be time well spent.

D. PURSUE OTHER INTERESTS

A major problem that is faced by many people who are very dedicated to their work is that they become so committed to their work that the rest of their life suffers. This, in turn, can lead to problems at work when feelings of exhaustion and discouragement set in. It is very important to have interests that you pursue outside of your work and that you make time for these interests. These help you to relax, to be with other people, to reduce stress, and to just have fun. Are you allowing enough time to pursue your interests outside of work? In the following spaces, list four outside interests that give you a break from your work.

1. _____

2. _____

3. _____

4. _____

5. _____

Now look back at your list. Have you spent time on any of these interests in the past week? If not you may want to manage your time so that you can pursue these interests.

Summary

You can be much more effective in your work if you take the time to think about your priorities, your values, your use of time, the enjoyable things that you do outside of work, and the need to control stress. Be a good friend to yourself. Give yourself a break once in a while. Make sure that you save time for the things that you like most, both on and off the job.

Routine Maintenance—
Your Two-Year Work Checkup

Just as you need to take in your car (or train) for routine maintenance, your work deserves a checkup at least every other year. Take some time to sit back and look at your work. How are things going? What are the positives and negatives? What, if anything, needs to be changed? This section will help you to examine your work in order to improve your satisfaction. Your routine maintenance has four major checkpoints.

- **The work environment**
- **People contacts**
- **The work itself**
- **Your expectations**

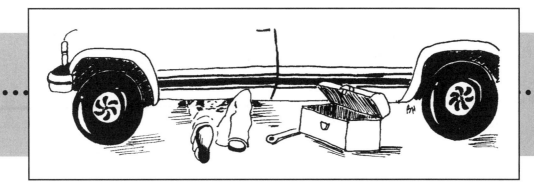

By looking closely at these four aspects of your work, you can isolate the areas with which you are unhappy and work to improve them. This may be more practical and more satisfying than simply giving up on your job and looking for a new one. Your objective in this evaluation is to weigh what you do not like against what you do like about your work. Even if your negatives *outnumber* your positives, the positive aspects of your work may *outweigh* all the negatives.

For example, a teacher's nine-month contract and benefits may outweigh the lack of flexibility of time during the workday. The challenge and excitement of work with a high degree of responsibility may outweigh the considerable time demands of the job. A total job-keeping and job-revitalization program demands that you undertake a careful analysis of your present work. It is not unusual for us to become disenchanted with our work as we fall into a routine and lose sight of some of the potential challenges in our work. Often we think the unknown is more attractive and appealing simply because it is unknown. This "grass is always greener" dream can cause further frustrations and anxiety because the unknown is not always better; rather, it can be worse. Change for the sake of change can lead to a career blunder. In order to avoid this problem, you may wish to evaluate your present situation, identify some possible options, and then make some tentative plans to improve your situation.

This section will help you to examine your work environment and to consider changes that you can make.

A. Your Work Environment

Your *work environment* is one component that you should carefully examine as part of your check-up. Consider your present work and make a check ($\sqrt{}$) in the column that best indicates your current level of satisfaction. Please feel free to add any other work environment characteristics that are unique to your situation.

Work Environment	Very Satisfied	Satisfied	Not Satisfied
Office location Pay Benefits Office policies Lunch arrangements and opportunities			
Time flexibility Vacations Sick leave Personal leave Promotion potential			
Travel opportunities Office arrangement Equipment quality Parking Surroundings outside Access to recreational facilities			
Air quality Cooling and heating systems Lighting Cafeteria and other on-site services Building security			
Supplies Maintenance Safety practices Commuting Decor and furnishings Restroom facilities A window in office Other:			

Now take a few minutes to assess what you can do to improve your work environment. Look at your checks in the Not Satisfied box and write those characteristics below. How can you creatively improve your work environment? Look for changes that you can make, either by taking action yourself or by working to change the system. If you can make even one or two changes, you will feel more in control of your environment.

I am not satisfied with

_____

_____

_____

_____

I could improve this by

_____

_____

_____

_____

B. YOUR PEOPLE CONTACTS

People contact is an integral part of most work. How much or how little people contact you have depends on you and what your work entails. Interpersonal skills are an advantage in just about any career. Who are the people with whom you have contact throughout your work day (or night)? Are you satisfied with the *amount* and *quality* of the contacts you have with those people or would you like to see some changes made? Rate your people contacts on the following chart and feel free to add any other groups of people you contact in your work.

People Contacts	Satisfied with Amount and Quality of Contact	Dissatisfied with Amount of Contact	Dissatisfied with Quality of Contact
Dealings with the public Customers Supervisor Supervisor's boss Coworkers in your immediate vicinity			
Support staff Maintenance personnel Personnel staff Interns Colleagues in other organizations			
Sales people Your own staff Office staff Upper management President or CEO			
Committees Colleagues in your organization Other:			

Now that you've checked those that apply to your work, list on the left in the following spaces the items that you've checked as "dissatisfied," either with the amount or quality of the contact. Think of ways that you can restructure your time in order to change the nature of these contacts, and write them in the spaces on the right. For example, if your supervisor always looks over your shoulder when you are working on a project, plan to discuss your current project and ask for her advice and opinions. If you are curious about how a peer in a similar company deals with his job, structure time for an exchange of information that could give you new insights and perspective on your own position.

Dissatisfied with contact   *I could improve this by*

_____   _____

_____   _____

_____   _____

_____   _____

_____   _____

C. YOUR WORK ITSELF

The next step is to look at your work itself. What do you do when you are at work? What are your rewards? What are your frustrations? How do you spend your time? Complete the following chart. Check (√) the response that *best* applies.

Your Work	Too Much	About Right	Not Enough
Independence Variety of tasks Challenge Tangible results Direction from supervisors			
Detailed job description Compliments from supervisors Competition with colleagues Distractions Time at my desk			
Opportunity to visit other offices Meetings Ability to be creative Repetitive tasks Clear procedures			

Your Work	Too Much	About Right	Not Enough
Sense of purpose Opportunity to be helpful Opportunity to use my skills Feeling that the organization cares about me Group projects			
Cooperative environment Pressure to get the job done Feeling a sense of accomplishment Volume of work Deadlines Other:			

Now list in the following spaces the factors about your work that you checked "too much" or "not enough." Try to think of at least one thing that you might do to improve the situation.

Too much or not enough   *I could improve this by*

_____   _____

_____   _____

_____   _____

_____   _____

_____   _____

_____   _____

D. YOUR EXPECTATIONS

Your expectations of your work have a profound effect on you. Those with very low expectations tend to be more satisfied with their work because they never expected much in the first place. On the other hand, those with high expectations may need to reevaluate their expectations and feelings about success.

What did you dream of achieving in your career and life when you were a teenager? What did you dream of becoming in your childhood? What were your expectations of yourself?

I dreamt I would be . . .

_____

_____

_____

_____

The dream of your youth can sometimes become an uncomfortable reality in adulthood if you haven't reevaluated your original career goals. By reevaluating your dream and by matching it more closely with your accomplishments you will have successfully dealt with an important adult developmental task. In the process of reevaluating your dream you may need to redefine your idea of success.

Success means different things to different people. Your values determine what success is to you. If you are interested in uncovering your values, you may wish to refer to Section I of this book. You may think success is managing a household, three children, and a part-time job; someone else may define success solely in terms of money, vacations, and luxury. In any career or life change, you may wish to examine more closely what your dream of accomplishment is, what your goals are, and how you would define success at this point in your life.

What expectations do you have for your work? What do you hope to accomplish? How important is your work to you? How much money do you hope to make? What position do you hope to reach?

My expectations

_____

_____

_____

_____

Look back at your expectations. Are they realistic, based on your present career, your education, your age, and the economy? If yes, go for it! If your expectations are not totally realistic, in what ways might you change these expectations? Don't forget to look at your *total lifestyle* for possible ways to fulfill your expectations.

Ways I might change my expectations

_____

_____

_____

_____

E. Expand Positives and Reduce Negatives

Now think of the three *most positive* and the three *most negative* things about your present work. Write them in the following spaces. If you are not currently employed, think back to a previous job.

Positives

1. _____

2. _____

3. _____

Negatives

1. _____

2. _____

3. _____

How do your positive and negative factors compare? Do your negatives overwhelm your positives, or do the positives make up for your negatives? Just how bad are your negatives? Are there any creative ways of dealing with your negatives? For example, if you dislike your supervisor, you may seek a transfer to a similar position within your organization. A change of scenery, coworkers, or supervisor may make a world of difference to your morale. What are some creative ways to deal with your negatives?

Try to think of at least two ways to *eliminate or reduce* each of your negatives.

Negative #1 _____

_____

Negative #2 _____

_____

Negative #3 _____

_____

Now try to think of at least two ways that you can *expand* each of your positives.

Positive #1 _____

_____

Positive #2 _____

_____

Positive #3 _____

_____

F. YOUR PERFECT WORK

Describe your perfect "dream" work. What would you do every day?

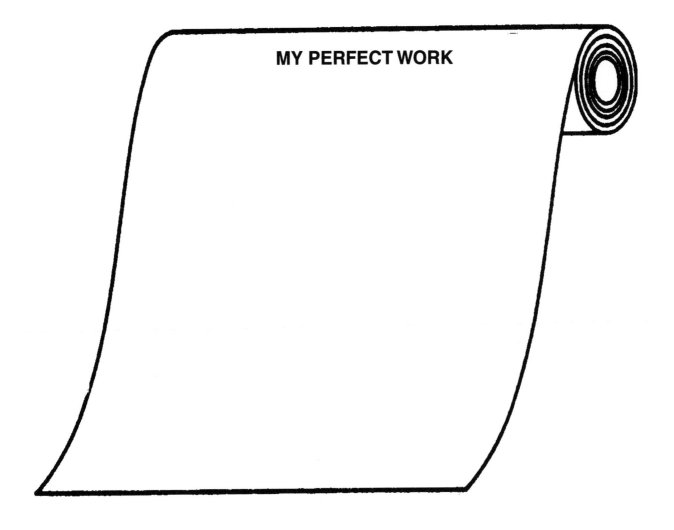

MY PERFECT WORK

Is there such a thing as a perfect job? a perfect life? What parts of your perfect dream work are most important to you? How can you integrate some elements of your dream work into your present work? I can integrate the elements of my perfect work into my present work by taking the following actions:

_____

_____

_____

_____

I can take the following actions to come closer in the future to having my perfect work:

_____

_____

_____

_____

It took me twenty years to become an overnight success.

—*Eddie Cantor*

The Payoff—Who Decides Whether You've Done Good Work?

A. Your Reward System

Everyone works in order to achieve certain rewards. The need for rewards will vary from person to person, both in the type and amount of the reward. In order to assess your work satisfaction, it is important to consider what type of rewards you need for your work to be fulfilling. Generally, rewards can be categorized as follows.

Extrinsic Rewards

These rewards come from *other sources*. They involve someone giving you something as a result of your work. They come from sources that you do not control. They come from other people, from systems, from personnel policies, and from other external sources. The following are examples of extrinsic rewards.

pay	letters of commendation
raises	positive job evaluations
promotion	bonuses
praise	paid leave
fringe benefits	thank yous
tangible results	awards for accomplishments

Intrinsic Rewards

These rewards come from within *you*. They are usually intangible and result from your own assessment of how well you have performed. While extrinsic rewards come from others, intrinsic rewards are dependent on your establishment of criteria for work success. The following are some examples of intrinsic rewards.

personal growth	solving a problem
pride in your work	self-expression
feeling of accomplishment	being creative
self-respect	using your skills and abilities
meeting a challenge	developing new skills
setting and achieving goals,	

Most work involves rewards of both types. It is important for you to assess the type of rewards that are most important to you and then to focus your work on achieving these rewards. Intrinsic rewards have the advantage of coming from within. You have more control over the rewards that you receive if you have established a good intrinsic reward system. However, everyone appreciates extrinsic rewards, and it is important that you know what you need. It may be possible to control some of the extrinsic rewards that are important to you by seeking feedback from others, by selecting work with tangible results, and by choosing a job with a large number of built-in reward systems.

The following questions are designed to help you assess what rewards are important to you. Try to be creative in exploring ways to increase both your extrinsic and intrinsic rewards.

Evaluating Your Extrinsic Rewards

1. Think about your present work and those jobs that you have had in the past. What type of extrinsic rewards—those rewards that come from others—are most important to you in order for you to feel that you've done a good job?

_____

_____

_____

_____

_____

_____

2. Now think again about your present work. (If you are not working at this time, think about your last job.) What kind of extrinsic rewards do you receive or have you received from others?

_____

_____

_____

_____

_____

_____

3. If certain extrinsic rewards are very important to you and you are not receiving them, how could you change your work so that you can receive more of these rewards?

_____

_____

_____

_____

_____

_____

Evaluating Your Intrinsic Rewards

1. Think about your present work and the jobs that you have had in the past. What type of intrinsic rewards—those that come from within you—are most important to you in order to feel that you've done a good job?

_____

_____

_____

_____

2. What kind of intrinsic rewards do you receive from your present work, or did you receive from your last job?

_____

_____

_____

_____

3. What action can you take to increase the intrinsic rewards that you receive from your work?

_____

_____

_____

_____

B. YOUR WORK SATISFACTION—IT'S YOUR DECISION

After looking at all aspects of your work life, the basic assessment of your satisfaction with your work is your responsibility. You can get help from others and explore alternatives, but you have to decide what you need to be satisfied with your work and whether your work can provide the satisfaction you want.

Some people seem to never be happy with their work. They always look only at the negatives, and all work has some negatives. These people spend a lot of time and energy complaining about their work without doing anything about it. Some people are willing to accept whatever comes their way and to turn over control of their work to others. Some people expect too much from their work, so much that no job could meet all of the needs that they hope to fulfill. Others expect very little from their work, seeing a job as just another part of their total lifestyle.

For many people, moving from one job to another fulfills a need for change and for some it can enhance work satisfaction. However, this may not always be the best approach. Often, one can benefit greatly by growing with a job and by seeking ways to increase job responsibilities and enhance work satisfaction. The previous pages in this chapter have been designed to help you make the most of your current work. At some point, it may be necessary to change jobs entirely in order to fulfill your needs. However, look at what you can do now to make the most of your work. An investment of time and energy in what you are doing now can have the potential of significant rewards.

> "When one door closes, another opens; but we often look so long and so regretfully upon the closed door that we do not see the one which has opened for us."
> —Alexander Graham Bell

1. What actions can I take to make the most of my work?

_____

_____

_____

_____

_____

_____

2. What are the risks involved in these actions?

_____

_____

_____

_____

_____

_____

3. Will these actions expose me to risk? Is the risk worth the payoff?

_____

_____

_____

_____

_____

They conquer who believe they can. He has not learned the lesson of life who does not each day surmount a fear.

—*Ralph Waldo Emerson*

Enhance Work Performance and Satisfaction

. . . .

 To make the most of my work, I need to take the following actions.

In the next week:

In the next month:

Within six months:

Within one year:

ADDITIONAL RESOURCES

Albright, Townsend. *How to Hold it All Together When You've Lost Your Job.* Lincolnwood, IL: VGM Career Books, 1996.

Berman, Eileen and Gordon, Elizabeth. *Dealing Effectively With Job Loss.* Authority Press, 1999.

Birkel, Damian J. and Miller, Stacey J. *Career Bounce-Back. Guide to Recovery and Reemployment.* New York: Amacom, 1998.

Casperson, Dana May. *Power Etiquette: What You Don't Know Can Kill Your Career.* New York: AMACOM, 1999.

Colgrove, Melba. *How to Survive the Loss of a Love.* New York: Bantam Books, 1991.

Charlesworth, Edward, and Nathan, Ronald. *Stress Management.* New York: Ballantine Books, 1985.

Chusmir, Leonard. *Thank God It's Monday.* New York: NAL, Dutton, 1990.

Covey, Stephen. *Seven Habits of Highly Effective People.* New York: Simon & Schuster, 1990.

Cox, Allan. *Straight Talk for Monday Morning.* New York: Wiley, 1991.

———. *The Crystal-Barkley Guide to Taking Charge of Your Career.* New York: Workman Publishing Co., 1995.

Davis, Martha. *Relaxation and Stress Reduction Workbook.* California: New Harbinger, 1988.

DuBrin, Andrew. *Your Own Worst Enemy.* New York: AMACOM, 1992.

Elkort, Martin. *Getting from Fired to Hired.* New York: Macmillan, 1997

Friedman, M. *Type A Behavior and Your Heart.* New York: Fawcett Publishing Company, 1985.

Glassner, Barry. *Career Crash—The New Crisis and Who Survives.* New York: Simon & Schuster, 1994.

Greenberg, Herbert M. *Coping with Job Stress.* New Jersey: Prentice-Hall, 1980.

Guterman, Mark S. *Common Sense for Uncommon Times.* California: CPP Books, 1994.

Hakim, Cliff. *When You Lose Your Job.* San Francisco: Berrett-Koehler Publishers, 1993.

Helmstetter, Shad. *What to Say When You Talk to Yourself.* Arizona: Grindle Press, 1990.

Hirsch, Arlene S. *National Business Employment Weekly—Love Your Work and Success Will Follow.* New York: John Wiley & Sons, 1996.

Holton, Ed. *The New Professional. Everything You Need to Know for a Great First Year on the Job.* Princeton, NJ: Peterson's Guides, 1991.

Hyatt, Carole, and Gottlieb, Linda. *When Smart People Fail.* New York: Penguin Books, 1988.

Josefowitz, Natasha. *Fitting In.* Massachusetts: Addison-Wesley, 1988.

Kevane, Raymond A. *Employment Power–Take Control of Your Career.* Seattle, WA: Peanut Butter Publishing, 1994.

Koonce, Richard. *Career Power: 12 Winning Habits to Get You from Where You Are to Where You Want to Be.* New York: AMACOM, 1994.

Lakein, Alan. *How to Get Control of Your Time and Your Life.* New York: New American Library, 1989.

Levinson, Harry. *Career Mastery.* California: Berrett-Koehler, 1992.

Lord, David. *National Business Employment Weekly Guide to Self-Employment.* New York: John Wiley & Sons, 1996.

Ludden, LaVerne. *Job Savvy: How to Be to a Success at Work.* California: JIST Works, 1998.

Lusk, Julie, ed. *30 Scripts for Relaxation, Imagery and Inner Healing.* Minnesota: Whole Person Associates, 1993.

Morin, William J. & Cabrera, James C. *Parting Company—How to Survive the Loss of a Job and Find Another Successfully.* New York: Harcourt & Brace & Co., 1991.

Mortell, Art. *The Courage to Fail.* New York: McGraw, 1992.

Olmsted, Barney, and Smith, Suzanne. *Job-Sharing Handbook.* Berkeley, California: Ten Speed Press, 1985.

Paulson, Terry. *Making Humor Work: In the Workplace.* California: Crisp Publications, 1989.

Pines, Ayala, and Aronson, Elliot. *Career Burnout.* New York: Free Press, 1989.

Potter, Beverly. *Beating Job Burnout.* California: Ronin Publishing Company, 1985.

———. *Preventing Job Burnout.* California: Crisp Publications, 1987.

———. *The Way of the Ronin: Riding the Waves of Change at Work.* California: Ronin Publishing Company, 1989.

Riehle, Kathleen A. *What Smart People Do When Losing Their Jobs.* New York: John Wiley & Sons, 1991.

Satterfield, Mark. *Career Etiquette*. Illinois: VGM, 1996.

Schechter, Howard. *Rekindling the Spirit in Work: How to be Yourself on the Job*. Barrytown, NY: Barrytown Ltd., 1995.

Schlossberg, Nancy. *Overwhelmed—Coping With Life's Ups and Downs*. New York: Dell, 1991.

Searing, Jill A., and Lovett, Anne B. *The Career Prescription—How to Stop Sabotaging Your Career and Put It on a Winning Track*. Englewood Cliffs, NJ: Prentice Hall, 1995.

Sher, Barbara. *Teamworks: Building Support Groups That Guarantee Success*. New York: Warner Books, 1991.

Stearns, Ann Kaiser. *Living Through Job Loss*. New York: Fireside, 1995.

Tubesing, Donald. *Kicking Your Stress Habits*. Minnesota: Whole Person Associates, 1993.

Waitley, Denis, and Witt, Rene L. *Joy of Working*. New York: Ballantine, 1986.

Whileman, Dr. Thomas, Verghese, Dr San and Peterson, Randy. *The Complete Stress Management Workbook*. Grand Rapids, MI: Zondervan Publishing House, 1996.

Yate, Martin. *Beat the Odds—Career Buoyancy Tactics for Today's Turbulent Job Market*. New York: Ballentine Books, 1995.

Ziglar, Zig. *Top Performance: How to Develop Excellence in Yourself and Others*. New York: Berkley, 1987.

SECTION SIX

Create Quality and Balance in Your Life

No matter how old you are, what career you have, what your background may be, what your family situation is, or who you are, it is essential that you *actively plan* the lifestyle that you want to live. Your career will play a very important role in your lifestyle, but there are many other factors to consider. Some may be as important or even more important than your career. Your interests, family activities and responsibilities, recreation, religion, community activities, friendships, and many other parts of your life all contribute to the definition of your unique self and help to determine your happiness and satisfaction with life.

Many people depend too heavily on their careers for their identity. These people may have major problems when they are confronted by career changes, job changes, or retirement. It is vital to maintain a balanced lifestyle, one that involves a variety of activities and interests. The lifestyle that you develop *now* will tend to stay with you as you go through life. If you eventually choose to retire, a balanced lifestyle can help you to deal with this transition. In the future, many people may be faced with the necessity of choosing a less than totally fulfilling career. A balanced lifestyle can help to compensate for this. It is important to build a pattern of activities and interests that you can take with you through life.

This chapter will help you to look at the factors that make up an enjoyable lifestyle and a long, healthy life. It will help you to look at the actions that you can take now to develop a well-rounded lifestyle. As you read this chapter, keep one principle in mind: *Don't wait until retirement to do what you want to do.* The lifestyle you develop now will grow with you for the rest of your years.

Your lifestyle is unique. As you read this section, consider the following factors, which may play an important role in your life satisfaction.

- Your career
- Your attitude toward life
- Your interests
- Your health
- Your physical activity
- Your diet
- Your family
- Your friends and colleagues
- Your finances
- Your personal growth
- Your fun
- Your challenges
- Your spiritual life
- Your continuing opportunity to learn
- Your physical surroundings

A Look into the Future

In this chapter we will consider the future. Try to project yourself years ahead and answer each of the following questions in the space provided below each question. Base your answers on what you *would like* to be doing in the future.

A.   You are 68 years old and it is Thursday. You are just waking up.

    1.   What will you do today?

    2.   With whom, if anyone, will you have lunch?

    3.   What will you do after six o'clock tonight?

    4.   What will you do tomorrow (Friday)?

    5.   What plans do you have for the weekend?

    6.   With whom are you living?

    7.   In what geographic area are you living?

    8.   In what setting and in what kind of housing are you living?

    9.   Are you working? If so, how does work fit into your life?

10. If you are working, what kind of work do you do?

11. What interests or hobbies do you have?

12. What contacts do you have with other people?

13. What are your major joys in life?

14. What aspects of your life are most important to you?

15. What do you need from others?

16. What do you have to give to others?

17. In what kind of physical condition are you?

18. What kind of family relationships do you have?

B. In the following spaces, try to summarize the answers you just wrote by asking yourself this question:

What do I want to be like at age 68?

_____

_____

_____

_____

_____

_____

C. Now ask yourself the following question.

What can I do now to start becoming the person I want to be at age 68?

_____

_____

_____

_____

_____

_____

It is important to start *now* to plan for the future, not only so that you have a better chance of becoming the person you would like to be, but also in order to begin doing some of the things that are most important to you now. Why wait? There is no time like the present. The following pages will help you to plan for a personally satisfying lifestyle that can take you into the years ahead.

Think Positively

Each person's needs are unique. What may be good for one individual may not be appropriate for another. Your lifestyle can correspond to your own preferences and values if you energetically pursue the activities that are important to you. Positive thinking is your key to developing a lifestyle that meets your needs.

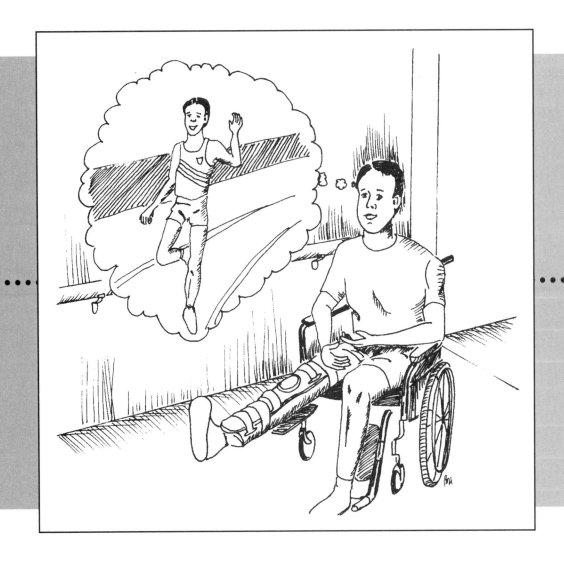

Have you ever met someone who is always looking at the world with a gloomy perspective? Some people prefer to dwell on the negative side of just about anything that happens in life. It is possible to find problems in almost anything. One can become reluctant to change because of the fear of potential problems. In order to appreciate life and to keep open to new relationships and experiences, think positively!

Try to get in the habit of looking at what you **can** do rather than what you cannot do. Look at what you **have** rather than at what you lack. When change takes place, concentrate on the gain that the change might bring rather than the loss. A positive attitude will help you to feel better about yourself and your choices. People will respond to you in a more positive way. You will probably be more successful on your job and you may well have a much better chance of staying healthy.

Erik Erikson, a noted psychoanalyst, described eight stages of human development. Each stage was characterized by a major task. The last two stages that Erickson described were generativity versus self-absorption and integrity versus despair.* In the task of generativity versus self-absorption, Erikson noted the importance of contributing to the growth and development of others, the community, the nation, and the world as opposed to being so wrapped up in one's self that there is little to give. In the last stage, integrity versus despair, Erikson described the importance of integrating one's life, including the rewards and disappointments, and moving on with a positive approach to life rather than despairing over lost opportunities.

A positive approach is critical in dealing successfully with these and other tasks that occur throughout life. Look at what can be accomplished rather than what cannot be accomplished. Is the glass of water half empty or half full? Consider the "half-full" side of life!

What parts of your life might benefit from a more positive approach right now?

_____

_____

_____

_____

_____

_____

---

*Ericson, Erik. "*Identity and the Life Cycle*" *Psychological Issues* I, 1959.

Know When It's Time to Change Work

Most of this book is devoted to helping you make career decisions. In Section V, you learned about doing a career checkup at least every two years. You also looked at ways to make your job better without leaving it. However, there may come a time when it is important to make a job change. The following questionnaire* may help in your decision making.

*Reprinted with permission of the American Public Welfare Association from *Public Welfare*, Vol. 39, No. 1. Copyright 1981 American Public Welfare Association.

Do You Dread Going to Work?

Rate each question on a scale of 1 to 5—with 1 meaning never; 2, rarely; 3, sometimes; 4, often; and 5, always:

Your response:

Do you:
_____ 1. Worry at night and have trouble sleeping?
_____ 2. Feel less competent or effective than you used to feel?
_____ 3. Consider yourself unappreciated or used on the job?
_____ 4. Always feel tired, even when you get enough sleep?
_____ 5. Dread going to work?
_____ 6. Get angry and irritated easily?
_____ 7. Have recurring headaches, stomachaches, or lower back pain?
_____ 8. Feel overwhelmed?

Are you:

_____ 9. Always watching the clock?
_____ 10. Avoiding conversation with coworkers?
_____ 11. Rigidly applying the rules without considering more creative solutions?
_____ 12. Increasing your use of alcohol or drugs?
_____ 13. Automatically expressing negative attitudes?
_____ 14. Excessively absent?

Does your job:

_____ 15. Overload you with work?
_____ 16. Deny you breaks, lunch time, sick leave, or vacation?
_____ 17. Demand long shifts and frequent overtime?
_____ 18. Pay too little?
_____ 19. Lack access to a social-professional support group?
_____ 20. Depend on capricious funding sources?
_____ 21. Not have enough funds to accomplish agency goals?
_____ 22. Lack clear guidelines?
_____ 23. Entail so many different tasks that you feel fragmented?
_____ 24. Require you to deal with rapid program changes?
_____ 25. Demand coping with negative community image and/or an angry public?

Now total the numbers in the response column

_____ Your Score: _____

What Your Score Means

25 to 35—You appear impressively mellow, with almost no job stress; you seem practically burnout-proof.

36 to 50—You express a low amount of job-related stress and are not likely to burn out. Look over those questions you scored 3 or above and think about ways you can reduce the stresses involved.

51 to 70—You seem to be under a moderate amount of stress on the job and have a fair chance of burning out. For each question you scored 4 or above, consider ways you can reduce the stresses involved. If possible, take action to improve your attitude or the situation surrounding those things that trouble you most.

71 to 90—You express a high amount of job-related stress and may have begun to burn out. Consider studying stress reduction, assertiveness, and burnout prevention. Mark each question you scored 4 or above and rank it in order of its effect on you. Begin with the ones that bother you most. For at least your top three, make a list of ways you can reduce the stresses involved and take action to improve your attitude, the situation, or both. If your body is reflecting this stress, get a medical checkup.

90 and above—You seem to be under a dangerous amount of stress and are probably nearing an advanced stage of burnout. Without some changes in your behaviors, attitude, and job situation, your potential for succumbing to stress-related illness is high. Consider taking classes in stress reduction and burnout prevention, seeking professional help, or both.

A high score on this questionnaire may indicate that a change is necessary to maintain your mental, physical, and emotional health. Use the career assessment techniques in Section V to determine if staying with your job and making changes would be preferable to leaving your job.

Work can be one of your most important sources of fulfillment. Your need for self-esteem and self-actualization can be met through work, as you saw in Section I. However, work can take on too important a role in life. For example, the workaholic who is compulsively devoted to a job and has few interests outside of work is in serious jeopardy when faced with a layoff or firing. The workaholic is out of balance. Since too much of anything, good or bad, can create problems, it is extremely important to develop interests and activities outside of work. Although work can fulfill a variety of needs, it is not necessary for work to fulfill all your needs. Important needs such as mental stimulation, socialization, and accomplishment can be fulfilled in or out of the work environment.

If you have balance in your life, and your work still causes a significant amount of stress or is unfulfilling to you, begin the career and life planning process as outlined in Section I. Self-assessment is appropriate any time in your life. If you go through the process and decide not to make a change, you will probably feel better about your job since you will have made a conscious decision to stay.

Develop Interests

Interests and hobbies can contribute significantly to your enjoyment of life and to your self-esteem. They can also provide a very important balance to life and a valuable contrast to work. Those who take the time to develop and pursue interests outside of work generally have higher satisfaction with life as they grow older. Interests and hobbies fulfill a variety of individual needs and are a source of just plain fun. For example, if you play a musical instrument as a member of a jazz group, you will fulfill needs for creativity and interaction with others. In addition, you can fulfill a need to challenge yourself by improving your musical skills. Such an activity may even help to fulfill your financial needs if your jazz group gets paid for gigs. Collectors of items such as baseball cards, china, or stamps can fulfill needs in traveling to conventions, for excitement in discovering rare treasures, or for challenge and interaction in bargaining with other collectors.

As you take your train trip to the future, make time for your interests and take time to develop new ones. A variety of interests can add vitality and richness to your life by providing outlets for creativity, challenges, mental and physical activity, social opportunities, a sense of accomplishment, growth, and even income. Use the following table to assess your interests and hobbies.

Pursuing Your Interests, Hobbies, and Activities

Check (√) the column that best represents your answer to each question.

	Yes	Somewhat	No
Do you have a variety of interests outside of work? Do you have hobbies? Do you actively pursue your interests or hobbies? Do you feel that you are able to spend the amount of time you want on your interests and hobbies?			
Do you feel that you have enough of a variety of interests and hobbies? Are many of the interests active (requiring your direct involvement) rather than passive (watching TV)? Do some of your interests involve other people? Do your interests and hobbies provide a good diversion from your work?			
If you are married, do you share a few interests and activities with your spouse? Do your interests and hobbies give you a sense of satisfaction and fulfillment? Do you have any interests or hobbies that could form the basis of a second career?			

If your answer was "somewhat" or "no" to any of the above questions, would you prefer your answers to be "yes"? If so, go back and place an X in the "yes" column.

In the following spaces, list what you can do now or in the future to turn your "somewhat" or "no" answers into "yes" answers.

_____

_____

_____

_____

_____

_____

_____

_____

_____

_____

_____

_____

_____

Take an Active Role in Staying Healthy

What could be more important to your quality of life than good health? A fatalistic attitude toward health stems from the belief that you have no control over your health. Nothing could be further from the truth. There are specific actions that you can take to increase your chances of staying in good health and of living longer. No matter what your age and lifestyle, you can become actively involved in giving yourself a better opportunity to be in good health. There are six major factors over which you have control.

A. The Importance of Physical Activity

Regular physical activity of some type can have a profound effect on improving your health and it can also increase the length of your life. A comprehensive study of 17,000 Harvard alumni by Dr. Ralph Paffenbarger demonstrated beyond a reasonable doubt that regular exercise decreases the risk of mortality from all diseases.* Many new studies have shown that even moderate exercise has great health benefits.** Although exercise cannot halt the aging process, it can slow it significantly. There is also evidence that regular exercise causes the brain to release endorphins, the body's own form of painkiller. This causes a feeling of well-being and gives a psychological lift both during and after exercise. According to the Paffenbarger study, the amount of exercise needed to produce benefits is the equivalent of burning off between 2,000 and 3,500 calories per week. This includes all exercise, not just special times that you devote to exercise, but also the regular walking, stair climbing, and other activity that you do in the course of your life every day.

A study published in the November 2, 1989 issue of the *Journal of the American Medical Association* shows that just a small amount of exercise reduces the death rate dramatically in the most sedentary individuals. In a long-range study of 13,344 men and 3,120 women, researchers found that the higher the fitness level, the lower the death rate tended to be. The primary benefit was in terms of reduced death rates from heart disease and cancer. Although the fittest individuals did the best, even those who have moderate physical activity had significantly lower death rates.***

The type of exercise seems to be less important than the fact that you do exercise. It is not essential that everyone jog, swim, bike ride, or skate. Simple walking can be an excellent source of exercise. The important factor is that you do exercise regularly, that it becomes a part of your regular routine, and that you look for ways to increase the amount of physical activity that you gain in your normal daily activities. To help you to evaluate the effects of various types of exercise, the following chart is provided:

---

* Higdon, Hal. "Newest Research Tells Us: If You Want Long Life—Exercise!" *50 Plus, August 1986, p. 17*
** Sussman, Vic. "No Pain and Lots of Gain" *US News and World Report, May 4, 1992, p. 86.*
***Health Magazine, Washington Post, November 7, 1989, p. 7.

Activity	Calories Used per Hour*
Walking (4 mph)	320
Tennis (singles)	440
Running (6 mph)	700
Bicycling (5 1/2 mph)	240
Swimming (freestyle—slow)	540
Dancing (medium speed)	250
Golf (walking briskly, carrying clubs)	300

It is important to find the activity or combination of activities that you can incorporate into your routine, and do them. In addition, there are other actions that you can take to alter your normal lifestyle to get more exercise. Here are a few:

B. Ten Ways to Increase Your Physical Activity

1. Wake up a half hour early and walk, cycle, jog, or swim before breakfast.
2. When you drive, park some distance away from your destination and walk briskly from your car.
3. Replace a big lunch with a light lunch and spend the extra time in physical activity, such as walking.
4. Walk up stairs instead of taking the elevator.
5. Walk up and down several flights of stairs after each hour of work.
6. Replace coffee breaks with exercise breaks.
7. If you are going a short distance, walk instead of drive.
8. When you sit for long periods of time, take a break, get some fresh air, and walk.
9. Instead of paying to have housework done, do it yourself, if it is a potential source of exercise.
10. Replace power tools and appliances with manually operated ones.

C. Diet

You are what you eat, and you age by what you eat. Overeating is a problem in American society, and it can affect your lifespan. Extra fat puts a tremendous burden on the heart. As you get older, your body requires fewer calories. A man who weighs 150 pounds at age 30 and

---

*These are estimates for a person of medium weight (about 150 pounds) and are given primarily to illustrate the differences between various types of exercise. For more specific information, consult one of the resources listed later in this chapter. Keep in mind that these figures can vary depending on an individual's weight and metabolism.

maintains a regular exercise program will weigh 200 pounds at age 60 if he does not reduce his calorie intake. The following table from the *American Medical Association Encyclopedia of Medicine* has been used as a standard guideline for ideal size–weight distribution.*

Men's Height (without shoes)	Normal Weight Ranges (without clothes)	Women's Height (without shoes)	Normal Weight Ranges (without clothes)
5'2"	113–143	4'10"	92–121
5'3"	116–146	4'11"	95–123
5'4"	119–149	5'0"	98–126
5'5"	122–153	5'1"	100–129
5'6"	125–157	5'2"	103–133
5'7"	128–161	5'3"	106–136
5'8"	131–165	5'4"	109–139
5'9"	134–170	5'5"	112–143
5'10"	137–175	5'6"	115–147
5'11"	141–180	5'7"	119–151
6'0"	145–184	5'8"	123–155
6'1"	149–189	5'9"	127–160
6'2"	153–194	5'10"	132–165
6'3"	158–200	5'11"	137–170
6'4"	163–206	6'0"	142–175

In addition to reducing excess calories, selection of the types of foods that you eat can enhance your health. There are many books and other resources on this subject and there are numerous studies underway that are designed to assess the effects of diet on health and longevity. It is important for you to remain current on the developments in this rapidly growing area. Some general guidelines for a healthy diet, based upon current research findings, are as follows.

1. Eat at least five servings of fruits and vegetables a day.
2. Take in no more than 25 percent of your daily calories from fat.
3. Eat at least six servings of grain products daily.
4. Eat less red meat and more fish and poultry.
5. If you eat dairy foods, choose ones that are low in fat.
6. Be informed about the benefits of certain vitamins and whether it is advisable to take vitamin supplements.

---

*Adapted from *The American Medical Association Encyclopedia of Medicine,* Charles B. Clayman, (ed.) New York: Random House, 1989, p. 1073.

D. DEALING WITH STRESS

Stress comes from a variety of sources, and what is stressful for one person may not be stressful for another. It is well known that too much stress or the inability to deal with it can have a negative impact on your health. It is important to be prepared for stress that may come from some unexpected sources, such as the loss of colleagues at work, the loss of a sense of purpose, and others. The following are some general guidelines for avoiding stress.

- Have a support system. Maintain contact with others. Participate in activities with others.
- Develop goals, both daily and long term. Have a reason to get up in the morning. Continue to challenge yourself.
- Have a variety of activities that give you a feeling of satisfaction and accomplishment.
- Continue to grow mentally. Read, take courses, join discussion groups.
- If confronted with a major stressing event, such as the loss of a spouse, seek help from others and from community support services.
- Try to look at the positive side of any change. Focus on what you can do, not on what you cannot do.
- Develop an optimistic approach to life. There is some evidence to indicate that people who look at the future from a positive point of view actually are healthier and live longer.

E. AVOIDING SELF-INJURIOUS BEHAVIOR

We have seen that through exercise, good diet, and positive lifestyle, it is possible to gain some control over your health and to develop the potential for a longer life. It is also possible to undermine your chances for good health and a long life. The following are examples of actions that work against the goal of a long and healthy life. These are self destructive and should be avoided.

- Smoking
- Excessive drinking or use of drugs
- Failing to wear a seat belt
- Reckless driving
- Sudden intense exercise without proper preparation (shoveling snow or running before getting in shape)
- Neglect of a physical problem or the failure to have regular check-ups

F. Medical Assistance

It is very important to obtain prompt medical assistance for health problems that emerge and to have regular checkups. Untreated medical problems can get worse, but problems found early can usually be corrected. It is essential to find a doctor in whom you have confidence. However, you cannot simply defer your medical concerns to a doctor. You have certain responsibilities. Among them are:

- Make a list of all your medical problems with appropriate details. Do not keep information from your doctor and be honest with her.
- Don't limit a visit to immediate problems. For example, if you have not had a routine checkup for some time, make arrangements to get one.
- Your relationship with your doctor is a partnership and you should work together to develop a health maintenance program that is right for you. You have primary responsibility for the success of this program.
- Do not avoid examinations or tests that may be necessary but unpleasant.
- Feel free to get a second opinion before surgery or other major medical interventions.
- If you don't understand something your doctor is doing or telling you, ask for an explanation or clarification. As a partner in your own health care, it is essential to get this information in order to make decisions or take action. You should know your condition and the treatment that will be required.

G. Use of Medicine*

Before using any medicine on a regular basis, you should check with your doctor. Certain nonprescription medicines can cause problems if misused. The following are some precautions.

- Do not assume that all commercial nonprescription medicines are safe to take just because the label indicates dosage and contents or if they are recommended by a pharmacist.
- Inform your doctor of all prescription and nonprescription medications you are taking. This may prevent one drug from harmfully combining with another.
- Do not accept without question the claims made for medicines in various types of advertising.

---

*Adapted from Germeroth, Stephen R., *Pre-Retirement Seminar*. Catonsville Community College, Chapter VI, p. 8.

- The use of mood-altering pills or sleeping pills should be monitored by your doctor.
- Although drugs must be screened and tested before they are available to the public, do not assume that all drugs are totally reliable.
- Many commercially available medications that deal with problems such as constipation and sleeplessness may not be as effective as a good diet and exercise program.
- Do not "try out" a prescription written for a friend or family member. Check with your doctor.

The following resource provides useful information on prescription drugs.

The Complete Drug Reference 2000 Edition. Consumer Reports Books, 9180 LeSaint Drive, Fairfield, OH 45014-5452.

H. Test Your Health Style

Now it's time to test *your* health style. Complete the following self-test developed by the Public Health Service and reprinted here with permission from the National Health Information Clearinghouse. The interpretation of your scores is on the back of the test.

healthstyle a self-test

All of us want good health. But many of us do not know how to be as healthy as possible. Health experts now describe *lifestyle* as one of the most important factors affecting health. In fact, it is estimated that as many as seven of the ten leading causes of death could be reduced through common-sense changes in lifestyle. That's what this brief test, developed by the Public Health Service, is all about. Its purpose is simply to tell you how well you are doing to stay healthy. The behaviors covered in the test are recommended for most Americans. Some of them may not apply to persons with certain chronic diseases or handicaps, or to pregnant women. Such persons may require special instructions from their physicians.

Almost Always / Sometimes / Almost Never

Cigarette Smoking

If you <u>never smoke</u>, enter a score of 10 for this section and go to the next section on *Alcohol and Drugs*.

1. I avoid smoking cigarettes. 2 1 0

2. I smoke only low tar and nicotine cigarettes *or* I smoke a pipe or cigars. 2 1 0

Smoking Score: _____

Alcohol and Drugs

1. I avoid drinking alcoholic beverages *or* I drink no more than 1 or 2 drinks a day. 4 1 0

2. I avoid using alcohol or other drugs (especially illegal drugs) as a way of handling stressful situations or the problems in my life. 2 1 0

3. I am careful not to drink alcohol when taking certain medicines (for example, medicine for sleeping, pain, colds, and allergies), or when pregnant. 2 1 0

4. I read and follow the label directions when using prescribed and over-the-counter drugs. 2 1 0

Alcohol and Drugs Score: _____

Eating Habits

1. I eat a variety of foods each day, such as fruits and vegetables, whole grain breads and cereals, lean meats, dairy products, dry peas and beans, and nuts and seeds. 4 1 0

2. I limit the amount of fat, saturated fat, and cholesterol I eat (including fat on meats, eggs, butter, cream, shortenings, and organ meats such as liver). 2 1 0

3. I limit the amount of salt I eat by cooking with only small amounts, not adding salt at the table, and avoiding salty snacks. 2 1 0

4. I avoid eating too much sugar (especially frequent snacks of sticky candy or soft drinks). 2 1 0

Eating Habits Score: _____

Exercise/Fitness

1. I maintain a desired weight, avoiding overweight and underweight. 3 1 0

2. I do vigorous exercises for 15-30 minutes at least 3 times a week (examples, include running, swimming, brisk walking). 3 1 0

3. I do exercises that enhance my muscle tone for 15-30 minutes at least 3 times a week (examples include yoga and calisthenics). 2 1 0

4. I use part of my leisure time participating in individual, family, or team activities that increase my level of fitness (such as gardening, bowling, golf, and baseball). 2 1 0

Exercise/Fitness Score: _____

Stress Control

1. I have a job or do other work that I enjoy. 2 1 0

2. I find it easy to relax and express my feelings freely. 2 1 0

3. I recognize early, and prepare for, events or situations likely to be stressful for me. 2 1 0

4. I have close friends, relatives, or others whom I can talk to about personal matters and call on for help when needed. 2 1 0

5. I participate in group activities (such as church and community organizations) or hobbies that I enjoy. 2 1 0

Stress Control Score: _____

Safety

1. I wear a seat belt while riding in a car. 2 1 0

2. I avoid driving while under the influence of alcohol and other drugs. 2 1 0

3. I obey traffic rules and the speed limit when driving. 2 1 0

4. I am careful when using potentially harmful products or substances (such as household cleaners, poisons, and electrical devices). 2 1 0

5. I avoid smoking in bed. 2 1 0

Safety Score: _____

What Your Scores Mean to YOU

Scores of 9 and 10

Excellent! Your answers show that you are aware of the importance of this area to your health. More important, you are putting your knowledge to work for you by practicing good health habits. As long as you continue to do so, this area should not pose a serious health risk. It's likely that you are setting an example for your family and friends to follow. Since you got a very high test score on this part of the test, you may want to consider other areas where your scores indicate room for improvement.

Scores of 6 to 8

Your health practices in this area are good, but there is room for improvement. Look again at the items you answered with a "Sometimes" or "Almost Never." What changes can you make to improve your score? Even a small change can often help you achieve better health.

Scores of 3 to 5

Your health risks are showing! Would you like more information about the risks you are facing and about why it is important for you to change these behaviors. Perhaps you need help in deciding how to successfully make the changes you desire. In either case, help is available.

Scores of 0 to 2

Obviously, you were concerned enough about your health to take the test. but your answers show that you may be taking serious and unnecessary risks with your health. Perhaps you are not aware of the risks and what to do about them. You can easily get the information and help you need to improve, if you wish. The next step is up to you.

YOU Can Start Right Now!

In the test you just completed were numerous suggestions to help you reduce your risk of disease and premature death. Here are some of the most significant:

 Avoid cigarettes. Cigarette smoking is the single most important preventable cause of illness and early death. It is especially risky for pregnant women and their unborn babies. Persons who stop smoking reduce their risk of getting heart disease and cancer. So if you're a cigarette smoker, think twice about lighting that next cigarette. If you choose to continue smoking, try decreasing the number of cigarettes you smoke and switching to a low tar and nicotine brand.

 Follow sensible drinking habits. Alcohol produces changes in mood and behavior. Most people who drink are able to control their intake of alcohol and to avoid undesired, and often harmful, effects. Heavy, regular use of alcohol can lead to cirrhosis of the liver, a leading cause of death. Also, statistics clearly show that mixing drinking and driving is often the cause of fatal or crippling accidents. So if you drink, do it wisely and in moderation. ***Use care in taking drugs.*** Today's greater use of drugs—both legal and illegal—is one of our most serious health risks. Even some drugs prescribed by your doctor can be dangerous if taken when drinking alcohol or before driving. Excessive or continued use of tranquilizers (or

"pep pills") can cause physical and mental problems. Using or experimenting with illicit drugs such as marijuana, heroin, cocaine, and PCP may lead to a number of damaging effects or even death.

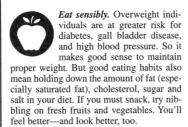 ***Eat sensibly.*** Overweight individuals are at greater risk for diabetes, gall bladder disease, and high blood pressure. So it makes good sense to maintain proper weight. But good eating habits also mean holding down the amount of fat (especially saturated fat), cholesterol, sugar and salt in your diet. If you must snack, try nibbling on fresh fruits and vegetables. You'll feel better—and look better, too.

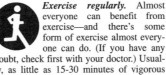 ***Exercise regularly.*** Almost everyone can benefit from exercise—and there's some form of exercise almost everyone can do. (If you have any doubt, check first with your doctor.) Usually, as little as 15-30 minutes of vigorous exercise three times a week will help you have a healthier heart, eliminate excess weight, tone up sagging muscles, and sleep better. Think how much difference all these improvements could make in the way you feel!

 Learn to handle stress. Stress is a normal part of living; everyone faces it to some degree. The causes of stress can be good or bad, desirable or undesirable (such as a promotion on the job or the loss of a spouse). Properly handled, stress need not be a problem. But unhealthy responses to stress—such as driving too fast or erratically, drinking too much, or prolonged anger or grief—can cause a variety of physical and mental problems. Even on a very busy day, find a few minutes to slow down and relax. Talking over a problem with someone you trust can often help you find a satisfactory solution. Learn to distinguish between things that are "worth fighting about" and things that are less important.

 Be safety conscious. Think "safety first" at home, at work, at school, at play, and on the highway. Buckle seat belts and obey traffic rules. Keep poisons and weapons out of the reach of children, and keep emergency numbers by your telephone. When the unexpected happens, you'll be prepared.

Where Do You Go From Here:

Start by asking yourself a few frank questions: *Am I really doing all I can to be as healthy as possible? What steps can I take to feel better? Am I willing to begin now?* If you scored low in one or more *sections* of the test, decide what changes you want to make for improvement. You might pick that aspect of your lifestyle where you feel you have the best chance for success and tackle that one first. Once you have improved your score there, go on to other areas.

If you already have tried to change your health habits (to stop smoking or exercise regularly, for example), don't be discouraged if you haven't yet succeeded. The difficulty you have encountered may be due to influences you've never really thought about—such as advertising—or to a lack

of support and encouragement. Understanding these influences is an important step toward changing the way they affect you. *There's Help Available.* In addition to personal actions you can take on your own, there are community programs and groups (such as the YMCA or the local chapter of the American Heart Association) that can assist you and your family to make the changes you want to make. If you want to know more about these groups or about health risks, contact your local health department or mail in the coupon on the right. There's a lot you can do to stay healthy or to improve your health—and there are organizations that can help you. Start a new HEALTHSTYLE today!

For more information, contact:

ODPHP Health
Information Center
P.O. Box 1133
Washington, DC
20013-1133

Maintain Good
Interpersonal Relationships

In Section II you identified your personal board of directors, your support groups, and your network of contacts. As you go through life, it is very important to maintain healthy interpersonal relationships by reaching out to others. Evaluating existing support and developing new sources of support are part of your lifestyle checkup. It is not necessary for you to have a wide variety of relationships. Usually the quality of the relationships is more important than the quantity. There is some evidence that those who are "joiners," who participate regularly in activities with others, are generally more satisfied with their lives and actually live longer.

Invest time and energy in your interpersonal relationships. If you are married or have a significant other, your relationship with your partner requires time, thought, adaptability, and flexibility. Maximize your positive relationships with family members and friends. If you find this difficult, seek help in order to build on your existing family relationships.

Look for activities and organizations that provide opportunities for interaction with others. Develop an accepting attitude as you deal with others. Be tolerant of your own and others' shortcomings and learn to be a good listener. The following table is provided so that you can evaluate your interpersonal relationships.

Improving Your Interpersonal Relationships

Please check the column that best represents your answer to each question.

	Yes	Somewhat	No
Do you participate with others in community or recreational activities? Do you interact with others at work? Do you have friends that you see regularly?			
Do you have regular contact with family? Do you have people that you can share your concerns with? Do you have people whom you can turn to for help?			
Are you able to spend as much time with your family as you wish? If you are married, do you communicate well with your spouse? If you are married, are you satisfied with your relationship with your spouse?			
Do you initiate contacts with others? Are you satisfied with the **quality** of the time you spend with family and friends? Do you rarely feel lonely?			

If your answer was "somewhat" or "no" to any of the above questions, would you prefer your answer to be "yes"? If so, go back and place an "X" in the "yes" column.

In the following spaces, list what you can do now or in the near future to turn your "somewhat" or "no" answers into "yes" answers.

_____

_____

_____

_____

_____

_____

_____

_____

Make the Most of Your Financial Resources

One key to a satisfying lifestyle is to feel in control of your finances. Money, as an extrinsic reward, is a primary value for many people and may be their main motivation for working. To others, intrinsic rewards, such as satisfaction and contribution remain more important motivating factors. For those who seek intrinsic and extrinsic rewards for work, it is essential to have sufficient financial resources to meet basic physical needs and to provide a certain degree of independence and security. No matter what your values may be and the role that money plays in your life, it can be helpful to follow some basic guidelines for maintaining financial stability.

1. **Define your financial goals.**

   Take some time to determine what is important to you and what you wish to accomplish with your resources. Do you want to own a home? Do you want a nest egg for retirement? Do you want to save for your own education or your children's education? Are there recreation or career-related activities that will strain your resources? Consider the kind of lifestyle that you want and set financial goals that will help you to attain that lifestyle.

2. **Make saving a regular way of life.**

   Most financial planning experts agree that it is important to save between 5 percent and 10 percent of your monthly paycheck. They advise you to pay yourself first, before paying the bills. Putting something—anything—aside on a regular basis establishes a pattern of saving. The more that you can save early in life, the better. You can establish the habit of saving and can benefit from long-term compounding of interest. Consider saving methods that are automatic, such as payroll deductions to credit union accounts, savings bonds, and other automatic investments.

3. **Take advantage of long-term compounding.**

   Most investments, when left to grow over time, can provide significant long-term rewards. Consider an investment of $1,000 that is left to compound at the very modest level of 7%.

$1000 @ 7% =	$1403	after	5 years
	$1907	after	10 years
	$2759	after	15 years
	$3870	after	20 years
	$5427	after	25 years

   Different investment opportunities provide varying rates of risk and of return. The most important fact is that early savings reap very significant long-term rewards.

4. **Plan ahead to meet financial goals.**

   If you have a young child and start early in the child's life to set aside funds for college, the money will grow and you will probably be ready to help your child with a variety of options when the time comes for college. If you value travel and plan to develop this interest in later years, it would be prudent to save regularly for a travel fund. It is often easier to save when the money is designated to meet a specific goal.

5. **Take advantage of company savings plans.**

Some organizations provide you with the opportunity to make tax-deferred contributions to retirement savings plans. Others provide programs that allow you to buy company stock at reduced rates. Many of these plans offer significant opportunities for long-term savings that are highly favorable compared with other types of investments. The convenience of automatic payroll deductions also encourages regular contributions. Consider these opportunities carefully as you evaluate your present job and before you change jobs.

6. **Maintain an emergency fund.**

Try to have a savings account that you can depend on for unforeseen expenses. These funds should be easily accessible and immediately available. Some financial planners suggest that this rainy-day fund should be approximately equal to six months' salary.

7. **Carry adequate insurance.**

The amount of insurance that you carry depends on your family commitments, your age, and other responsibilities. There are resources on financial planning that can give guidelines on the amount of insurance for your specific situation. Take advantage of company-sponsored insurance programs, because life and health insurance are usually offered at lower rates. If you are the primary wage earner, consider the purchase of long-term disability insurance. This type of insurance, which is overlooked by many, guarantees income should you be unable to work. Carefully examine and choose insurance products that are available on the open market. Become informed about the relative merits of different types of insurance.

8. **Take advantage of your company's pension plan.**

Most organizations require contributions to their pension plans, but some give you options for contributions and even the type of plan to which your contributions would go. Consider issues such as time required for vesting, investment of funds, and transferability of the plan to another work setting. Too many people passively accept a plan without investigating it. Do research and stay informed about your pension plan options. If you do not have a pension plan available through your place of employment, establish your own.

9.   Take responsibility for your own long-term financial needs.

Do not assume that your pension plan and social security will fulfill your financial needs as you approach retirement. Plan to supplement these earnings with your own savings. A variety of savings plans are available and some, such as individual retirement accounts (IRAs) or Keogh plans for the self-employed, provide significant tax benefits.

10.   Live within your means.

Periodically evaluate your financial situation. Where does your money go? Does the way you spend your money reflect your values? Could you spend less in one area to provide more resources for another more important area? Have you developed a budget? If not, would a budget help you to regulate your monthly expenses? Do you tend to overspend by credit card use? It is easy to fall into patterns of spending money without having the resources available. Take time on a regular basis to analyze your finances.

These are ten simple suggestions for making the most of your financial resources. There are many books, magazines, and other resources on financial planning, investment strategies, and budgeting. Use available print resources, workshops, classes, and professional consultants as you develop your financial plan and take control of your financial destiny.

Continue to Learn

No matter what your age or life stage, it is important to continue to learn. The opportunities for continuing education for adults are growing daily. College is no longer the exclusive realm of the 18- to 21-year-old age group; adults by the millions return to college for a variety of reasons. Adults of all ages, ethnic origins, cultural heritages, and socioeconomic levels are back in the classroom learning a wide variety of subjects. Learning opportunities are found not only within colleges, but in organizations, on videotape, through the mail, on computers, in informal groups, and through professional associations. Continued learning is becoming popular and crucial for success for a variety of reasons.

A. ADVANTAGES OF CONTINUED LEARNING

Lifelong learning helps you to:

- Change careers or jobs
- Learn or update skills
- Pursue interests
- Meet people
- Develop support systems
- Teach and mentor others
- Use existing skills and knowledge
- Create balance in your life
- Keep involved with the changing world
- Keep mentally and physically active
- Expand your knowledge
- Take a study trip
- Exchange ideas
- Meet challenges
- Take a risk
- Increase self-esteem
- Earn a degree or another degree
- Enjoy life

B. BARRIERS TO CONTINUED LEARNING

Although continued learning provides so many opportunities for growth, many people do not take advantage of them. Barriers seem to block the way to continued learning. These barriers include believing the following myths.

- Intelligence declines with aging.
- Adults cannot compete in the classroom with younger students.
- Institutions are not interested in the adult student.
- Learning is for others, not yourself.
- Having a degree already exempts you from learning.
- Brain cells are dead and cannot be revived.
- Anxiety will prevent learning.
- There is no time to learn.
- Learning is too much work and too difficult when you work full time.

These myths are internal barriers that can distract you from your next step on your career path or avocational pursuits. The barriers are in your mind and can be overcome if you are motivated to keep learning. Stretching your mind can pay off in a big way. Given the technologies of today and the pace of changing technologies for tomorrow, continuing to learn is the only way to meet future challenges.

C. OPPORTUNITIES FOR CONTINUED LEARNING

As you go through life, consider a variety of ways to continue to learn for career and lifestyle purposes. The following are some continuing education options:

- College and university courses
- Home-study programs
- Adult education programs
- Corporate training programs
- Hobby groups
- Musical groups
- Technical certification programs
- Study-travel groups
- Learning with a friend
- Teaching
- Tutoring
- Elderhostel programs
- Workshops
- Reading
- Writing

How can you take advantage of opportunities for continued learning? What are some ideas that you have for learning? In the following spaces, list the five areas that you would like to expand through learning in the next year. Put a check mark (√) next to the ones that are job or career related. If your answers are all job related, then add one or two that are specifically for fun.

1. _____

2. _____

3. _____

4. _____

5. _____

Your Lifestyle Checkup

The following pages contain a guide for a lifestyle checkup. Every so often, it is important to evaluate how things are going in your life. This book contains many checklists and exercises designed to help you assess a variety of factors. This lifestyle checkup summarizes this section and ends the book. Review this checkup periodically. If you wish to make some changes, go to the appropriate chapter in this book for detailed assistance in reviewing your options.

A. YOUR WORK

It is important to periodically assess the evolution of your career. To do this, turn back to Section V and complete Chapter 24, Routine Maintenance—Your Two-Year Job Checkup. When you are finished with your checkup, answer the following questions:

1. Do you want to change your work? _____

   If yes, what are your alternatives? _____

   _____

   _____

2. Do you want to stay in your career but change jobs? _____

   If yes, what are some alternatives? _____

   _____

   _____

3. Do you want to change the setting in which you work? _____

   If yes, what are some alternatives? _____

   _____

   _____

4. Do you want to change the type of people you work with? _____

   If yes, what kind of people do you want to work with? _____

   _____

   _____

5. Do you want to keep your job but change your duties? _____

   If yes, what are some alternatives? _____

   _____

   _____

B. YOUR FAMILY

Evaluate your family life. Consider the possibility of enhancing relationships, time spent, communication, and the support that you give and receive. Family relationships are dynamic and ever changing. Include your extended family as you answer the following questions.

1. What are the sources of satisfaction in your family life?

    _____   _____

    _____   _____

    _____   _____

    _____   _____

2. What are the sources of frustration in your family life?

    _____   _____

    _____   _____

    _____   _____

    _____   _____

3. Would you like to change your family life? If so, in what ways?

    _____   _____

    _____   _____

    _____   _____

    _____   _____

4. How many of these changes can you actually make? When and how will you make these changes?

    _____   _____

    _____   _____

    _____   _____

    _____   _____

5. Is there anything about your relationships with your friends that you would like to change? If yes, what changes would you like to make?

_____

_____

_____

C. YOUR VALUES

What are your life priorities at the present time? Is your career of primary importance? How about the time you spend with your family? Do you have outside interests, community activities, or creative outlets? Do you spend time in volunteer work, have a second job, or go to school? There are always many factors in your life that compete for your time and attention. What you value most often determines how you will spend your time. You are always making value decisions, and an awareness of what values are most important to you can help you to live a more harmonious and less stressful life. When you know which values have a higher priority, you can more easily make life's major and minor decisions. Your values do change as you go through the various life stages. If you are currently seeking some change in your career or lifestyle, it may be due in part to the fact that some of your values may have changed. What was important to you in the past may be less important now. You may want to devote greater attention in your life to new activities or to some of the things you did not have as much time for in the past.

1. What aspects of your life are most important to you at the present time?

_____   _____

_____   _____

_____   _____

_____   _____

2. Now take these and place them in order, with the most important first.

_____   _____

_____   _____

_____   _____

_____   _____

3. Have your values changed over the past five to ten years? Are things that were important then less important now? Have other things taken on greater importance? In what ways have your values changed? List those things that have become more important and those that have become less important to you.

More important

_____

_____

_____

_____

Less important

_____

_____

_____

_____

D. YOUR PHYSICAL CHARACTERISTICS

Studies have shown that men are healthiest from ages 15 to 25 and women from ages 15 to 30. The more serious physical problems associated with aging, such as arthritis, rheumatism, heart ailments, and the like do not normally begin until around age 65 for women and 60 for men. However, physical changes that take place earlier can have an effect on your daily life. Vision peaks in the late teens, declines slightly in the twenties, remains stable through the mid-forties, and then declines steadily. Hearing peaks around age 10, remains high through the forties, and often declines rapidly after age 60. Taste, smell, and touch remain relatively stable, although there may be a slight decline in later life. Contrary to common belief, mental faculties do not generally deteriorate with age unless there is illness. Although individuals ages 18 to 25 do best on IQ tests, the wisdom and experience that comes with increasing age compensate for reduced speed in learning. Physical strength and stamina decrease with age, although physical activity can play an important role in slowing this process.

It is important for you to evaluate whether any physical changes you may be undergoing have a bearing on your current experience. A physically demanding job may become difficult to maintain. A high-paced job with long hours may cause you to have physical problems. You may have to adjust some of your leisure activities to reflect your changing physical capabilities. If so, it is important to replace these activities with something, and not to simply give them up. If you have been experiencing any physical problems, it is important to have them evaluated by qualified personnel. Consider the influence on your physical health as you make any decision to change your lifestyle or career.

1. What physical changes have you experienced that may have an effect on your job or your leisure activities?

   _____   _____

   _____   _____

2. What physical problems may be related to your work or lifestyle?

   _____   _____

   _____   _____

3. How would you resolve a conflict between what you want to do and what you are physically able to do?

Want to do	*Able to do*	*Resolution*
_____	_____	_____
_____	_____	_____

4. What kind of action is necessary to accommodate your physical condition?

Medical assistance _____

Job change _____

Lifestyle change _____

E. YOUR PSYCHOLOGICAL CHARACTERISTICS

What is your outlook on life? Are you bored with your work or lifestyle? This can happen after you have worked for a number of years. Do you find yourself generally frustrated and feel that you are not worth as much as you once were? If your work seems to leave you dead-ended, this can have a negative effect on your self-confidence. If you previously devoted most of your efforts to your job, you may now need to branch out in different directions.

Do you feel that you have lost time when you compare yourself with someone else your age? This is a common concern, because it is based on our societal values, which tend to indicate that certain things are done at certain ages. Feeling that you are out of step with where you should be at your age can lead to a lack of self-worth and a sense of hopelessness. It is important to remember that you need to evaluate your own lifestyle and what you yourself want to do. Comparisons with others, unless you derive support and inspiration from them, can be self-defeating. There is a distinct danger in approaching life changes with a negative, apprehensive, or defeatist outlook. If you can prepare yourself to approach these changes as opportunities for growth, your happiness and self-worth can increase.

1. What are some of the things that you often find yourself worrying about?

2. How would you describe your outlook on life? Positive? Negative? In what ways?

Some positive approaches I take   *Some negative approaches I take*

_____   _____

_____   _____

_____   _____

_____   _____

3. What concerns can you actually change or do something about?

Concern   *Solution*

_____   _____

_____   _____

_____   _____

_____   _____

F. Your Leisure

Do you have much leisure time? How do you spend your leisure time? Many of the hours that you have for leisure are actually taken up by household chores, eating, sleeping, personal care, and other programmed activities that you must do. Leisure time is time available to you to do what you wish. You are free to schedule it or not schedule it, depending on your own preferences. If you are unhappy with your current lifestyle, look at how you are spending your time. Do you have time available to pursue your own interests independent of your job and the demands of others? It may help to assume greater control of your nonwork time and make sure that you block out time for yourself. In addition, evaluate the type of activity that you normally do in your leisure time. Sewing, for example, can be a good leisure time activity if you truly enjoy it and derive satisfaction from it. To others, sewing may simply be work and must be done out of necessity. If you enjoy working on your car and find it relaxing, it is a valuable leisure activity. However, if you feel you must do it to save on repair bills, this activity takes on quite a different meaning.

It is important for all people to have some balance in their lives, and fulfilling leisure activities can be very valuable. This is especially true as you progress through the developmental life stages and begin to look for other areas of fulfillment besides work and family. Interests that you enjoy pursuing for their own sake can play a significant role in your ability to lead a satisfying life. These interests can take many forms, can be done alone or with people, can be active or passive, and can be expensive or of little or no cost. What is important is that you enjoy doing them for their own sake.

1. Write in the spaces below four of your most satisfying leisure activities at this point in your life.

   _____   _____

   _____   _____

   _____   _____

   _____   _____

2. Next to each item just listed, indicate approximately when you last did this activity.

3. How might you change the way you spend your time so that you can more often do the things you like to do?

4. What are some other things that you would like to do in your leisure time, but do not do now?

   _____   _____

   _____   _____

   _____   _____

   _____   _____

G. YOUR PHYSICAL SURROUNDINGS

One possibility for change is the physical environment in which you work and live. Do you basically like the type of work you do but find yourself unhappy with the people with whom you work, the place where you work, or the distance you travel to work? If so, you may wish to consider looking for a job where you would be doing the same type of work but in a different setting. Compared with other job changes, this would be an easier change to make because it would not involve obtaining new job skills. Another source of dissatisfaction can be the home or neighborhood in which you live. If your values conflict with those of your neighbors, if you feel isolated, or if the apartment or house in which you live is not appropriate to your needs, this can have a distinctly negative effect on your general life satisfaction. Consider your options for making a change.

The third source of dissatisfaction can be the geographic area in which you live. Consider your interests and the lifestyle you want. Would you be happier in a warmer climate, in a more rural environment, in a small town, in a large city? If you have the option of moving, is this something you would like to consider? How important is closeness to family and friends? At times people tend to place too much emphasis on their residence or area they live as a source of dissatisfaction when there are really other problems that must be dealt with, but your physical environment *can* be a major factor in considering any change. A change in your environment could have positive effects on your lifestyle satisfaction.

1. What do you like about the setting where you work, your home, and the geographic area where you live?

Work	*Home*	*Geographic area*
_____	_____	_____
_____	_____	_____
_____	_____	_____
_____	_____	_____
_____	_____	_____

2. What don't you like about the setting where you work, your home, and the geographic area where you live?

Work	*Home*	*Geographic area*
_____	_____	_____
_____	_____	_____
_____	_____	_____
_____	_____	_____
_____	_____	_____

3. What changes in these three aspects of your physical environment can you realistically consider?

Work	*Home*	*Geographic area*
_____	_____	_____
_____	_____	_____
_____	_____	_____
_____	_____	_____
_____	_____	_____

H. INFLUENCE OF OTHERS

What influence do others have over how you live your life or whether you can change your career? There are some very legitimate concerns when you consider the influence of others. Family financial responsibilities are a reality, although too often these are used as an excuse to not even consider a major change. If you are unhappy with your career, talk it over with your spouse and family. Your happiness may be more important than stability, and they may be willing to make some sacrifices to help you achieve greater happiness. It is also important, if you are married, to make major decisions with your spouse. Friends and other family members can also provide excellent support, if their primary concern is your satisfaction and happiness.

Too often, however, the influence of others can be a negative factor in making a change. You may find yourself comparing where you are in your life and what you have with others your age. This can be a needless source of anxiety. You may be too willing to let friends tell you what they think would be best for you. Some help can be useful, but you *must* make the decisions. Members of your extended family may like to have you around, but your own life fulfillment may be increased by moving from the area. Some people may value stability and, even though they are well-meaning, may attempt to impose those values on you. It is important that you not allow direct influence or perceived influence to be imposed on you when it comes to finally making a decision. Consider the advice of others who have your best interests at heart, but also consider their reference points. Then make your decision.

1. Who *has* influence over you, and in what ways?

    Who   *In what ways?*

    _____   _____

    _____   _____

    _____   _____

    _____   _____

2. Who *should* have influence over you, and in what ways?

    Who   *In what ways?*

    _____   _____

    _____   _____

    _____   _____

    _____   _____

3. Do you want to change the influence that other people have over you, either by becoming less dependent on some or by gaining new sources of support from friends or family? If yes, what changes would you like to make?

    _____

    _____

    _____

Summary—Lifestyle Checkup

If you have identified some changes that you want to make, now is the time to plan your action. Look back at your options and write them on the following chart.

1. Complete the following chart, indicating what changes you want to make and when you want to make them.

Changes I Want to Make	Now	Within the Next Month	Within the Next Year	In Five Years
a.				
b.				
c.				
d.				
e.				
Others:				

2. Rank these changes.

Priority #1 _____

Priority #2 _____

Priority #3 _____

Priority #4 _____

Priority #5 _____

3. Now develop a plan of action. How will you go about making your top priority change?

#1 _____

_____

_____

How will you go about making your other priority changes?

#2 _____

_____

_____

#3 _____

_____

_____

#4 _____

_____

_____

#5 _____

_____

_____

What Kind of Help Do You Need in Making These Changes?

1. **Self-Evaluation**

   If, for example, you want to change your career but are unsure about alternatives, you might want to consider Sections I through III of this book. You might also want to enroll in a career exploration course, or seek individual counseling. Both are available at the counseling service of your local community or four-year college, at community agencies, or at private counseling services.

2. **Information**

   You will need information in order to make changes. At the end of this chapter is a bibliography of written resources that may help you. The career resources center in your local library or college can be a good source of information on careers, educational opportunities, and leisure activities.

3. **Support from Others**

   You should use family and friends as sources of support. Test out ideas and share your decision-making process with those whom your decision will affect. Get help from those whose opinions you value. Remember that you will make the final choice, but the involvement of others can be of great help.

4. **Identify Realistic Options**

Some changes may be very difficult to achieve because they conflict with your responsibilities. They may involve major adjustments in your life and in the lives of your family members. Determine which changes can be realistically made and work on them. If you can first make some changes that seem minor, these may make quite a difference in your life so that you do not have to make a major change that would cause a great deal of upheaval for yourself and your family.

5. **Decision Making**

You can deal effectively with change and make decisions. See Section II of this book. Remember that even if, after considering a change, you decide not to change, it is still a decision that you reached. You will be better off for having considered your alternatives.

6. **Nothing Is Forever**

Have confidence in your ability to make decisions and to make changes. Do not become overly concerned about making the right change. Have confidence in your ability to make decisions. Remember that change can bring about growth. Even though one change may not work out, you can simply change again. By knowing yourself better and by knowing how to make decisions, you can gain greater control over your life.

SUMMARY

Create Quality and Balance in Your Life

 As you go through life, set aside the time to evaluate where you are and where you want to go. Think about charting new directions, about laying some new track and driving your train down that track. These new directions may be career related or may involve other parts of your life. Avoid just going along the tracks without making any decisions and without pulling over to think about where you have been, where you are right now, and where you want to be. Keep control of your train trip throughout life. Make sure that your trip reflects your priorities. Be willing to consider and implement changes and even chart a new course. Appreciate all the aspects of your trip, not just your career, as you take charge of the direction and quality of your journey.

ADDITIONAL RESOURCES

Briley, Richard G. *Are You Positive?* New York: Berkley Publications, 1991.

Brilliant, Ashleigh. *I Feel Much Better, Now That I've Given Up Hope.* California: Woodbridge Press, 1984.

————. *I Try to Take One Day at a Time: But Sometimes Several Days Attack Me at Once.* California: Woodbridge Press, 1988.

Brody, Jane. *Jane Brody's Good Food Book.* New York: Bantam, 1987.

Chapman, Elwood. *Attitude: Your Most Priceless Possession.* California: Crisp Publications, 1988.

Cohen, Marjorie. *Work, Study, Travel Abroad: The Whole World Handbook.* New York: St. Martin's Press, 1992–1993.

Eisenberg, Gerson G. *Learning Vacations.* New Jersey: Peterson's Guides, 1989.

Feingold, S. Norman. *Futuristic Exercises: A Work Book for Emerging Lifestyles and Careers in the 21st Century and Beyond.* Maryland: Garrett Park Press, 1989.

Fischer, Edward. *Life in the Afternoon.* New Jersey: Paulist Press, 1987.

Haponski, William C., and McCabe, Charles E. *New Horizons: The Education and Career Planning Guide for Adults.* New Jersey: Peterson's Guides, 1985.

Harty, Terry, and Harty, Karen Kerkstra. *Finding a Job After 50.* Hawthorne, NJ: Career Press, 1994.

Haynes, Marion. *Personal Time Management.* California: Crisp Publications, 1987.

Helmstetter, Shad. *What to Say When You Talk to Your Self.* Arizona: Grindle Press, 1986.

Jeffers, Susan. *Feel the Fear and Do It Anyway.* New York: Columbine Books, 1988.

Lenz, Elinor. *Rights of Passage.* Virginia: Impact, 1992.

Martin, Renne. *A Survival Guide for Women.* Washington, DC: Regnery-Gateway, 1991.

Mason, L. John. *Stress Passages.* California: Celestial Arts, 1988.

Moore, Marti. *Crossroads: A Back to School Career Guide for Adults.* Rhode Island: The Carroll Press, 1980.

Raber, Merrill, and Dyck, George. *Mental Fitness: A Guide to Emotional Health.* California: Crisp Publications, 1987.

Reicher, Gayle, and Burke, Nancy. *Active Wellness: 10 Step Program for a Healthy Body, Mind & Spirit.* New York: Time Life Custom Publishers, 1999.

Rich, Phil, Copans, Stuart and Copans, Kenneth. *The Healing Journey Through Job Loss: Your Journal for Reflection and Revitalization.* New York: John Wiley & Sons, 1999.

Richardson, John M. *Making It Happen: A Positive Guide to the Future.* Massachusetts: Roundtable Publications, 1982.

Ryan, Regina, and Travis, John. *The Wellness Workbook.* California: Ten Speed Press, 1988.

Savageau, David *Places Rated Almanac.* Foster City, CA: IDG Books Worldwide, Inc., 2000.

Schlossberg, Nancy. *Overwhelmed—Coping with Life's Ups and Downs.* New York: Dell, 1991.

Schlossberg, Nancy K., and Robinson, Susan Porter. *Going to Plan B—How You Can Cope, Regroup, and Start Your Life on a New Path.* New York: Fireside, 1996.

Scollard, Jeannette. *Risk to Win.* New York: Macmillan, 1989.

Simon, Sidney. *Getting Unstuck: Breaking through Your Barriers to Change.* New York: Warner Books, 1989.

Smith, Hyrum W. *10 Natural Laws of Successful Time and Life Management.* New York: Warner Books, 1995.

Sweetgall, Robert et al. *Fitness Walking.* New York: Putnam Publisher Group, 1985.

Thomas, Marian. *Balancing Career and Family.* Kansas: National Press, 1991.

Tubesing, Donald. *Seeking Your Healthy Balance.* Minnesota: Whole Person Associates, 1993.

Waitley, Denis. *Seeds of Greatness.* New York: Pocket Books, 1988.

————. *The Psychology of Winning.* New York: Berkley, 1984.

Whileman, Dr. Thomas, Werghese, Dr. San, and Petersan, Randy. *The Complete Stress Management Workbook.* Grand Rapids, MI: Zondervan Publishing House, 1996.

Appendix A
Continuous Career
Options Listing

Add and delete career possibilities as you continue to do your research and informational interviewing. Keep track of your progress by reviewing this master list of careers. Happy career planning, now and in the future.

_____   _____

_____   _____

_____   _____

_____   _____

_____   _____

_____   _____

_____   _____

_____   _____

_____   _____

_____   _____

_____   _____

_____   _____

_____   _____

_____   _____

_____   _____

_____   _____

Bibliography

In addition to the following listing of sources used in this book, there are numerous resources listed at the end of each chapter, including an annotated bibliography at the end of Section III.

Bloomfield, Harold et al. *How to Survive the Loss of a Love.* New York: Bantam Press, 1977.

Bolles, Richard N. *The Three Boxes of Life.* Berkeley, California: Ten Speed Press, 1981.

———. *What Color Is Your Parachute?* Berkeley, California: Ten Speed Press, 2000.

Bramhall, Martha. "Do You Dread Going to Work?" *Public Welfare Journal,* Winter 1981.

Bridges, William. *Job Shift: How to Prosper in a Workplace without Jobs.* Reading, MA: Addison-Wesley Publishing Co., 1994.

Clayman, Charles B. (ed.). *The American Medical Association Encyclopedia of Medicine.* New York: Random House, 1989.

Covey, Steven. *First Things First.* New York: Simon and Schuster, 1995.

Dixon, Pam. *Job Searching Online for Dummies.* Foster City, CA: IDG Books Worldwide, Inc., 1998.

Erikson, Erik. "Identity and the Life Cycle." *Psychological Issues* I, 1959.

Fine, Sidney. *Dictionary of Occupational Titles* (4th ed). Washington, D.C.: U.S. Department of Labor, Employment and Training Administration, 1977.

Germeroth, Stephen R. *Pre-Retirement Seminar.* Catonsville Community College, n.d.

Gilligan, Carol. *In a Different Voice.* Cambridge, Mass: Harvard University Press, 1983.

Glassner, Barry. *Career Crash—The New Crisis and Who Survives.* New York: Simon & Schuster, 1994.

Gonyea, James. *Career Selector 2001.* Hauppauge, N. Y.: Barron's Educational Series, Inc., 1993.

Gorman, Tom. *Multipreneuring.* New York: Fireside, 1996.

Graber, Steven, Blackett, Thomas F., Sampson, Heidi E. *Adams Electronic Job Search Almanac 2000.* Holbrook, MA: Adams Media Corp., 2000.

Herr, E.L., and Cramer, S.H. *Career Guidance and Counseling through the Lifespan.* Boston: Scott, Foresman and Co., 1988.

Holland, John L. *Making Vocational Choices: A Theory of Careers.* Englewood Cliffs, New Jersey: Prentice-Hall, 1985.

Hudson, Frederic M. *The Adult Years—Mastering the Art of Self-Renewal.* San Francisco: Jossey-Bass, 1991.

Krannich, Ronald L., and Krannich, Caryl Rae. *Best Jobs for the 21st Century.* Manassas Park, VA: Impact Publications, 1998.

Lathrop, Richard. *Who's Hiring Who.* Berkeley, California: Ten Speed Press, 1981.

Levinson, Daniel J. *The Seasons of a Man's Life.* New York: Ballantine Books, 1979.

Maslow, Abraham. *Motivation and Personality* (2nd ed.). New York: Harper & Row, 1970.

Myers, Isabel Briggs, with Myers, Peter B. *Gifts Differing.* Palo Alto, California: Consulting Psychologists Press, 1980.

Osipow, Samuel H. *Theories of Career Development.* Englewood Cliffs, New Jersey: Prentice-Hall, 1983.

Rifkin, Jeremy. *The End of Work.* New York: G.P. Putnam's Sons, 1995.

Satir, Virginia. *Self-Esteem.* California: Celestial Arts. 1975.

Schlossberg, Nancy. "A Model for Analyzing Human Adaptation to Transition." *The Counseling Psychologist,* Vol. 9, no. 2, 1981.

Schlossberg, Nancy; Troll, Lillian; and Leibowitz, Zandy. *Perspectives on Counseling Adults: Issues and Skills.* Monterey, California: Brooks/Cole Publishing Company, 1978.

Sheehy, Gail. *Passages: Predictable Crises of Adult Life.* New York: E.P. Dutton and Co., Inc., 1977.

Simon, S.B. *Getting Unstuck: Breaking Through the Barriers to Change.* New York: Warner, 1989.

Super, D.E. "A Lifespan, Lifespace Approach to Career Development." *Journal of Vocational Behavior,* 16 (30), 1980.

Thompson, Larry. "Living Longer Fitter." *The Washington Post Health Magazine,* November 7, 1989.

Tiedeman, D.V., and Miller-Tiedeman, A. "Career Decision-Making: An Individualistic Perspective," in D. Brown and L. Brooks (eds.) *Career Choice and Development. Applying Contemporary Theories to Practice.* San Francisco: Jossey-Bass, 1984.

Van Gennep, Arnold. *The Rites of Passage.* Chicago, University of Chicago Press, reprint 1960.

Veninga, Robert L., and Spradley, James P. *The Work/Stress Connection: How to Cope with Job Burnout.* Boston: Little, Brown and Co., 1982.

Wolfinger, Anne. *The Quick Internet Guide to Career and Education Information.* Indianapolis, IN: VIST Works, Inc., 2000.

Index